D0466282

WOOD HOUSES

WOOD HOUSES

By Ruth Slavid

ABBEVILLE PRESS PUBLISHERS NEW YORK LONDON

First published in the United States of America in 2006 by Abbeville Press, 137 Varick Street, New York, NY 10013

First published in Great Britain in 2006 by Laurence King Publishing Ltd
www.laurenceking.co.uk

Printed in China

First Edition
10 9 8 7 6 5 4 3 2 1

Library of Congress Cataloging-in-Publication Data

Slavid, Ruth.
Wood houses / by Ruth Slavid. — 1st ed.
p. cm.
Includes index.
ISBN-13: 978-0-7892-0888-0
ISBN-10: 0-7892-0888-1
1. Building, Wooden—History—21st century. 2. Architecture, Domestic.
I. Title.

NA7173.S63 2006
728'.37—dc22

2006011321

Front of jacket image: Riddell Residence, Wilson, Wyoming, Will Bruder Architects, photo by Bill Timmerman, see pp. 114–117

Back of jacket image: Accordion House, Årjangs Commun, Värmland, Sweden, 24H> architecture, photo by Christian Richters, see pp. 42–47

Book Design by Neil Pereira
Jacket design by Misha Beletsky

For bulk and premium sales and for text adoption procedures, write to Customer Service Manager, Abbeville Press, 137 Varick Street, New York, NY 10013 or call 1-800-ARTBOOK.

Contents

Introduction

Above: The Stiftsgården Palace in Trondheim is unusual in that it is an eighteenth-century monumental building in wood, a reflection of Norway's readily available timber and of its lack of other resources.

There is a marvellous miniature painting in the Bedford Hours, created in Paris in about 1423, of the construction of Noah's ark. With nothing about it to suggest that what is being built is going to be a ship, what we see is effectively a three-storey timber frame with a pitched roof. Noah directs a team of workmen who are perched on the roof, carrying planks up a ladder, drilling holes or, in the foreground, using a plane, an axe and a saw on the raw material. Along with their colourful tunics and leggings, some even wear tool belts that would scarcely look out of place today.

There is no need to pretend that the Master of the Munich Golden Legend, who was responsible for this particular illustration, had any particular insight into the timber skills of early biblical times. What we can see, however, is the high level of skill with wood that was available in Europe in the fifteenth century, and a range of activity that is still familiar today. A self-builder would probably nod knowingly, wishing that he could have such a dedicated team. Give or take a little mechanization and the use of some manufactured timber products, not an enormous amount has changed.

Today's statement, 'Manual construction of log houses: Log house is a solid construction. Massive constructions of the house are reliable, whereas the microclimate of premises makes a great contribution to the cosiness of the house and health of people living therein' comes from the website of Petras Ubartas, an architect from Vilnius in Lithuania (hence the imperfect English) who specializes in log cabins and is exporting his designs across Europe, most recently to Spain. Despite his Masters in architecture, his constructions would doubtless be very recognizable to the workmen in the Bedford Hours.

The Log Home Builders' Association of North America claims: 'Our mission is to help people learn how to live debt free and avoid becoming trapped by a 30-year mortgage. One or two people can build a real handcrafted log home, log cabin, house, lodge, or cottage from logs very quickly easily, and inexpensively, using simple hand-tools that will fit in a car trunk. In fact, it is often possible to build very beautiful log homes without a mortgage (and without log home kits).' The only aspect of the design of these buildings at which those fifteenth-century craftsmen might raise an eyebrow is the lack of sophistication. And, perhaps, the rugged, anti-establishment individualism, which is such a far cry from the cooperative ethos of the guild system.

Archaeologists, of course, can look much further back for examples of timber housing. Whereas countries such as Egypt and several Far Eastern countries moved directly from the most primitive shelters to the use of mud bricks, for much of the world, and particularly for northern and central Europe, timber was the material of the first 'proper' houses. In forested areas it was abundant; it was strong; and it was relatively easy to work.

Among the earliest known timber dwellings are those at Terra Amata near Nice in the south of France. Built during the Palaeolithic period, between 450,000 and 380,000 BC, they consist of shallow dwellings 8–15 metres (26–50 feet) long and 4–6 metres(13–20 feet)wide. Large poles in the centre support the roofs, with smaller poles and rock walls around the edges.

Sir Banister Fletcher's *A History of Architecture* identifies the continuing evolution of timber houses through such projects as Nea Nikomedia in Macedonia, northern Greece, built in about 5800 BC. This has rectangular dwellings built from timber, with an infill of reeds and an internal plaster surface of mud and chaff. Later, wooden longhouses were built in locations ranging from Holland to the Ukraine.

In China, at Banpocun, houses built in about 4000 BC were circular and partially sunk into the ground. Four centre posts supported a conical wattle and daub roof which sloped almost to the ground, supported at its edges by slender posts. Later the Chinese introduced a great deal of standardization into building design, with wooden houses whose elements were connected by mortice and tenon joints that were well able to withstand earthquakes.

As architecture became more sophisticated, so more demanding and durable materials such as stone and brick were used for monumental buildings, but timber remained the vernacular one and was used in most housing. Indeed, in countries such as Norway, where other materials were in very short supply, the more widespread use of timber persisted. As late as the eighteenth century, buildings as grandiose as the Stiftsgården Palace in Trondheim were built of wood. Similarly, countries like Japan clung on to their timber architecture.

In England some distinctive examples of timber construction had developed. One example was the cruck frame, a kind of wishbone of heavy timber that seems to echo the Gothic arch or an upturned boat. And in the United States many of the early colonial houses, even the more grandiose, were of wood. But generally, because of the relatively modest status of this material, houses were demolished, occasionally burnt, or simply remodelled until their timber origins disappeared.

The invisibility of the timber house was finally confirmed with the advent of the Modern Movement in the early part of the twentieth century. The newest, most elegant designs were in those enticing new materials, steel and concrete and glass. It was not that timber houses ceased to be built, but that they ceased to be at the cutting edge of architecture.

However, there was another, more humanist tradition still coexisting with the harder edges of Modernism, with timber playing a part. We can see this in some of the houses of Frank Lloyd Wright and in Alvar Aalto's Villa Mairea at Noormarkku in Finland (see pages 8 and 9). This tradition slumbered for a few decades before re-emerging.

Several strands in today's development in houses can be traced back to Walter Segal and his self-build housing movement. The German-born

Above: This depiction of Noah's Ark in the Bedford Book of Hours gives a fascinating insight into fifteenth-century craftsmanship.

architect, brought up in a utopian community in Switzerland's Ticino region, spent his working life in the United Kingdom. The origins of self-build date back to a temporary house Segal built for himself, his partner and children in 1960 in Highgate in London. Intended to be used only while the 'proper' house was under construction, it had a lightweight timber frame and standard cladding elements. Foundations were virtually non-existent – simply paving slabs. This design, which attracted considerable attention from the architectural community, evolved into an ever simpler approach that Segal used on several projects. As it was refined, occupiers were able to undertake more and more of the construction work themselves, which both saved them money and gave them a sense of involvement with, and control over, their destinies.

Many of the ideas associated with Segal's self-build continue in a lot of timber housing today: the individual control, the idea of 'touching the ground lightly', and the nascent environmental approach, which has now become more sophisticated. The 'stick-build' approach with small timber elements was suited to people with little access to a construction plant, although many today would argue that it is unnecessarily complex, and that larger-scale elements, although involving some mechanical lifting, make life much simpler.

Another important project in the return to serious consideration of timber by architects was the Sea Ranch condominium in California (see page 12). Designed in the mid-1960s by Moore, Lyndon, Turnbull & Whitaker, it comprises a cluster of homes, timber framed and clad, harking back to ideas of agricultural buildings but forming a defined community in its windy, seaside environment. Its importance today lies in its recognition that timber could be used in a contemporary idiom, and in the reference to barns and to other rural buildings that has become so prominent in wooden houses now. Today, post post-Modernism, there is little shame in mixing the modern with historic references.

Above: Taliesin West (1937 onwards) at Scottsdale, Arizona, is one of several houses in which Frank Lloyd Wright used timber, continuing a humanist tradition that contrasted with the sterner diktats of the Modern Movement.

Practices such as Robert Harvey Oshatz Architect revived a romantic, organic tradition with projects such as the Mount Crested Butte residence in Colorado, built in the mid-1980s (see page 11). Oshatz studied and worked with Frank Lloyd Wright, but adopts a far more flamboyant and curvaceous style than anything his mentor created. At Mount Crested Butte he designed a high-elevation home built out from a central pole for two brothers obsessed with skiing. It uses a variety of levels and has an undulating roof that has led locals to dub it the 'snow clam'.

Building It

If there is a renaissance today in the use of timber for houses, it reflects a huge range of approaches and designs. Wood may be selected for environmental reasons, for lightness, for a connection with nature, for ease of working or simply for its sensuous properties. And there are almost as many different approaches to building with timber as there are aesthetics of the houses that result.

Most important, still, is the timber frame, and this is certainly the type of construction that is used most widely in commercial housing projects. Traditionally, timber houses were built with large wooden elements, laboriously connected with heavy joints. Innovation came in the early nineteenth century with the development in the United States of the balloon frame. First used in Chicago, it replaced the heavy frame walls that were built whole on the ground and then lifted into place with a much lighter solution. It was based on much lighter pre-cut 5- x 10-centimetre (2- x 4-inch) studs positioned 40 centimetres (16 inches) apart and held together by factory-produced nails. Thanks to the large number of studs, the frame could withstand heavy wind loads despite its inherent lightness. With factories producing nails, and mills cutting wood in standard dimensions, a lot of the skill was removed from the process of frame production – so much so that many workers in America built their own homes.

Top: Alvar Aalto's Villa Mairea (1937–9) expresses timber externally in the cladding and window frames.

Above: Inside Villa Mairea, one gains a true appreciation of the extent to which the material is used.

While the use of lightweight frames has persisted, the European model of a platform frame, originally developed in Scandinavia, has largely superseded the balloon frame even in its home in North America.

Balloon frames are continuous throughout the height of the building so that floors are let into the members of the frames, minimizing vertical movement. In contrast, with platform frames the ground-floor walls are built off a timber platform. This makes it possible to build the walls on site and tilt them up – a return, of course, to an earlier approach, but using much lighter elements and mechanization. Indeed, the increasing move to off-site construction, coupled with the ready availability of small cranes on site, is in many cases removing the imperative to build with small elements. For instance, 40 per cent of wood construction in North America is prefabricated – 30 per cent of wall systems and 75 per cent of roofs. This helps to deal with falling skill levels and removes the uncertainty of on-site work. It also means that the larger those individual elements are, the faster and more assured construction will be once they arrive at the site.

There is, therefore, something of a backlash against the idea of using a multiplicity of tiny elements. For example, the truss-rafter roof, while relatively inexpensive and lightweight, occupies the whole roof space. In contrast, a more massive form of construction makes better use of the space by allowing it to be opened up, giving the householder more flexibility. Similarly, more massive structural walls can be expressed on the interior of a building. In the case of a system like the relatively heavyweight wall and floor panels from the German company Lignatur, these can combine a structural role with acoustic properties.

How Green Is It?

Part of the resurgence in timber's popularity as a material for housing is thanks to its environmental credentials – it is the structural element with the lowest embodied energy; it is a 'renewable natural resource'; it is not toxic. However, any architect who wants to address the issue of sustainability seriously is faced with a minefield of choices in making a selection of materials of any kind. How far has a material travelled? How sustainably was it sourced? How will its inherent properties affect the performance of the building in terms of energy consumption and carbon-dioxide emissions?

One of the main issues with timber is its sourcing. Ethically there is, of course, a vast difference between using timber from properly managed forests whose owners treat questions of regeneration, biodiversity and environmental good neighbourliness seriously and, in the worst instance, using wood that has been hacked out of virgin rainforest.

It is therefore essential that wood, particularly hardwood, is certified. There are a number of certification schemes and, as with many worthy ventures, no love lost between the main bodies. The chief schemes are the Forest Stewardship Certification (FSC), mostly used by English-speaking nations, and the Programme for the Endorsement of Forest Certification (PEFC), which is more appropriate for many European countries that have large numbers of small, family-run timber producers. It is a fair rule of thumb that most softwoods (the main materials used for building frames and so on) will have been sourced sustainably whatever the paperwork says. With hardwoods, however, and particularly tropical hardwoods, it is essential to follow proper procedures to ensure they have been produced in an environmentally sustainable manner.

There are two main problems. One is that in countries that are making great advances in responsible production there may also be a number of cowboy producers who are still exporting. It is important, therefore, to have a proper chain of custody for timber, a means of discovering exactly where it came from. The second problem is that discovering the origins of the timber in manufactured products may be more difficult than tracing the source for raw lumber – an issue that is compounded by contractors searching for the lowest prices and attempting to replace the elements contained in an architect's specification. In both instances the golden rule is: if in doubt, don't. As with all areas of environmental uncertainty, if a product's pedigree is questionable it should be avoided. Almost always, an acceptable alternative will exist.

In more general terms, the environmental credentials of timber are excellent. The European Commission estimates that, on average,

Opposite top: Robert Harvey Oshatz revived a romantic, organic tradition when he designed this house at Mount Crested Butte, Colorado, in the mid-1980s.

Opposite right: The two main lightweight framing systems are balloon frame (left), and platform frame (right). The latter form has come to dominate.

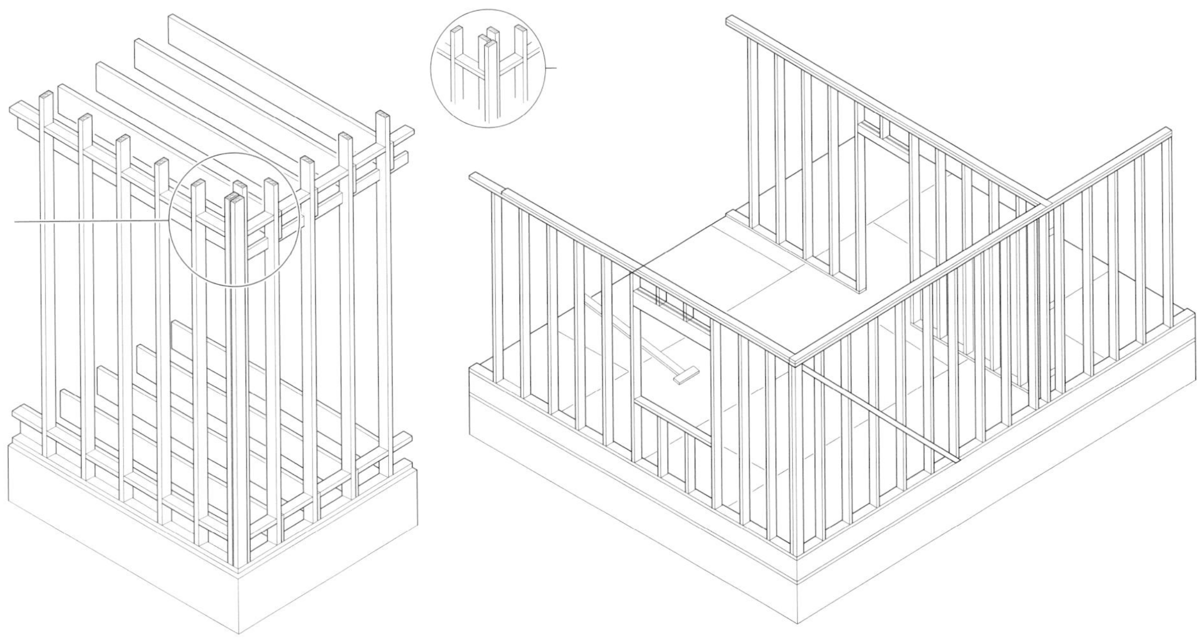

Above: The Sea Ranch condominium in California, by Moore, Lyndon, Turnbull & Whitaker, was radical in its reference to agricultural buildings.

substituting 1 cubic metre (35 cubic feet) of wood for other materials will result in a saving of 0.8 tonnes of carbon dioxide. Timber also has inherently good thermal properties and avoids the potential pitfalls of thermal bridging that can occur with steel.

Will It Burn?

Since everybody knows that wood is a good material with which to build a domestic fire or a bonfire, there is a popular perception that timber-framed buildings are likely to burn down. But, like so many things that seem to be just common sense, this is wrong. Large, heavy wooden elements are one of the most successful fire-resisting choices that can be made. In a fire the outer layer of a piece of timber will char, and the charring will provide protection for the rest of the member. Burning will therefore be extremely slow and, as the properties of timber do not change greatly with heat, there will not be the danger of catastrophic collapse that can occur when, for example, steel beams pass a critical temperature and, losing much of their strength, buckle. As long as the design allows for the effective reduction in cross-section that charring involves, timber will provide excellent structural stability.

However, a lightweight timber frame is more problematic. The narrow cross-section means that the percentage lost to charring will be far greater. Nevertheless, there are relatively simple approaches that can make this type of construction safe. To a great extent these involve enclosure with fire-resisting materials, such as gypsum plasterboard.

With multi-occupancy, multistorey structures, the behaviour of timber in a fire has been more of a concern. One of the major considerations has been compartmentation – the ability to restrain the fire within a section of the building. This and other structural issues have been tackled extensively in research.

For example, at the start of the twenty-first century, work at the United Kingdom's Building Research Establishment involved the construction and extensive testing of a full-scale, six-storey timber-frame building. This proved that structural stability could be obtained and, even more important, that the building could achieve a high level of fire performance. This removed restrictions on the use of timber as a construction method above a height of 11 metres (36 feet), and has resulted in projects such as the six-storey timber-framed student accommodation at the University of Swansea in Wales, designed by Architype and completed in 2004.

At the University of Canterbury in Christchurch, New Zealand, Professor Andy Buchanan produced a report on the behaviour of timber in fire, which concludes: 'Timber buildings can be designed and constructed to be just as safe as buildings of any other materials, recognizing that the selection of materials is only a small part of the overall process of providing fire safety in buildings.'

Among his other recommendations is an enhanced use of sprinklers in domestic buildings. This was one of the strategies adopted when a pair of five-storey buildings in Melbourne, Australia, was extended upward by adding another three storeys. The design for the Bourke Street Apartments, by Hayball Leonard Stent Pty Ltd Architects, had to be realized in timber because it was the only material that was light enough not to overload the original structure (see page 15).

Top: Architype took advantage of less rigid restrictions to build six-storey timber-framed accommodation at the University of Swansea, Wales.

Above: Tests at the Building Research Establishment in the UK demonstrated that tall timber-framed structures could withstand fire.

By using fire-resistant plasterboard and fibre-cement sheet between the new and adjacent construction, the architects were able to show that their building would satisfy the fire and acoustic requirements of the Australian building code.

Fire is a particular issue in parts of Australia because of the danger of bush fires. However, research by the Commonwealth Scientific and Industrial Research Organisation (CSIRO), the country's chief research organization, has shown that the effects of the fires are relatively misunderstood. A very small proportion of building damage occurs through 'flashover' in the midst of a raging inferno. Much more happens up to several hours later, especially if a house is unoccupied, as a result of the falling and accumulation of wind-borne burning debris. CSIRO has therefore developed a series of recommendations, such as avoiding the use of re-entrant corners on the plan and ensuring that windows can keep out debris. It cautions against the use of external timber decks; and recommends that external timber doors should have metal kick plates so that any build-up of smouldering debris will be against metal rather than wood. With precautions such as these, there is no reason why the overall construction should not be in timber.

As with so many other issues, satisfactory fire resistance can be achieved with the proper detailing and execution of a building. Concern about fire is certainly no reason to rule out the use of timber.

In the City

So, timber ticks all the right boxes environmentally, and it can stand up to fire, but there may be doubts about how appropriate its use is in an urban situation. This is the flip side of its inherent appeal as a material for holiday homes, in the country and by the sea. It may look great in its flip-flops and sun hat, but can it wear pinstripes with conviction?

The answer is yes, because so many different types of timber housing are possible today. And while there is great concern about re-creating density in cities, this is no longer accompanied by an evangelical belief in the importance of high-rise construction. The recent research into medium-rise timber construction, as described above, increases the material's potential for use in towns.

For many architects, timber's environmental credentials provide the driving force for its adoption. For example, Thomas Spiegelhalter Studio used timber extensively to build solar-powered housing, first in Freiburg, Germany, and later at Ihringen (see page 16). More recently, in 2005, as part of research at the University of South Carolina, where he teaches, Spiegelhalter was constructing fast-build experimental multistorey timber housing in Los Angeles.

Similarly, in the United Kingdom Bill Dunster designed BedZed, the embodiment of his environmental principles, just outside Croydon using timber as the main structural material (see page 17). Although subsequent analyses showed some flaws in the realization of the project, it won numerous prizes and helped to shift perceptions. An approach that had previously appeared to be the result of fringe enthusiasm could be accepted as a mainstream way of tackling concerns about sustainability. And BedZed, as part of an unromantically urban area that is included in the sprawl of south London, is certainly no rustic retreat.

It is not just proselytizing environmentalists who see timber as a reasonable material to use in cities. During a talk at London's Tate Modern in summer 2005 Jacques Herzog, of the Pritzker Prize-winning practice Herzog & de Meuron, condemned the paucity of talent evident in much United States architecture today. But, he said, 'America has all those small wooden houses which are OK.'

In many cities of the world timber is a traditional material for houses. Now that we no longer subscribe rigidly to a Modernist agenda that decrees that all reference to the past is anathema, putting new timber houses against these existing ones can be seen as appropriate, without the need for pastiche.

Above: Hayball Leonard Stent Pty Ltd Architects used sprinklers and rigid compartmentalization to meet regulations when it put a lightweight timber extension on top of two existing buildings in Melbourne.

A Timber Aesthetic?

What should a twenty-first-century wood house look like? This is a question without meaning. Architects have to deal with the individual aspirations of clients, and also with issues of context and availability of materials. Some timber houses will have been designed from a deep-seated belief that wood is the only material to use. In other cases, the decision to choose it will have evolved alongside the design. There are houses built by people who have cut down their own trees and created every element themselves, including timber pegs to hold the structural elements together. There are others that use extensive prefabrication and sophisticated manufacturing techniques, and where timber is only a part of an extensive palette of materials.

In an age where we fear homogeneity, imposed by the influence of multinational companies, we should celebrate diversity and regional variation. And timber certainly lends itself to this, with different species of tree prospering in different environments, and with no two pieces of wood being identical.

This is not a pattern book for designing houses in wood. And beyond their shared use of a single, if diverse, material many of the buildings have little in common with each other. But, as some of the best recent exemplars of wood houses, the projects illustrated here provide a celebration of what can be done with something that, while undeniably traditional, is also beginning to seem increasingly modern. Using a material that gives so much instinctive pleasure through touch, vision and smell, the houses were designed to provide pleasure to their occupiers, to visitors and to passers-by. And, I hope, now to the readers of this book.

Above: Thomas Spiegelhalter Studio pioneered new forms of environmentally friendly timber housing with its solar-powered homes at Ihringen, Germany, in 1999.

Opposite: Bill Dunster's award-winning BedZed housing scheme (2001) in the London suburb of Croydon showed that environmental responsibility could be part of the mainstream, and that timber is at home in towns.

MARKETING SUI

If you want to escape city life – to get away from it all whether for a short break, a holiday, a weekend or possibly for ever, a wood house seems to push all the right buttons. No matter how contemporary its design and up to date its construction, it has enough links with the concept of 'natural' materials and with tradition to feel romantically right. And if it is actually in woods, then so much the better.

Its appeal is even enshrined in song. Line Renaud's *Ma cabane au Canada* is a deliciously romantic evocation of a woman retiring with her lover to a cabin in the woods, with squirrels on the doorstep and heavy winter snowfalls. It finishes:

> A quoi bon chercher ailleurs
> Je sais bien que le bonheur
> Il est là
> Dans ma cabane au Canada
>
> (What is the point of looking elsewhere? I know that happiness is there, in my log cabin in Canada)

The architects of the houses in this section have sought to grasp some of this appeal, in buildings that make the most of their natural surroundings while still reflecting the contemporary world in the artistry and ingenuity of their designs.

Brian MacKay-Lyons' houses (see page 20) are distinctively Canadian, although something more than cabins. And they draw not so much on the country's forestry tradition as on the history of boat-building in his native Nova Scotia, a history that means skills in working wood are prevalent. MacKay-Lyons has developed a distinctively local sensibility and built his houses in places with wonderful views, often of the sea. Some of his clients have been particularly rugged, welcoming the outdoors into their homes in ways that others might consider uncomfortable. But his obviously manufactured artefacts sit beautifully within the landscapes, allowing the inhabitants to interact with the external world, while still maintaining a very Canadian sense of privacy.

If some of MacKay-Lyons' clients are prepared to compromise with comfort, this is even more the case when buildings are intended to be holiday homes, where the lack of comfort may often be part of the appeal. So Schmidt, Hammer & Lassen's summer house in Jutland, Denmark (see page 26) dispenses almost entirely with notions of privacy, and has everybody sleeping on shelves. But those shelves open to the outside world, bringing more advantages than disadvantages. Similarly, Saunders and Wilhelmsen have designed a holiday home that makes as much use of the outdoor space between its two volumes as it does of the interior (see page 48).

Both these projects strive for an elegant simplicity, realized superbly in a building designed by Henning Larsen near the coast of Zealand in Denmark (see opposite). This rather mysterious-looking, metal and larch box, almost transcendent in its simplicity, is that increasingly common combination – a holiday home that can double as an office.

There is more complexity in the Onominese Retreat that Betsy Williams designed with Cornelius Alig in Michigan as a lakeside holiday home (see page 30). Again this is partly used for work, with an artist's studio above the garage, and the complexity is all in the planning and not in the materials and finishes – nor in the way of life, since this house does not even have a mail delivery.

These houses all emphasize the ability to open up to nature, to make the most of a delightful but brief northern summer. But others are made of sterner stuff, and offer the pleasures of country retreats in all weathers. Balance Associates' cabin (that word again) in Washington (see page 36) is able to cope with heavy snows in winter as well as offering delightful summer living. In Sutherland, in the north of Scotland, Gokay Deveci has designed a simple cabin for the artist Lotte Glob that is framed in timber with a copper roof (see opposite). Its insulation will withstand cold winters and the structure must be able to resist winds of up to 320 kph (200 mph).

Similarly, Gisle Løkken has designed a house in Skarsfjord, Norway, that also needs to be tough despite its delicate appearance (see opposite). True, it is a holiday home; but, given that it is within the Arctic Circle, it needs to be able to cocoon its user even in the summer period. In the USA, Dan Rockhill and Associates have designed the Terrace House for a very different environment – as a series of objects miles from anywhere on the seemingly endless Kansas plains (see page 52).

None of these buildings bears any resemblance to the *dragspelhuset* (Accordion House) two Dutch architects have built in woods in Sweden (see page 42). Again largely a summer retreat, it does not in any way embrace the ideas of simplicity in design and appearance reflected in the other houses in this section. Instead, it is determinedly odd, zoomorphic and almost menacing. If you came upon this unexpectedly your thoughts might again turn to song. But this time it would not be a romantic ballad, but that children's old favourite, *The Teddy Bears' Picnic*. The song, although lighthearted, draws on our other, more atavistic feelings about woods and the houses we find within them – the stuff of mythology and fairy tales. After all, we all know that you may be able to get away from it all – but you can never get away from yourself.

Chapter 1
Retreats

Top: Gokay Deveci has designed this house for Lotte Glob to cope with the rugged climate of the north of Scotland.

Above left: Henning Larsen's transcendently simple house in Zealand, Denmark, doubles as an office.

Above right: Gisle Løkken's summer house in Norway has to protect its owner from Arctic weather.

Messenger House II

Upper Kingsbury, Nova Scotia, Canada 2003
Brian MacKay-Lyons Architect

If you want a home in a dramatic location in Canada, Brian MacKay-Lyons Architect is certainly the practice to design it. The architect, based in Halifax, Nova Scotia, understands how to create houses that are just civilized enough. Their uncompromising geometry does not compete with the natural environment but somehow is not alien to it either. MacKay-Lyons is unapologetic about employing an architecture that builds on Nova Scotia's boat-building tradition (150 years ago half of all the sailing ships in the world were built there).

Timber is also the most suitable building material for the area's climate, where there are large swings not only in temperature but also in humidity. 'Wood is the only material that has the plasticity to deal with the climate,' MacKay-Lyons says.

The fact that boats have traditionally been built up from a series of small elements gives Nova Scotia a claim, he believes, to be the inventor of the lightweight timber frame. This is a technology that MacKay-Lyons embraces as being both flexible – a few ribs can usually be knocked out without any damage – and environmental: small elements can come from rapidly grown and easily replaced timber. The other great advantage to the use of wood in Nova Scotia is that the boat-building tradition means that there are large numbers of highly skilled carpenters.

Although it is now diversifying into some larger buildings types, the practice has built its reputation on a series of timber houses that have several common themes. In addition to the use of wood, these include slightly complex entrance sequences that maintain the occupants' privacy, and what MacKay-Lyons describes as 'shrink-fit' skins.

One of the latest in the practice's portfolio is Messenger House II, an extremely clever design. Created as a retirement home for a client described as having 'high aspiration but a low budget', it has a twisted geometric form that takes best advantage of the site and the views. Instinctively, one feels there is something 'just right' about the geometry, although it is not immediately clear what. In fact, the building pulls off that magic trick of having a section and plan that are identical.

This is not just an architectural fancy, but also assists in the construction process. With light-framed wood houses, MacKay-Lyons believes that the logical construction process is to build the ground floor (in timber of course) and then use this as a working deck on which to assemble the frames, prior to tilting them into position. At Messenger House II, he says, once the deck was constructed there was 'no need for any measurement. If the frame filled the floor, it was right.'

The house sits on a glacial hill top, called a drumlin, overlooking the Nova Scotia coast. Although it looks as if it is a single monolithic volume, in fact it combines three elements. Permanent quarters are at the south-eastern end of the building with the master bedroom, unusually, on the ground floor, enjoying the best view over Gaff Point. At the other end are guest spaces and a shed. And between the two is the large space of the 'great room' plus a glazed courtyard. There is another division, with the inhabited spaces on the south-western side and the servant spaces to the north-east.

MacKay-Lyons has described Messenger House II as a development in his quest for 'plainness'. This

Far left: Horizontal steel 'columns', which are circular in section, brace the structure in the great room.

Left: Sloping walls reflect the twisted geometric form of the building.

Opposite: 'Shrink-fit' timber cladding is ideal in a climate that experiences extreme variations of temperature and humidity.

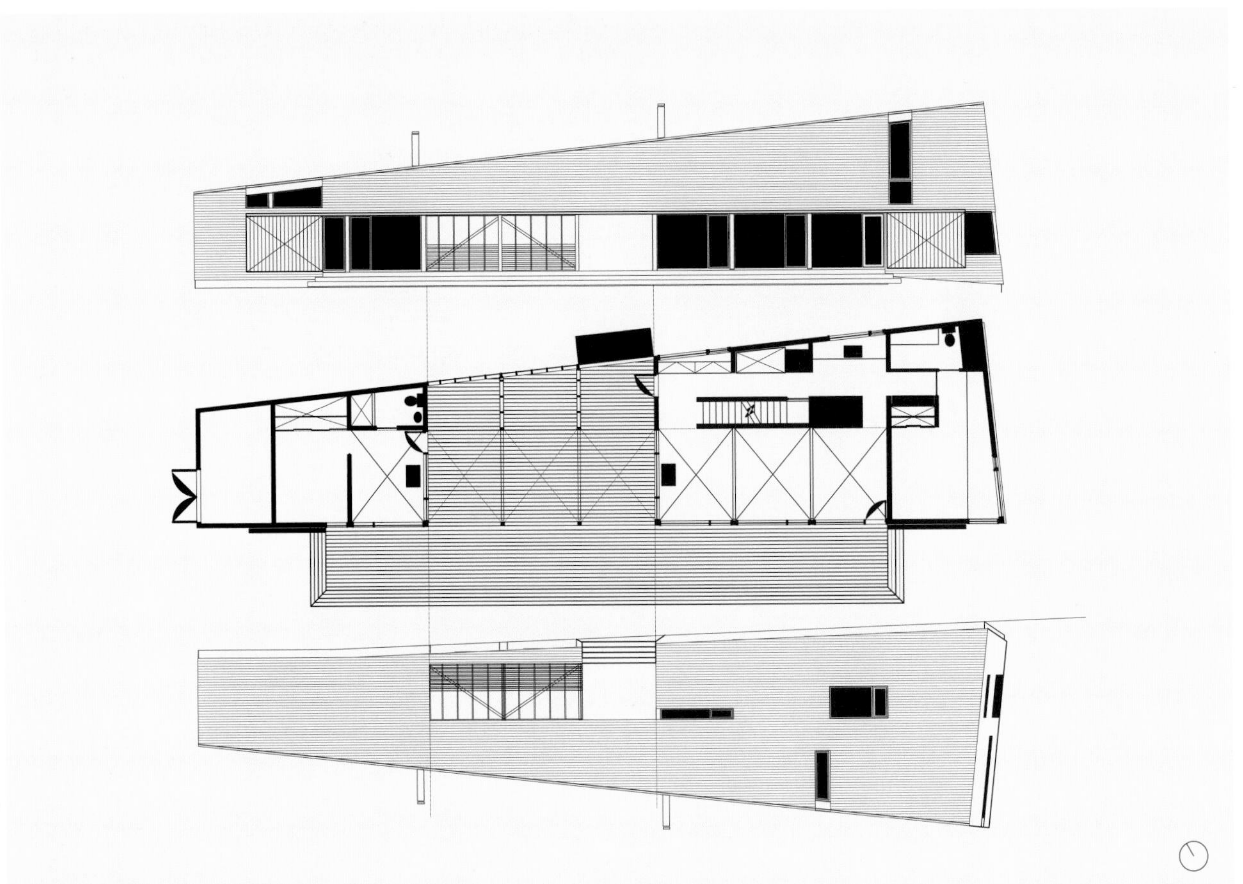

Top: By matching elevations to the plan, walls could be built on the base plate and tilted into place.

Above: The south-west façade benefits from solar gain, but barn doors can be closed over the glazing.

is expressed through the simple structural form, which also helped to make the house relatively inexpensive. It is built up around a central spine of 50-millimetre x 150-millimetre (2-inch x 6-in) timber framing at 600 millimetres (23½ inches) on centre. Cobalt blue shear walls, timber bracing and some horizontal steel columns, most evident in the open spaces, deal with the transverse wind loads. The columns are circular in section, which helps, says MacKay-Lyons, to emphasize the fact that, despite their horizontal orientation, they are columns, and not beams, dealing with direct loads.

The 'shrink-fit' effect is enhanced by the fact that the roof does not have overhanging eaves. This is counter-intuitive, MacKay-Lyons admits, but in Nova Scotia, 'if you want a building to leak you put eaves on it'. The reason is that heavy snowfalls are likely to be followed by a thaw, and then by another freeze. The result, too often, on an overhanging roof is the creation of an ice dam, with a build-up of water behind it – a sure-fire way of discovering if there is any weakness at all in the roof structure.

With the more open side of Messenger House II facing south-west, there is the opportunity to take advantage of solar gain. But, because the weather can often be fierce, barn doors can close across the glazing of the 'great room'. Otherwise, the building has a deliberately taut skin, with aluminium-framed windows, a Galvalume roof and eastern-white-cedar shingles. MacKay-Lyons has explained that he sees these as an ideal material for use in an exposed coastal environment: 'We use them like feathers on a duck – tightly spaced, woven corners, and in four layers.'

This interesting analogy should not, however, be allowed to disguise the fact that there is nothing soft and feathery about the house. It sits in its exposed location looking as if it has been there for ever, and as if its carefully crafted form is in fact the result of a battle with the elements. Boat sheds in the intertidal zone of Nova Scotia have become twisted in a similar way as they have tussled over the years with the wind and the water. This house looks like one that could not be blown away, and is poised to give as good as it gets.

Brian MacKay-Lyons had a hard time at architecture school, where his teachers believed his attachment to local traditions was at odds with the most progressive developments in international architecture. 'They called me a hick,' he says. 'But it is better to be a first-rate hick than a third-rate international architect.' Messenger House II provides further validation of his determination. If only there were more such first-rate hicks around.

Above: The south-west side of the courtyard allows views of the Nova Scotia landscape.

Above: Eastern-white-cedar shingles, ideal for exposed coastal sites, are used for the cladding.

Top: Messenger House II sits in its surroundings like a structure that has, over time, been twisted by the wind.

Above: The north-east side of the building is dedicated to servant spaces.

Summer House

Jutland, Denmark 2001
Schmidt, Hammer & Lassen

There is an odd romanticism about holidays, which means we often welcome inconveniences we would resent at home. Frequently, it is a feeling that we are playing at life – building fires, wearing very few or very old clothes – which evokes a sense of childhood innocence for adults and children alike. And one aspect of this is the idea of being tucked away to sleep, almost as if you were a doll that was being put away in a drawer.

Think of the couchettes on European trains, of those tiny Japanese hotels where people sleep in slots, of any small space with bunk beds. The idea behind these is evoked by a summer house at Juelsminde in Jutland, designed by Schmidt, Hammer & Lassen for partner Bjarne Hammer. Idyllically sited on the tip of a promontory, only minutes from beaches in two directions, this is an ideal environment for city dwellers to spend a few weeks playing at the simple life. Originally the land housed just a couple of shacks where holidaymakers, cosy in bunk beds behind flimsy walls, could feel at one with nature.

The new house, although infinitely more elegant and civilized, enshrines a lot of this simplicity. It is effectively two single-storey rectangular timber volumes, one jutting into the other, with a total area of 84 square metres (900 square feet). The larger volume contains the open-plan living space, operating as living and kitchen area. The entire long south-west façade consists of 11 glazed panels, framed in Oregon pine, that can open up entirely to the patio beyond. On the north-east side is the smaller volume, made separate by the fact that it is necessary to step up to reach it. It is lower than the larger one, so it has clerestory glazing above. Most of its length is occupied by six sleeping 'shelves', effectively three sets of bunk beds, with the rest of the space comprising a bathroom plus cupboard. Again, the outer façade is fully glazed, for maximum contact with nature, and each of the lower bunks, plus the bathroom, has a door to outside so occupants are free to go out whenever they wish.

Timber has been used extensively both inside and out, with larch slats and cladding deliberately creating the sense of a wooden casket. In contrast to the intended solidity of the sleeping structure, the ceiling to the main space is a series of slender slats running longitudinally, adding an air of refinement to the very simple space. This is accentuated by the use of pale concrete for the kitchen counters, plus a polished concrete inlay in the floor of the communal room.

The architect has described this as, 'a Nordic summer house under a deep blue sky surrounded by green foliage'. Given that this is northern Europe the deep blue sky cannot be guaranteed; but the green foliage can since this is very definitely a summer house, a place to recharge the batteries before returning to daily life. And that daily life is doubtless lived in a house with personal possessions and private space, with doors to slam or hide behind. But for those lovely weeks of carefree summer, these simple boxes in Jutland provide a wonderful way to live.

Above: Glazed panels, framed in Oregon pine, can be folded away to open the south-west façade.

Above: The simple cladding of larch slats on the exterior evokes the appearance of a wooden casket.

Opposite top and centre: Two views of the south-west façade, by day and by night, which opens onto the patio.

Opposite bottom: Plan and section showing the simple relationship between the two single-storey rectangular volumes.

Overleaf: The interiors offer basic yet evocative living conditions that bring to mind the nostalgia of childhood holidays.

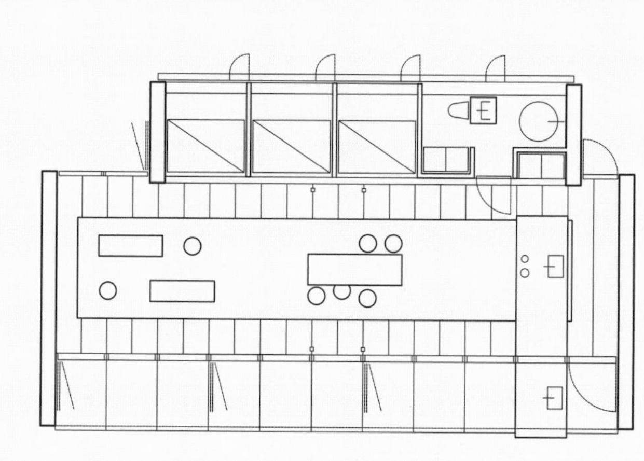

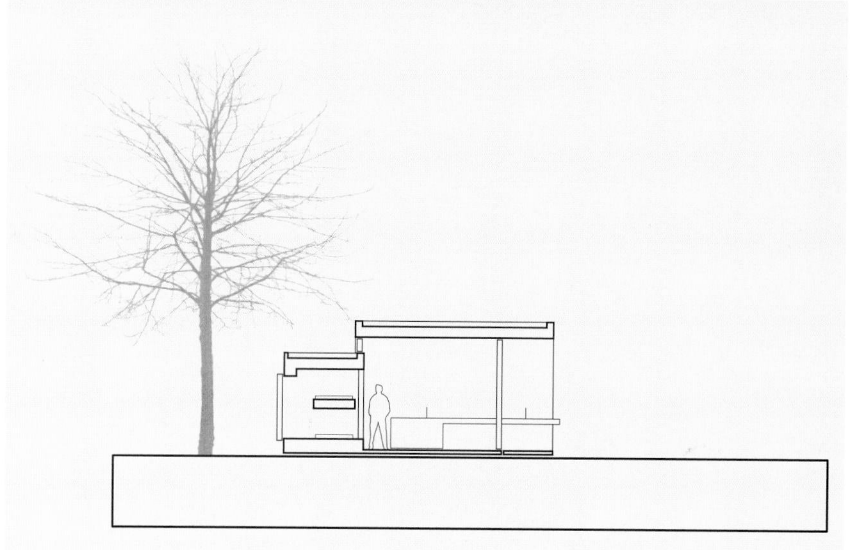

Onominese Retreat
Leelanau Peninsula,
Michigan, USA 2002
Betsy Williams with Cornelius Alig

The most challenging client for an architect must be another architect, so praise is due to Betsy Williams for not only taking on a project for an architecturally trained client, but for also turning it into a collaboration. The result, the Onominese Retreat on the Leelanau Peninsula of north-western lower Michigan, does not bear witness to a clash of egos. Instead, it shows a laudable absence of these in its creation, while providing for the very specific requirements of the client.

The couple – a developer and an artist – had been looking for a holiday home in the area for ten years when they finally found the site they had been looking for on a series of tiers above Lake Michigan. The house was placed below an existing meadow and a road, joining it to a path that winds down to the shore. Williams broke it up into three separate elements: a two-storey house with living space and children's bedrooms above; an adjoining raised 'tower' with a basement recreation room, the master bedroom and a guest bedroom; and, further away, a garage with a studio above it.

In keeping with the client's desire for simple living (no air-conditioning, no cable, no mail delivery), the building makes reference to local fishing shacks and farm buildings in terms of form and materials. Most of the structure is conventional timber framing, but with glulam beams supporting the main floor and roof. External sloping struts support the overhanging eaves.

Cedar cladding stained a blue-grey colour is used both vertically, in some cases interlocked with horizontal battens, and horizontally, giving some contrast to the otherwise inexpressive walls. The cool dark colour of the external walls also forms a counterpoint to the warmth of the fir window frames and doors, and the pine used on the undersides of the projecting roofs. Simple slats form primitive brises-soleil over the north entrance and to the loggia at the top of the tower. This lookout justifies the tower, which is a slightly surprising solution in such a rustic setting. However, it allows guests to sleep in a room that enjoys excellent views, and to extend their pleasure when they step out onto the loggia.

Internally, finishes are also simple with birch plywood ceilings and perforated birch, and cherry, cabinets. Floors are predominantly lino, but timber is used on some passageways and on the stairs.

The clients have introduced their own innovations within Williams' design, but she has given them a simple, robust background against which to work. Since energy conservation was a consideration windows are not large, so this is in no way a transparent building – indeed, it presents a slightly stern face. However, it offers plenty of external space in which to enjoy nature. It is not a house designed to dictate to a client, but one within which life can be lived in an interesting manner.

Opposite: The tower provides a guest bedroom with views of the countryside that can be further enjoyed from the loggia.

Above left: The main two-storey building contains living space on the ground floor with children's bedrooms above.

Above right: Stained cedar cladding adds interest to the exterior through varying its use, vertically and horizontally.

Above: Glulam beams support the roof and main floor, while fir is used for the window frames and doors.

Above left: The first-floor study is only partly enclosed to enhance the sense of space.

Above right: Situated above the garage and removed from the main house, the studio benefits from privacy.

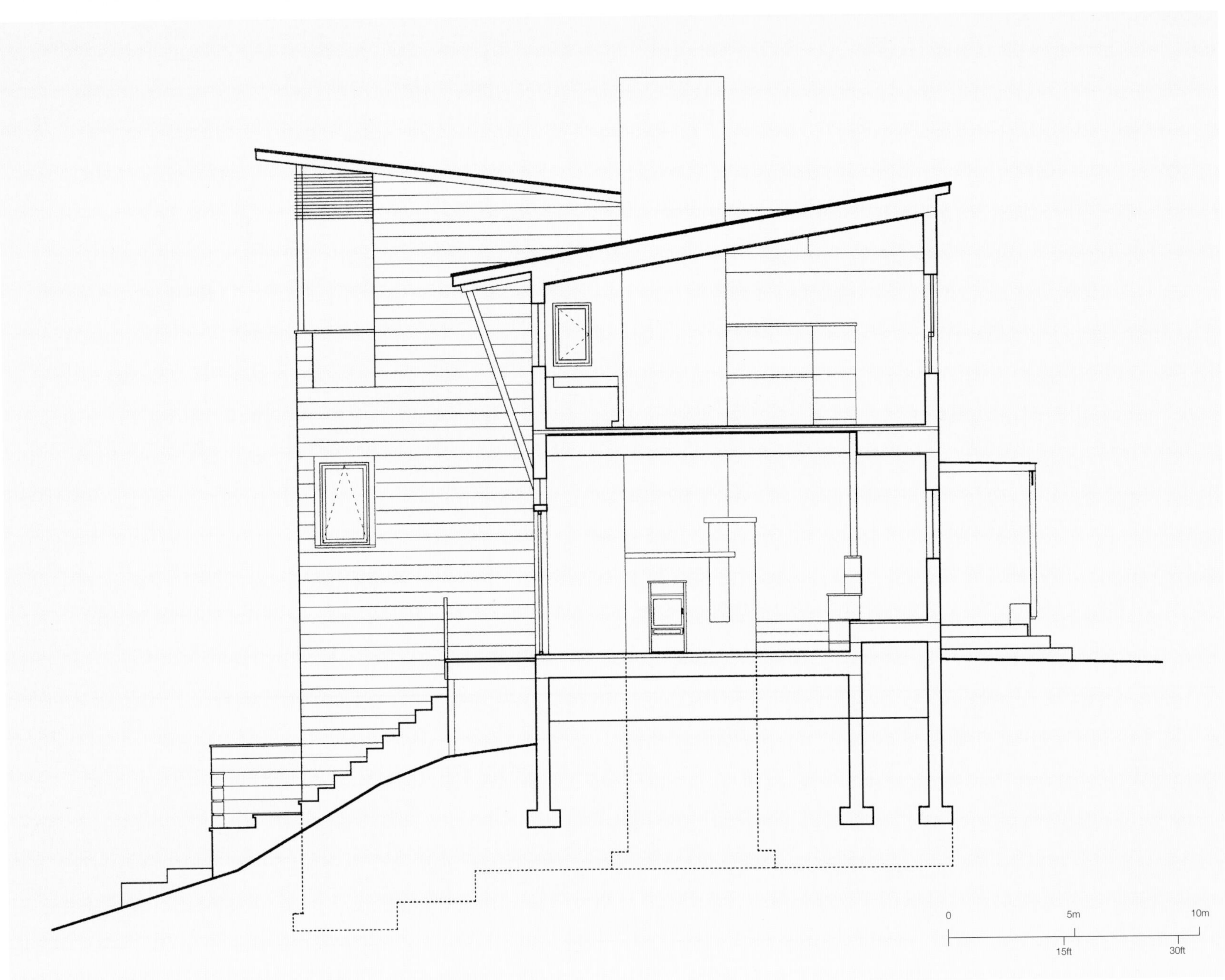

Above: A section through the main house shows the tower sited behind it.

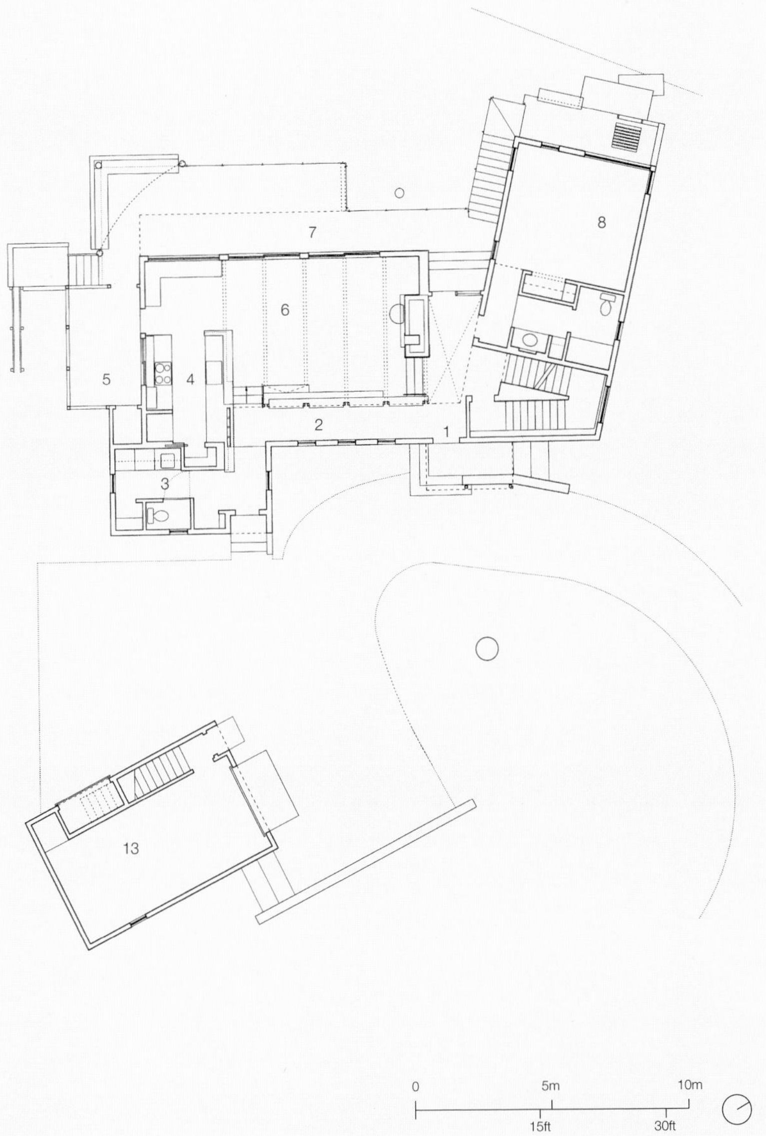

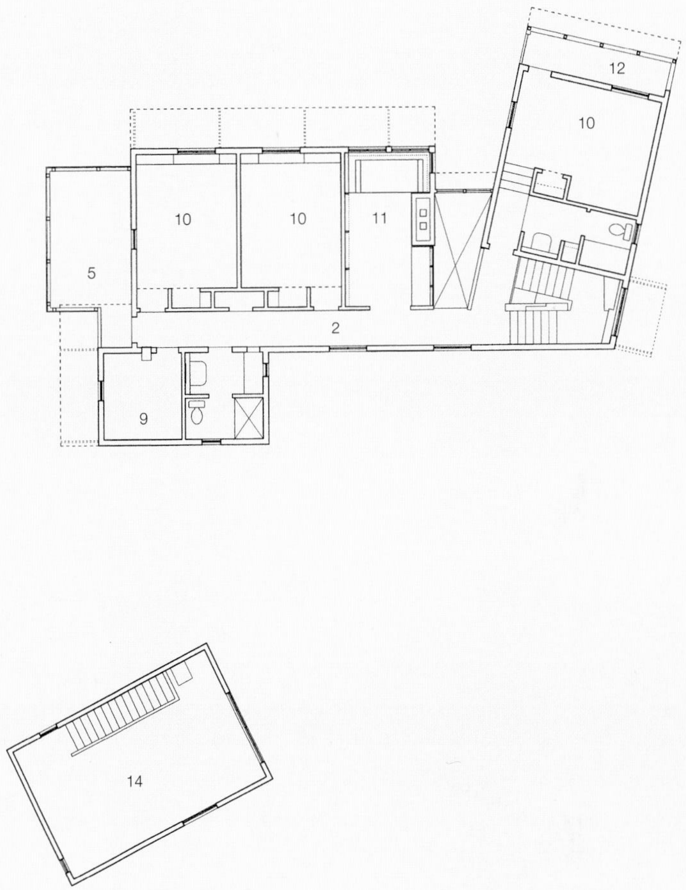

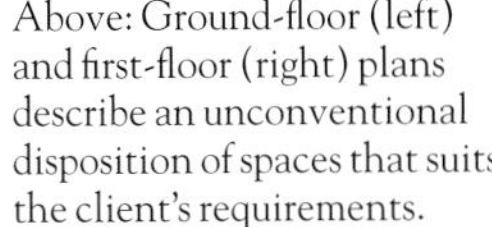

Above: Ground-floor (left) and first-floor (right) plans describe an unconventional disposition of spaces that suits the client's requirements.

1. entrance; 2. hall; 3. laundry; 4. kitchen; 5. porch; 6. living room; 7. deck; 8. master bedroom; 9. storage; 10. guest bedroom; 11. study; 12. loggia; 13. garage; 14. studio.

Cabin in the Cascades Mountains

Elbow Coulee, Washington State, USA 2001
Balance Associates

On a snowy day in the Cascades Mountains of Washington State (and there are plenty of snowy days), look in the right direction and you may see no more than two white hillocks on a hillside. These hillocks, however, are in fact the house and garage of the Cabin at Elbow Coulee, designed as a year-round retreat for a couple who love this beautiful but demanding landscape.

There are two big responsibilities when building here, on the edge of the North Cascades National Park. One is to have as little impact as possible on the natural environment. The other is to make sure the house can be lived in all year round – no small challenge when winter temperatures frequently drop to -14°C (-7°F) and summer ones can surpass 38°C (100°F). The solution that Balance Associates produced is one that satisfies the client's requirement to be in touch with the external world, and to be as environmentally responsible as possible.

The two buildings are sheltered by sloping roofs. They make use of passive solar heating for the winter, and also have a high thermal mass to damp down diurnal temperature variations – even in summer, the evening temperature can be near freezing as the site is 700 metres (2,300) feet above sea level.

The 7-hectare (17-acre) site is at the transition point between grassland steppe and ponderosa pine forest and has a stream, Thompson Creek, running along its length, roughly parallel to Elbow Coulee Road which itself runs along the lower, southern boundary. Siting the buildings so that they faced in this direction allowed glazing to face largely south and east to make the most of the sun's heat, with the insulated roofs, further insulated with snow in winter, providing thermal protection from the cold and sunless north. The architect also chose a position 60 metres (200 feet) from the stream, where there would be minimal impact upon it, and where it would not be necessary to cut down trees.

Because the buildings sit on a slope, it made sense to create the house on two levels. The design therefore incorporates two retaining walls. The first supports an external cantilevered deck and the open-plan area for living, cooking and eating. At the back of this space is another concrete retaining wall, supporting bedrooms, a bathroom, and a utility room and sauna, plus smaller external areas.

Above the level of the retaining walls all construction is in wood. The design had to cope with snow loads of up to 342 kilograms per square metre (70 pounds per square foot) live load, plus wind loads and earthquake loads. Whereas the roof of the garage slopes back into the hillside, the roof of the house slopes forward, roughly parallel to the hill. The architect therefore decided to design it so that it would retain winter snow, rather than dumping it all onto the main, southern patio area.

Design of the structure was made more complex by the near-total transparency of the lower, front part of the house, particularly the southern façade which has two lift-and-glide wood-framed glazed doors, 2.5-metres (8-feet) wide. The upper, more enclosed area, coupled with the roof, therefore supplies the dimensional stability. All the exterior walls at this level are plywood shear walls. The roof, also plywood-sheathed, also acts as a shear panel.

Above left: Roundwood posts support the back of the main roof and enhance the building's rustic appearance.

Above right: Glazing allows the lower, front part of the house to be almost entirely transparent.

Above: Sitting on a slope, the house is built sensibly on two levels. The rear part has its own external space.

The structure of the roof consists of 13-centimetre (5⅛-inch) and 3-millimetre x 38-centimetre (⅛ x 15-inch) glulam beams, which are 2.5 metres (8 feet) apart. In keeping with the client's desire to use rough-seeming materials to give a rustic appearance, the purlins between the beams are 15-centimetre (6-inch) logs. These are the thinnings from lodgepole pine plantations. On the external areas the purlins are placed directly on top of the beams, but in the internal ones a space has been created for insulation. The ceiling finish is of rough-sawn plywood. Again in keeping with the rugged aesthetic, the outer roof finish is of corrugated metal.

The architect designed the gutter/snow-brake system to be as inconspicuous as possible by incorporating it within a trellis. Made from a 10- x 10-centimetre (4- x 4-inch) steel angle, it catches the meltwater and directs it to catch basins at either side of the house. Self-heating tape prevents the snow melt freezing again in the gutter.

The cladding of the house is with timber that was salvaged from a drainage ditch. As well as having excellent environmental credentials, this means it has already weathered over a period of about 60 years, and therefore that its appearance in future will be stable. Having been cleaned and sealed, it should need little further maintenance.

In contrast to the relatively rough appearance of the main structural components, there is considerable elegance to the framing of the glazing which was done with carefully selected oak strips. Because of the remoteness of the house and the large size of some of the elements, these were manufactured on site.

Other elegant internal fixtures, such as the stairs, also make use of manufactured wood, in this case Parallam, a trade name for PSL (parallel strand lumber). While this may seem to contrast with the rough-hewn aesthetic, it fits with the client's environmental philosophy since elements such as this, and the glulam that has been widely used, make use of relatively small timber components. They therefore use wood more efficiently, and preclude the need to cut down mature trees.

Exposed-concrete floors and the exposed surfaces of the rough-cast concrete retaining walls add to the thermal mass of the building, and so help to reduce the total heating load. The overall effect is of a building that it must be a joy to occupy. Externally it is a little awkward, particularly in the roundwood supports for the back of the main roof, but it achieves its aim of having a minimal impact on the environment. In winter, at least, it virtually disappears into it.

Above: In summer the open façades to the south and east of the building link it to the external environment.

Above: The framing to the glazing provides an elegant counterpoint to the rough-hewn exterior.

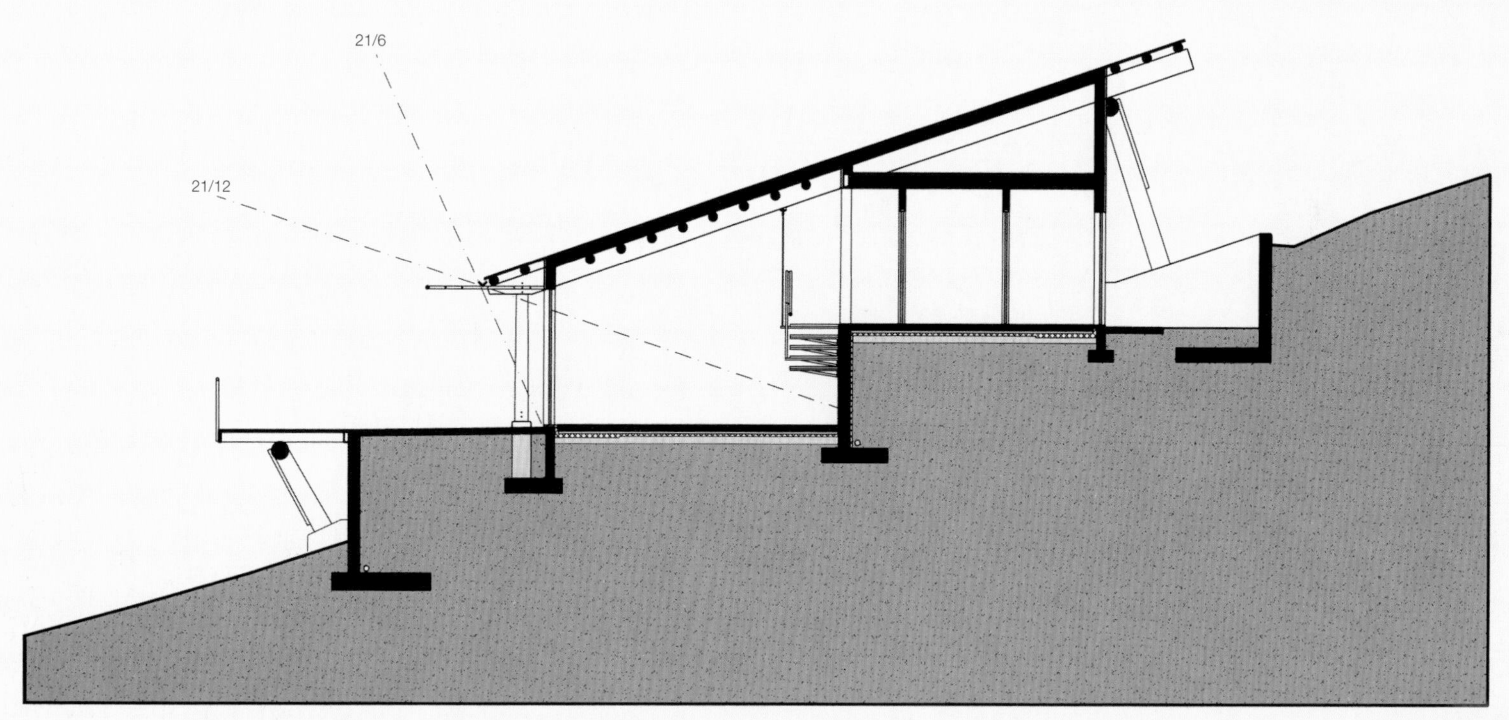

Above: The sun's angle at midsummer and midwinter shows the front space shaded in summer but sunny in winter.

Above: In winter the house and the garage, seen in the foreground, blend into the landscape.

Accordion House

Årjängs Commun,
Värmland, Sweden 2004
24H> architecture

If you have ever worried that woods could contain unaccountable, menacing creatures, you should steer well clear of Lake Övre Gla in Sweden at dusk – at least unless you are aware of what has been built there. The 'dragspelhuset' (Swedish for 'accordion house' because it can become bigger and smaller), designed by two young Dutch architects, is one of the most zoomorphic buildings in existence. With the lights on inside, this scaly creature, reminiscent of a pangolin, looms out of the gloom with its giant glowing eye, and a slightly comical horn that suggests it may have some rhinoceros in its ancestry.

In fact it is just a house and is entirely unthreatening. But it has a pedigree as curious as its appearance – it is a house by architects keen to use local materials and technology, yet who acknowledge both Frank Gehry and Sweden's ice hotel as influences. The duo, Maartje Lammers and Boris Zeisser, now run a practice in the Netherlands called 24H> architecture, but have previously worked for Koolhaas and Mecanoo. Their projects for other clients range from urban planning to retail interiors and hotel receptions, and their interests include buildings whose functions can change, sometimes within the course of a single day. In an oblique manner, this thinking also affects their rustic retreat.

The starting point for the project was a nineteenth-century fisherman's cabin on the shores of the lake, in the Glaskogen nature reserve. Lammers and Zeisser kept this hut virtually unchanged, just insulating it and taking out elements like an unworkable kitchen. It then became the sleeping quarters for their new enterprise, painted a deliberately dark blue to encourage their young daughter to go to sleep on the light Swedish summer nights.

Alongside the cabin they constructed their extendible extension, a form that can never have appeared in those woods before, yet one that is intended to blend in with the surroundings and partially disappear in summer. Built with a curved frame made from local, rotproof timber, the new part of the house can extend in summer to increase its area from 54 to 72 square metres (580 to 775 square feet). The extendible section, which contains most of the windows, is moved in and out in an appropriately low-tech manner – using a system of ropes and pulleys. When extended, it cantilevers out over a stream. This extension area contains a stove, and seating fitted into permanent slots in the floor. Further back, in the permanent part of the building, are the kitchen and dining areas.

Above left: Whimsical lighting introduces a deliberate note of incongruity to the rustic setting.

Above right: The extendible 'head' of the building, moved using ropes and pulleys, cantilevers over a stream.

Above: The zoomorphic *dragspelhuset* is an extension to the cabin and intended to blend in with the woodland.

Above: Reindeer skins line the curved frame of the extendible section. Furniture is fixed into slots on the floor.

The permanent section is lined with slender timber laths that run along the length of the structure, with some unevenness as the laths have to find their way around the complex curves. The extension, in contrast, is lined with reindeer skins, a concept that Lammers and Zeisser adopted from Sweden's far chillier ice hotel. Another distinction between the two sections is that the direction of the floor planks changes from lengthways to crossways at the junction.

With the fur on the inside, what goes on the outside of this creature? It is clad in timber shingles that run roughly horizontally, but bunch and hump over the building's contours, also changing in size. In this case the architects were determined not to use local materials. Shingles cut from Swedish timber are relatively soft and require painting every year if they are to endure. This is not an ideal solution either for architects enamoured of the idea of expressing the nature of their materials, or indeed for occasional visitors. So instead they specified red cedar shingles from Canada, which can deal with exposure without the need to paint. But it is interesting to see that within a couple of years a colour contrast began to emerge between the shingles on the main part of the new building, which are exposed all year round, and those on the extension, which is retracted, hence protecting them, in the winter.

First appearances may emphasize staying in touch with the natural world, evidenced by the rough nature of the cladding and the construction, some way from the house, of a uteda, a traditional, primitive Swedish privy. This is, after all, an area that is attracting large numbers of Dutch and Germans from their crowded towns and overworked landscapes, to enjoy the pleasures of a relatively untouched environment. But the choice of Canadian shingles is just one example of the presence of a more sophisticated architectural intelligence at work.

The form of the building may seem almost random, but it is, in fact, very carefully thought out to allow one part to nest within another, and to ensure that connections between sections are not blocked when the extension is retracted. And internally, among all the wood and the skins, there is some rather whimsical lighting by Ingo Maurer and also by Eelco Baststra, a Dutch designer who finds much of his work in the glitzy environment of cruise ships. This is certainly not the source one would expect for accessories in a domestic Swedish cabin; but the architects enjoy this manner of confounding expectations in their paid work, and are not likely to turn their backs on it altogether even when relaxing in the woods.

Above left: Providing superb views over Lake Övre Gla, most of the windows are sited in the extendable section.

Above right: The irregularity of the building's form partly camouflages it among surrounding trees.

Overleaf: Plans and sections of the house show it in both its retracted and extended state.

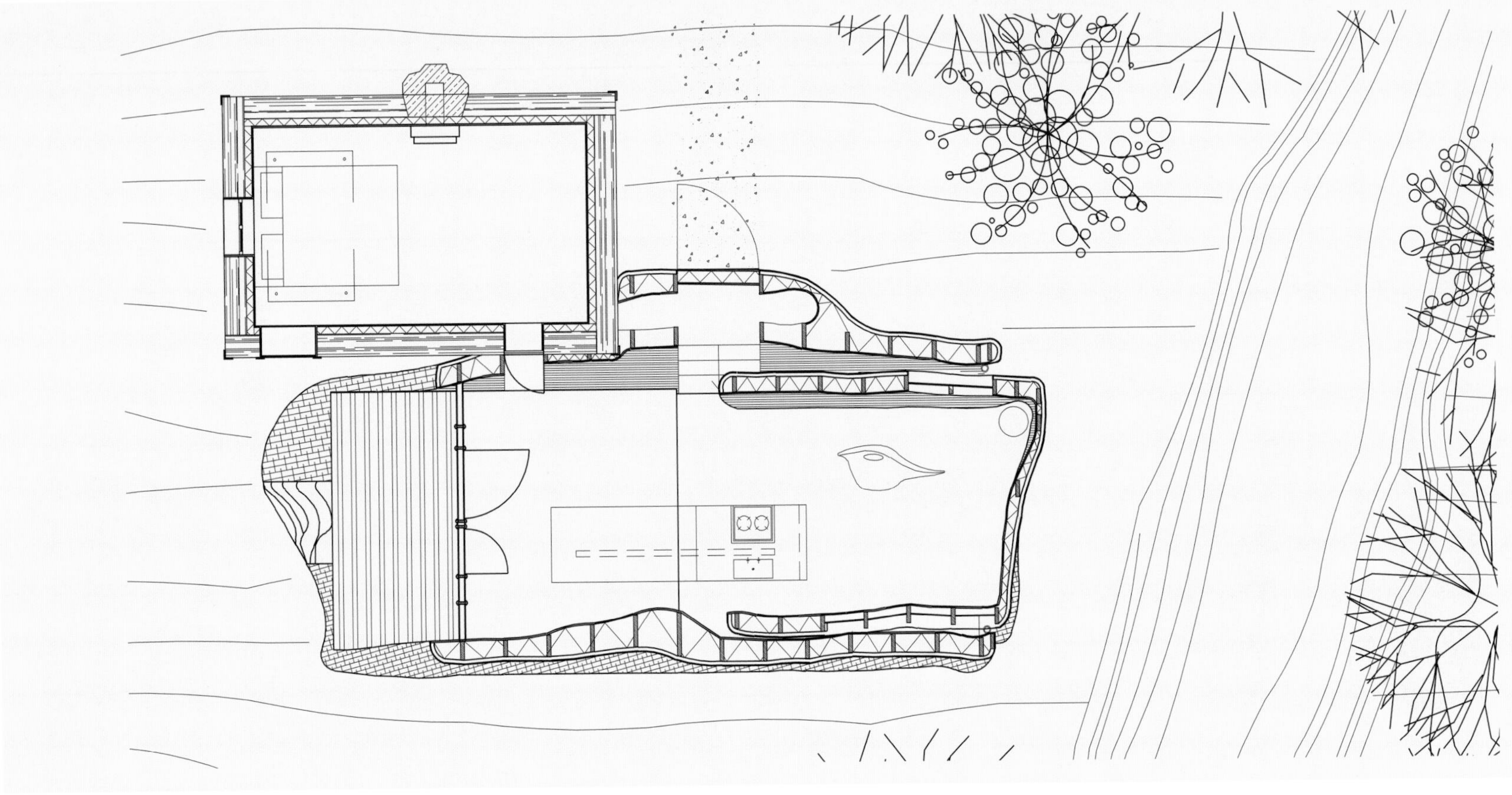

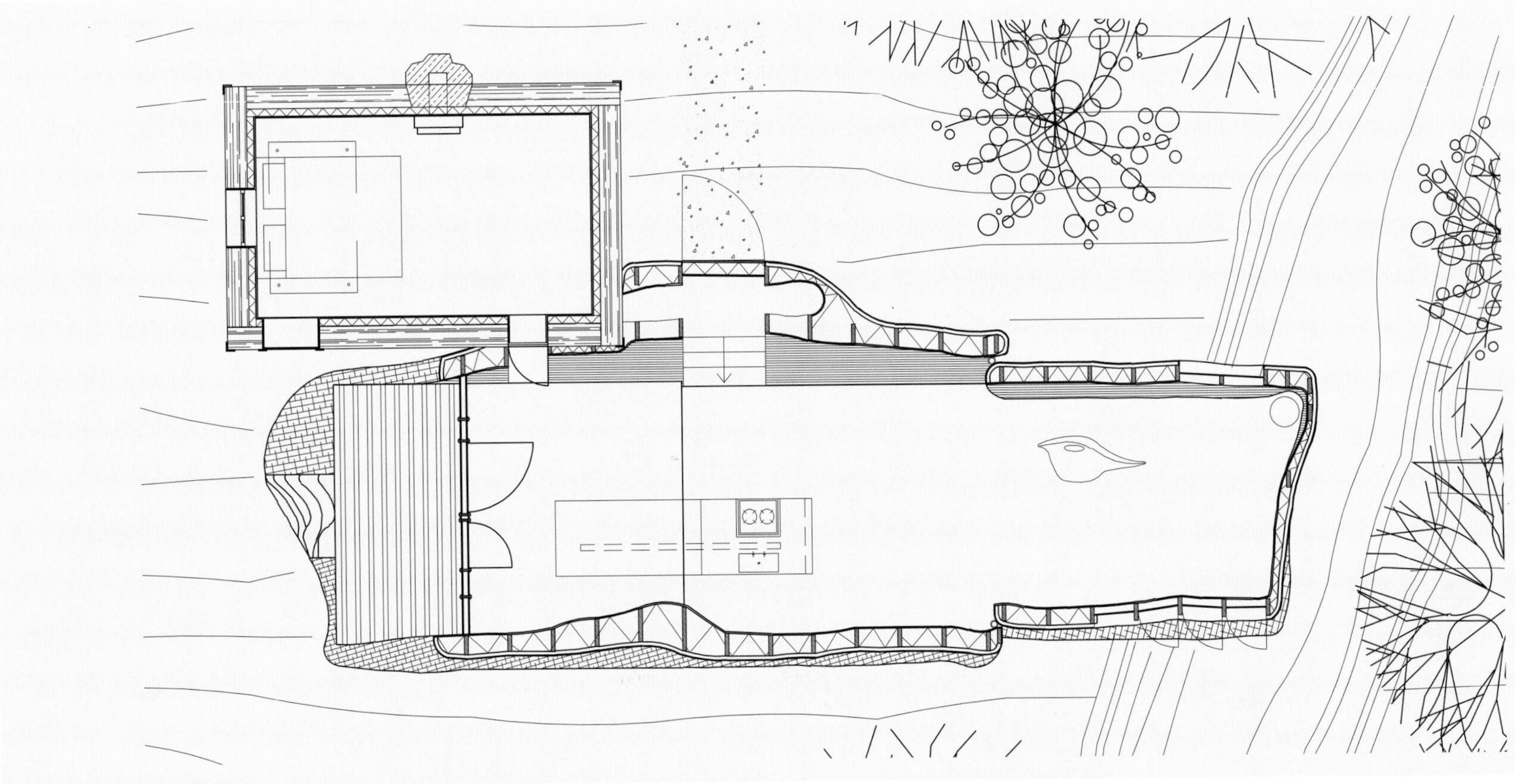

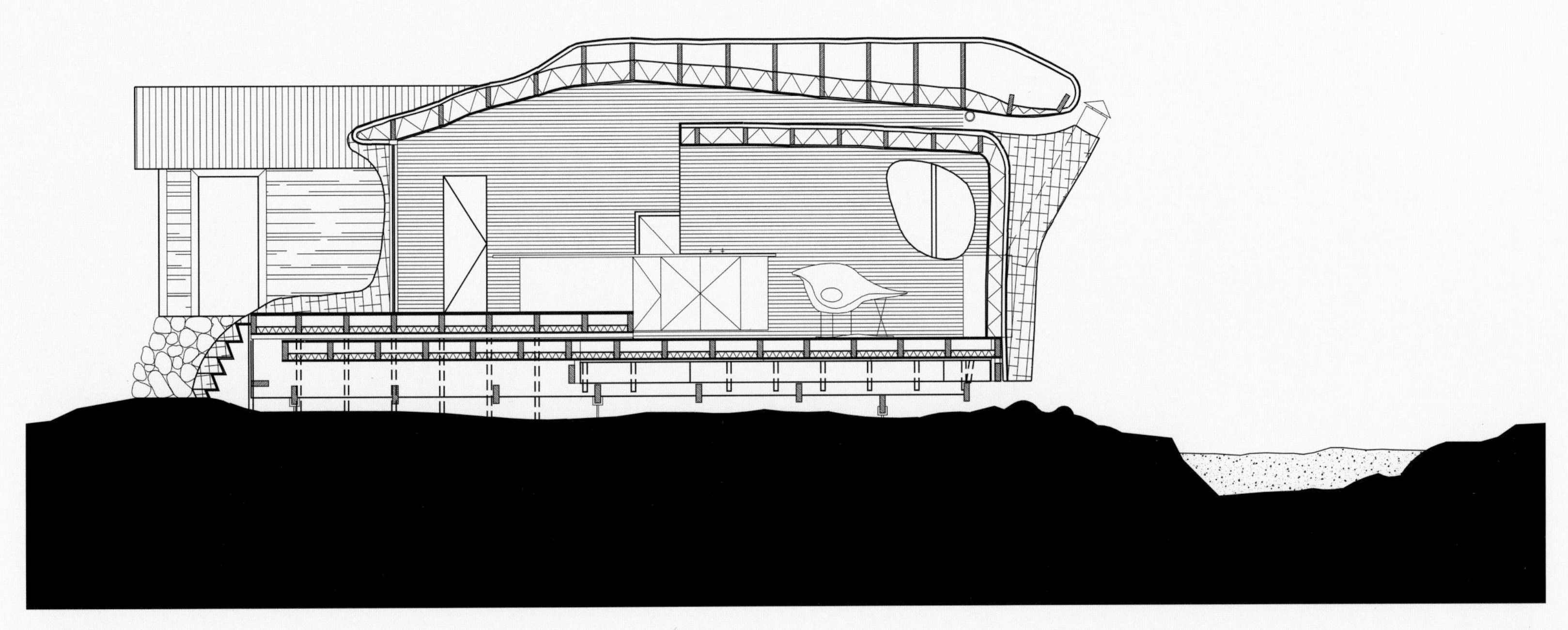

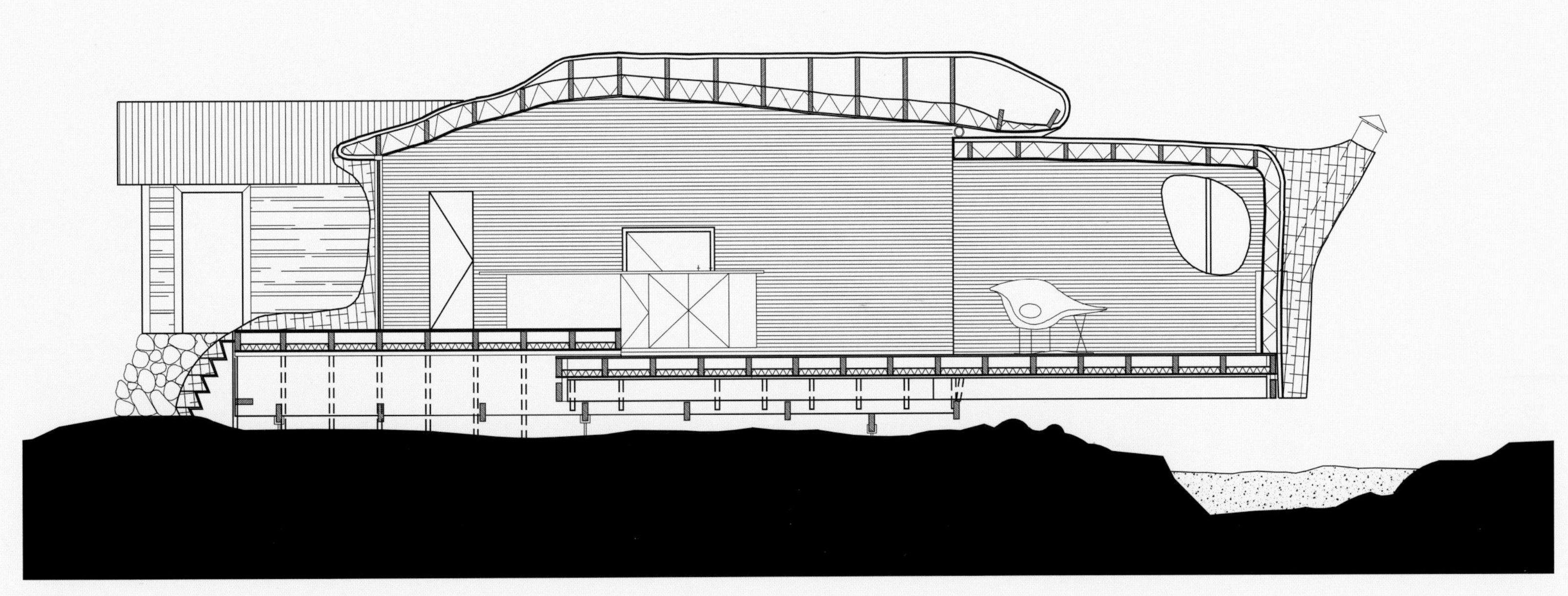

Summer House
Åland, Finland 2002
Saunders and Wilhelmsen

The concept of a summer house in northern European woods can seem so simple and natural that one might think it happened almost without thought, just arising from a local tradition of building with wood. So it is a little surprising to learn that such a house, in a pine forest on one of Finland's Åland Islands, was designed by two young architects based in Norway, one of whom is originally Canadian and the other of whom gained much of his experience in Germany.

But look again and it becomes clear that this is not the simplicity that comes from knowing nothing else. It is a simplicity that grows from a distillation of ideas, a deliberate choice rather than an absence of choice. And it is none the worse for that.

Saunders and Wilhelmsen consists of Todd Saunders, an architect and environmental planner from Canada, and Norwegian Tommie Wilhelmsen, who spent several years in Frankfurt with Behnisch, Behnisch and Partner. The two set up in practice in Bergen, Norway, at the start of the century when they were just a couple of years on either side of 30, and immediately began work on a rash of projects, many of them self-generated.

Although officially in Finland, the Åland Islands are easily accessible from Stockholm in Sweden, and are largely Swedish speaking. They are also self-governing, with their own stamps. This seems just the right environment for the cross-cultural partnership of Saunders and Wilhelmsen to build their first building in – and 'build' is the correct term, since one of the duo's beliefs is in the importance of taking part in the construction process. In this case, they worked with four of their students from Bergen University's school of architecture.

The house, set only 40 metres (44 yards) from the sea, is effectively a pair of boxes, but these are united by sitting on a common timber platform that

Above: Believing in taking part in building their designs, the architects were closely involved in the construction process.

creates an open dining space between the two elements. This effectively doubles the area of 42 square metres (450 square feet). In fact, the architects envisaged the whole as a continuous long folding wooden structure that creates the enclosures, the deck and even a roof garden.

The pine for its structure comes from a local sawmill, and is clad with birch boards on top of birch ply. A much finer treatment is used for the façades than for the enclosing 'boxes' with their rounded corners, producing the impression of a manufactured artefact as much as a house. One of the boxes contains sleeping accommodation, the other a kitchen – this is relatively simple rustic living, not a sophisticated retreat. And each has a staircase, allowing access to the roof which gives magnificent views in this predominantly flat and watery environment.

The practice is committed to the idea of environmental building. Insulation is with linseed fibres, and the external timbers are treated with linseed oil – no alien chemicals here. The house is raised on pilotis, to ensure as little interference with tree roots as possible.

Although it sits so well in the northern European tradition of summer escapes in woodland, the house has a degree of thinking behind it that makes it unsurprising that another of the practice's declared commitments is to experimental design. Saunders and Wilhelmsen are working on other summer homes, but also on changing people's attitudes to student housing. The fruit of cross-cultural thinking, the summer house at Åland may one day be seen not just as an appealing object in the landscape, but also as the starting point of an interesting and complex oeuvre.

Above left: The façades of the pair of boxy forms give the impression of a manufactured artefact.

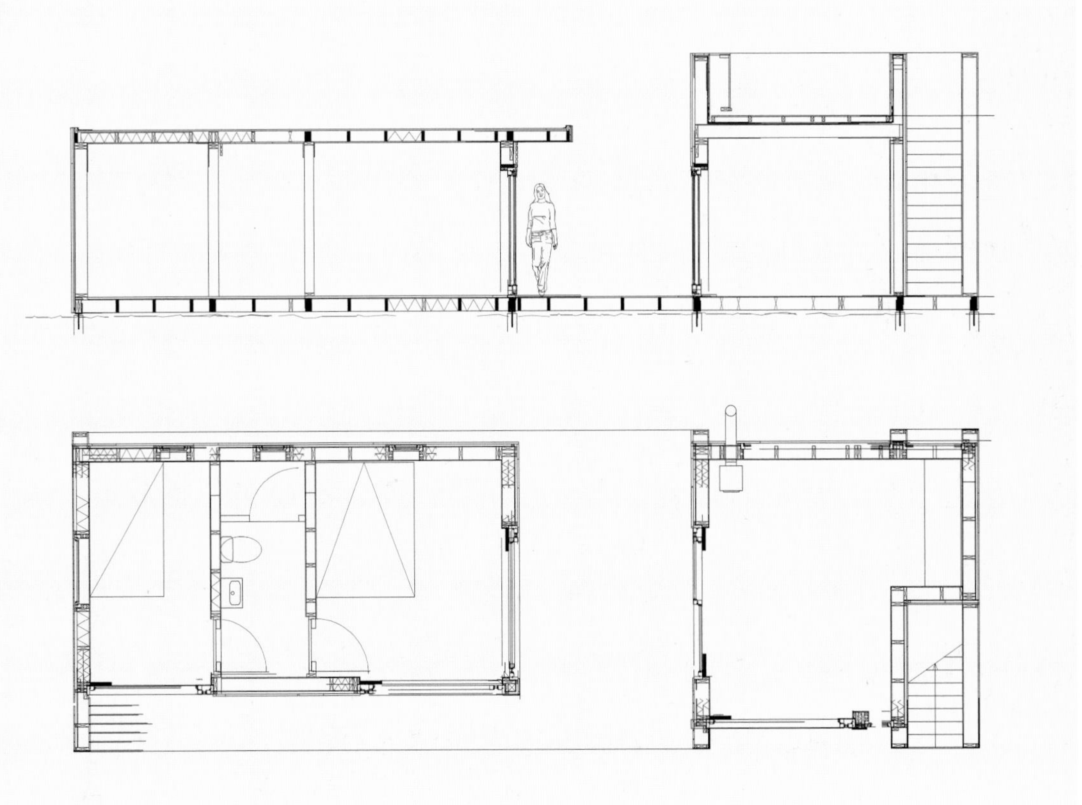

Above right: Section (top) and plan of the house – the space between the two elements forms an outdoor room.

Top and above: The house is intended as a summer residence but its simple forms sit well in the winter landscape.

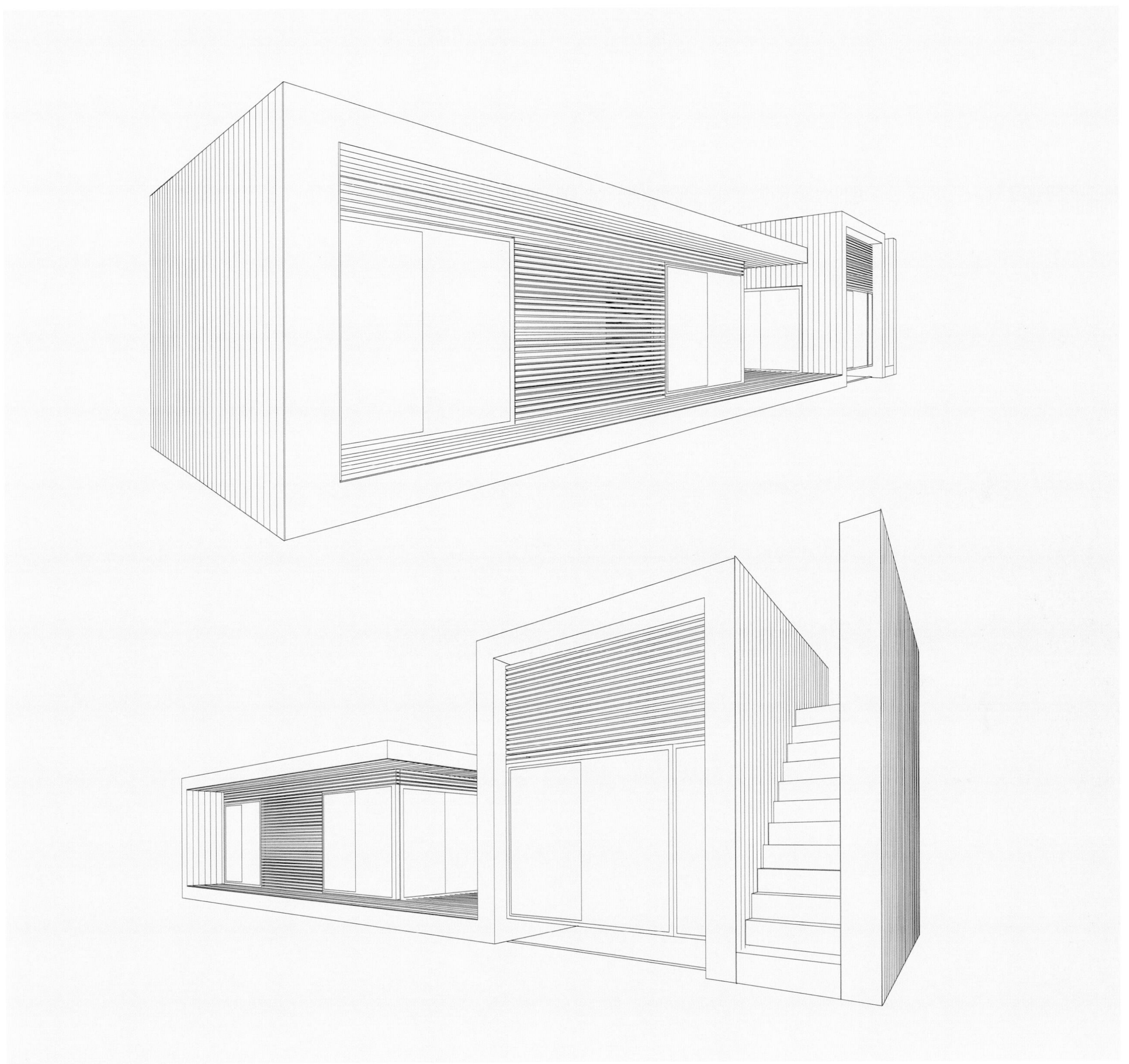

Above: Visuals emphasize the contrast between the coarser elements and the finer treatment used for the façades.

Terrace House

Baldwin, Kansas, USA 2002
Dan Rockhill and Associates

Set on the seemingly endless flat plains near Baldwin in east Kansas, Terrace House, designed by Dan Rockhill and Associates, belies its name and in fact consists of three linked buildings in a compound. There are two horizontal structures, one containing an office and a master bedroom, and the other a bedroom for teenage children. Between them is a tower, 10.6 metres (35 feet) tall, which draws on the vernacular buildings of the Pawnee Indians. Unusual among the plains Indians for the fact that they lived in permanent settlements, the Pawnee built large oval lodges that housed between 30 and 50 people. These were constructed from posts, willow branches, grass and earth.

This version is evidently more modest in scale, and slicker in design, but it keeps to the idea of timber construction, using massive Douglas fir posts to support it. And, like the Pawnee structures, it is lit from above, with a massive skylight. This provides a dramatic environment in which all the communal activities of the house take place. The exterior of the tower is clad in slate.

Overall, the effect of the building is of a campus of three unusual but very deliberate structures, sitting strongly on the prairie landscape. Those who do not grasp the allusions to Native American buildings may well think of the language of grain elevators.

There are almost no right angles in the project, making for interesting interior spaces but also proving a challenge to build. And for Rockhill this was not a challenge that he would pass on to a contractor. Most unusually today, his practice not only designs but also carries out all its own building work, rooting itself strongly in the materiality of what it designs.

Although most projects are relatively modest, and are within Rockhill's adopted state (he used to teach in upstate New York), their commitment to their environment coupled with a determination to have an entirely contemporary approach, are giving his work a significance that extends well beyond his geographic limitations.

Above: The house forms an interesting collection of objects on the featureless prairie of eastern Kansas.

Opposite top: The central tower derives from the communal buildings of the Pawnee Indians.

Opposite bottom left: Translucent materials are used wherever possible to maximize the amount of light in the building.

Opposite bottom right: A complex structure of Douglas fir supports the tower, which has a skylight at the top.

Opposite: All communal activities take place in the tower building.

Above left: Framing with Douglas fir is also used elsewhere in the complex.

Above right: Geometry is complex enough that it gives an initial impression of randomness.

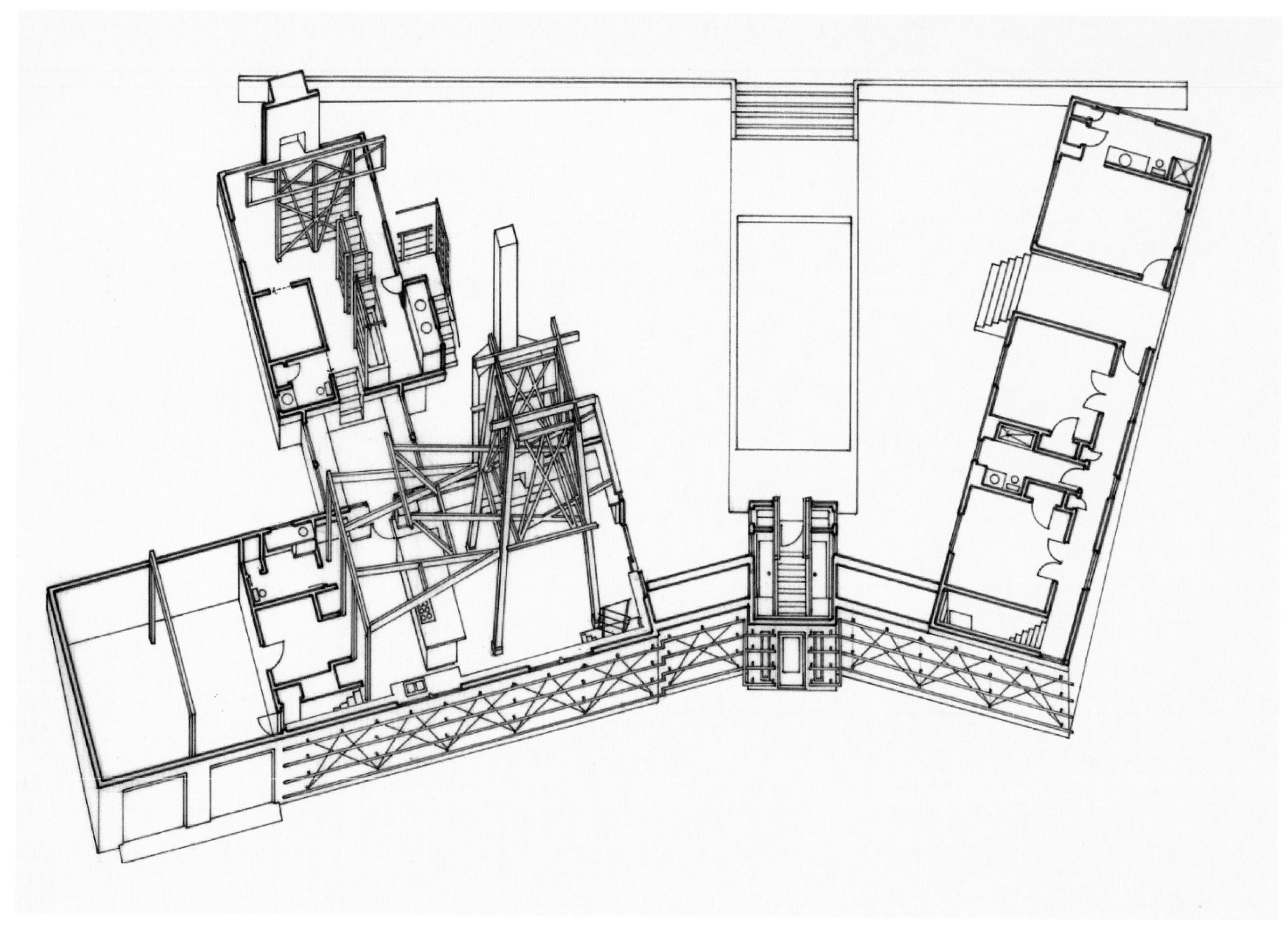

Above: Three disparate elements combine to form the 'campus' of the house.

Opposite: Construction is deliberately massive, with all elements expressed clearly.

We all know that a high-quality diamond does not need an elaborate setting, and, similarly, the beautiful surfaces of timber can benefit from being used with the utmost simplicity. In some cases this can come from imitating agricultural buildings as, for instance, English architect James Gorst has done with his house at Whithurst Park in West Sussex (see page 70), which makes reference to the English hay barn. But Gorst himself has shown, in another project, that this simplicity does not have to make such an explicitly agricultural reference. At Wakelins in Suffolk he has refurbished a fifteenth-century house but also given it a strikingly modern addition (see opposite). This, clad in European oak boarding, shows how flush windows and simple cutaway corners serve to emphasize the pleasure that one takes in the properties of the materials.

Brückner & Brückner used a similar simplicity for the house it designed at Bärnau, Oberpfalz, in Germany (see page 66). Again, the form is as simple as possible, with larch rather than oak cladding playing the starring role. This house shuts up almost completely, allowing one to appreciate a sculptural object of timber and a contrasting slab of granite.

A similar impression of a simple box with entirely flush glazing is created in a very elegant building in Seekirchen near Salzburg, Austria, designed by Johannes Ebner and Franz Grömer (see opposite). Clad in unsawn vertical strips of larch, it exhibits one of the paradoxes of houses of this type. Despite its relatively closed appearance from outside, from the interior the existence of glazing pushed right out to the outer edge of the skin gives the inhabitants an extraordinary feeling of freedom, of being in touch with the external world.

The Maison Goulet in Canada (see page 60) exhibits the kind of willed austerity so often found in architects' own houses, where there is no need to compromise with the sentimental wishes of clients. Here the simplicity lies above all in the extensive use of plywood for the interior, a material that many see as either temporary or cheap, but which has its own stark beauty when detailed with care and a good eye.

At the Bunch Residence in California (see page 74) the simplicity is more in the boldness of the concept and the external appearance than in the design itself, which, internally, is both rich and complex. But by putting the house just below the only level part of the site, the architect has allowed it to be a hidden gem. Its relatively small and very simple public façade allows visitors the maximum degree of surprise and delight when they actually penetrate the building.

All these houses, though, with their plumbing and heating and electricity, are more sophisticated than that children's favourite, the tree house. At a time when we are all keen to 'get in touch with our inner child' this form is becoming popular as a leisure indulgence for adults, either publicly provided or as the private plaything of the rich. An excellent example is the tree house in Tuscany (see page 78), designed by one (former) rock musician for another.

The tree house as an indulgence is generally limited to Europe and North America, where near-universal affluence makes it seem romantic to hark back to simpler times. But there are people for whom this type of dwelling is basic to their lifestyle. For instance, photographer Roland Garve has documented the relatively elaborate tree houses that are built and occupied by the Korobai of New Guinea. These are fascinating and the way of living they reflect can be appealing. But in most of Africa life is too tough to make this kind of nostalgia attractive. So when Ethiopian architect Ahadu Abaineh designed a 'tree house' on the outskirts of Addis Ababa, it was of a very different kind (see opposite). This was not a house built in a tree, but a house built from trees. Abaineh sees growing trees as a way of both restoring the urban ecological balance and of creating inexpensive homes that do not use environmentally destructive materials. His house has a tree at each corner, with untreated timber poles forming the rest of the structure. The other materials are mud infill for the walls and an overhanging roof of corrugated metal. This not only keeps the walls dry, but also channels rain to water the trees. If the idea were widely adopted it would result in simple but civilized homes sited in groves of trees – a far cry from the kind of urban squalor to which the poor and newly arrived are too often subjected in cities across the world.

Chapter 2
Simple Houses

Top: At Wakelins in Suffolk, England, James Gorst shows that straightforward pleasure in materials can create an appealing counterpoint to an existing building.

Above left: Ahadu Abaineh's 'tree house' on the edge of Addis Ababa incorporates growing trees in the structure.

Above right: Johannes Ebner and Franz Grömer designed this house in Seekirchen, Austria to allow the occupants to feel in touch with nature.

Maison Goulet

Sainte-Marguerite-du-Lac-Masson
Quebec, Canada 2002
Saia Barbarese Topouzanov

Above: A change in level across the site made it possible to create a semi-basement studio and workshop.

When architects design homes for themselves they can bring their most uncompromising principles into play. It was fortunate, therefore, that when Mario Saia, senior partner of Montreal-based Saia Barbarese Topouzanov, chose to design a second home for himself and his wife he did so on a site that encouraged this kind of rigorous approach.

Near Entrelacs in the Laurentian Mountains north of Montreal, the site slopes downwards towards Lake Grenier in the south. With the most obvious place to build being a relatively narrow rock-shelf part-way down the site, construction of a long narrow house, facing south, became a logical solution. As a result the architect has created a building that, externally, mimics traditional construction but, internally, plays some clever spatial games.

With a total floor area of 230 square metres (2,500 square feet), the house is like a bar, more than 18 metres (60 feet) long and 5.5 metres (18 feet) deep. It is timber framed, clad with zinc and has an aluminium pitched roof. Internally, however, the dominant material is beautifully matched and crafted Douglas fir plywood.

With the entrance at the 'back' northern side of the house, there is a near-continuous wall of glazing on the southern side at ground-floor level. Windows are framed with white oak. The central, living space is double height and somewhat cathedral-like as it rises into the pitch of the roof. At the eastern end are a fireplace and chimney, dividing the living area from the kitchen. To the west there is another fireplace at the far end of the house, but before getting to this you step into a 'terrace', a single-height sitting space that seems both very open, because it is almost entirely enclosed in glazing, and yet contained because of the lower ceiling height. The effect is of being in a glazed pod projecting from the house itself, a good compromise in this cold climate between a feeling of being in touch with the beauties of nature and of being cocooned from its harsher aspects.

There is an internal rear wall in the living space, behind which are two timber staircases. One leads up to the bedrooms at the western end of the building, the other to an office at the eastern end. Unusually, there is no link between the two sets of rooms at this level, an idea that at first seems perverse until you realize the value there can be in a separation between spaces intended for repose and for work.

There is a slope across the site as well as from front to back, making it possible to insert a studio and workshop at the eastern end of the basement with their own direct access to the outside world.

The predominance of the plywood cladding creates a glowing space, but one that can occasionally trouble the eye because the surfaces have no depth. In contrast, however, large slabs of stone clad the chimneys and also form the flooring for the entire ground floor. The upper level is floored with birch. Acknowledgment of the harshness of the climate comes with the installation of a ventilation system that, in winter, circulates warm air from the ceiling to a stone base where it is converted to radiant heat. This is a house that needs to close up and protect its inhabitants when it is cold, where they can take comfort in their existence within their elegant timber box. In summer, however, it opens up to take the best advantage of its magnificent setting.

Above left: Near-continuous glazing at ground-floor level on the southern side makes the best use of sunlight.

Above right: The stone chimney is a reminder of the importance of heating in this cold climate.

Top left: Twin timber staircases lead to upper-floor spaces that are not connected to each other.

Above left: Double height and a sloping roof give a cathedral-like feel to the main living space.

Top right: Finely crafted wood walls contrast with the random stone paving covering the entire ground floor.

Above right: A small internal window on the upper level allows views of the central living space.

Top left: Even the tiling in the bathroom is in keeping with the overall colour scheme.

Above left: The kitchen is inserted behind the main fireplace that divides it from the living area.

Top right: A fireplace also creates a focal point in the first-floor study, and provides welcome warmth in winter.

Above right: Regularly framed windows echo the verticals of the trees in the surrounding landscape.

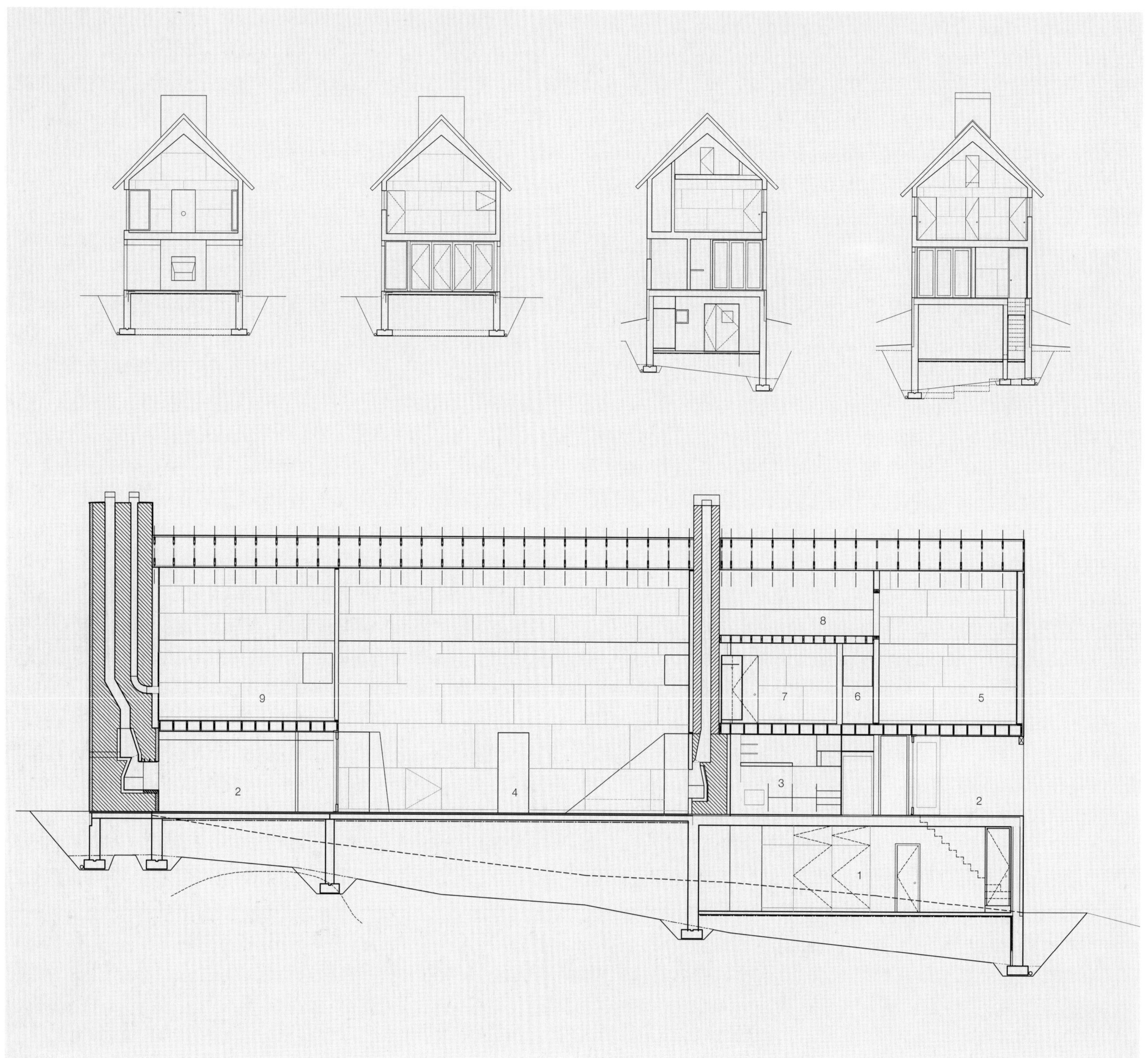

Top: Cross-sections through the two-to-three storey house.

Above: Longitudinal section. 1. workshop; 2. terrace; 3. kitchen; 4. living; 5. master bedroom; 6. bath; 7. bedroom; 8. mezzanine; 9. study.

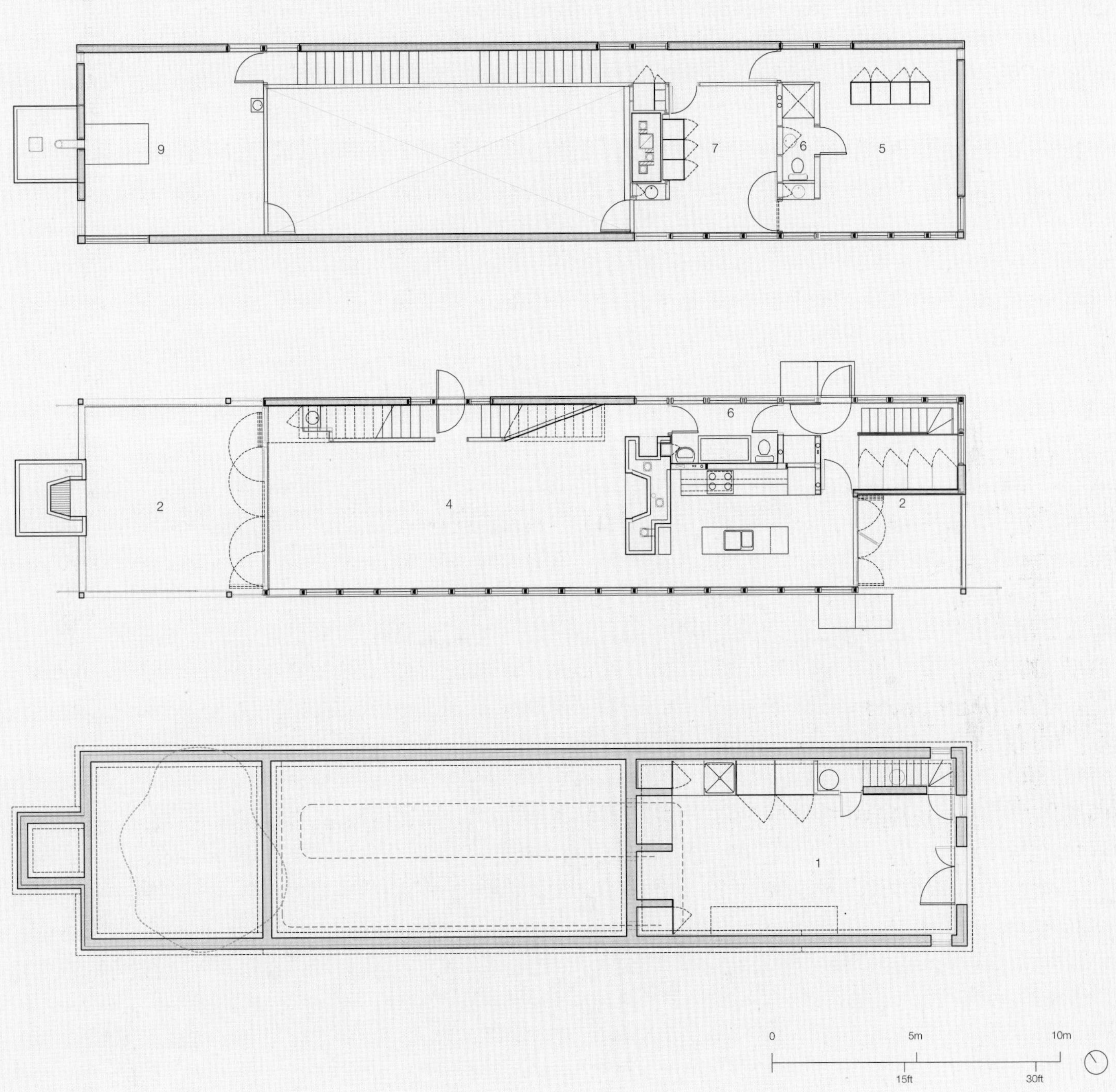

Above: From bottom, the basement, ground-floor and first-floor plans of the house.

Family House

Bärnau, Oberpfalz, Germany 2002
Brückner & Brückner

In a landscape of woods, fields and fish ponds stands this impenetrable but not unwelcoming object – a house, constructed of two materials, that allows its residents views out over the landscape but does not give much away to the passer-by. Architects Brückner & Brückner designed the house for a fish farmer who wanted to be near his work. Ironically, the only site that was available for construction was itself a pond – but one not suitable for commercial exploitation as the nature of the ground meant the water kept seeping away. The house was therefore built within the curtilage of the pond, with only the areas around the house filled in.

With the house sitting at the foot of the Oberpfalz woods, timber on its own would have been an eminently suitable material, but the architects enhanced the composition significantly by adding a second material to the exterior. This is locally produced granite, in a rectangular block that rises almost to the eaves on the principal façade. The effect is to anchor the building visually to the ground, and to provide a pleasing and uncompromising geometric arrangement. The entrance door is to one side of this block, which has glazing above it bringing light into the master bedroom and to the upper-floor corridor.

Larch is used for the rest of the cladding, and with geometric gable ends and no overhanging eaves the effect is of a single sculptural object in the landscape, enhanced by windows set in the same plane as the cladding, with minimal external frames. Although the house opens up more on its other long side, with near storey-height windows allowing the users to spill out from the dining/living area, this does not negate the slightly enigmatic presence of the building.

Internally, however, it is a series of relatively conventional but well-considered spaces, with extensive use of timber on floors, stairs, some walls and the window and door surrounds. The occupying family is placed comfortably within the landscape while retaining its separateness both from nature itself and from other people.

Above left: The end gable presents an enigmatic face that does not betray a residential purpose to the outside world.

Above right: Larch, locally produced granite and glazing combine to create a pleasingly geometric structure.

Right: Windows are set in the same plane as the cladding, enhancing the effect of a simple geometric form.

Top left: The basement, with its stark geometric planes, has a tough, uncompromising feel.

Above left: Delightfully framed windows provide views of the landscape that are accessible even to children.

Top right: Timber is also used internally in order to create a warm but simple, geometric effect.

Above right: The staircase offers a pleasing contrast between the horizontal cladding and the verticals of the balustrade.

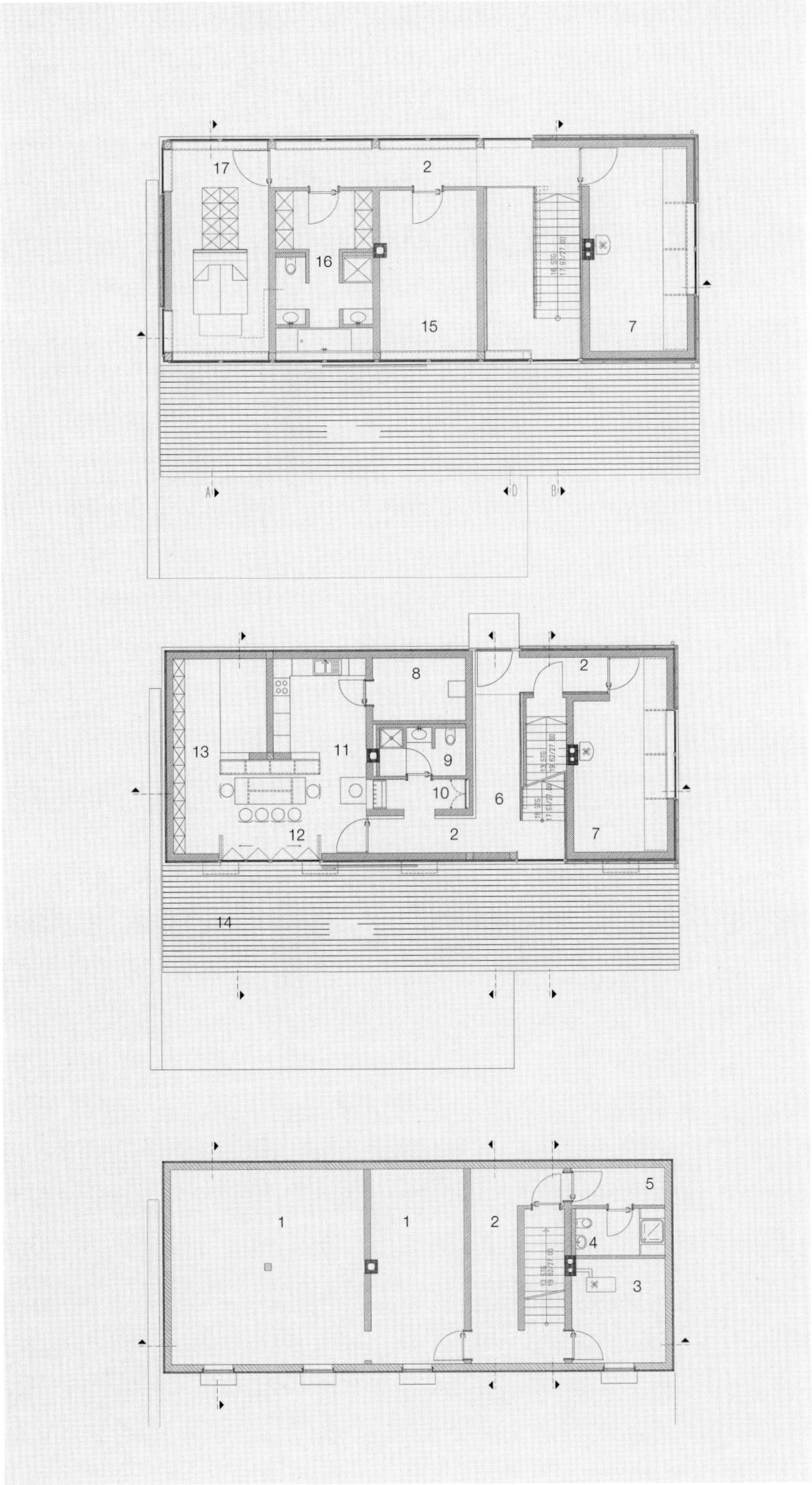

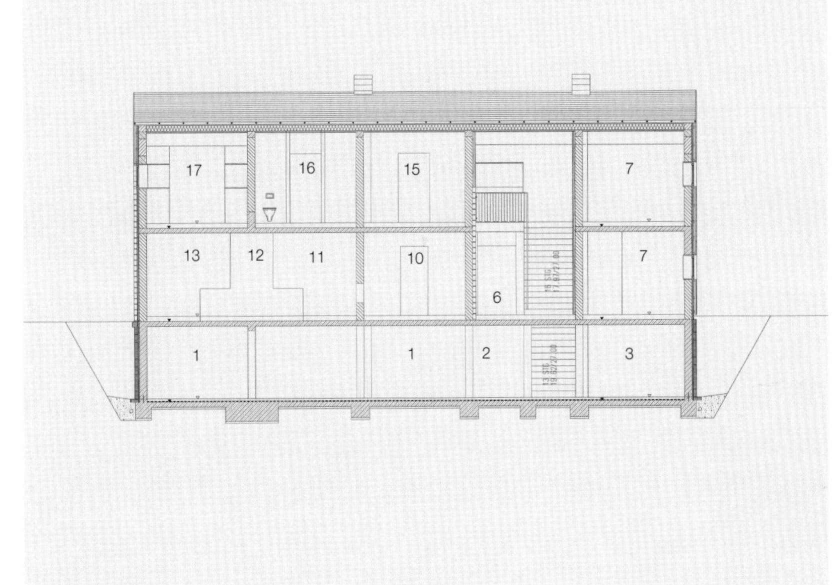

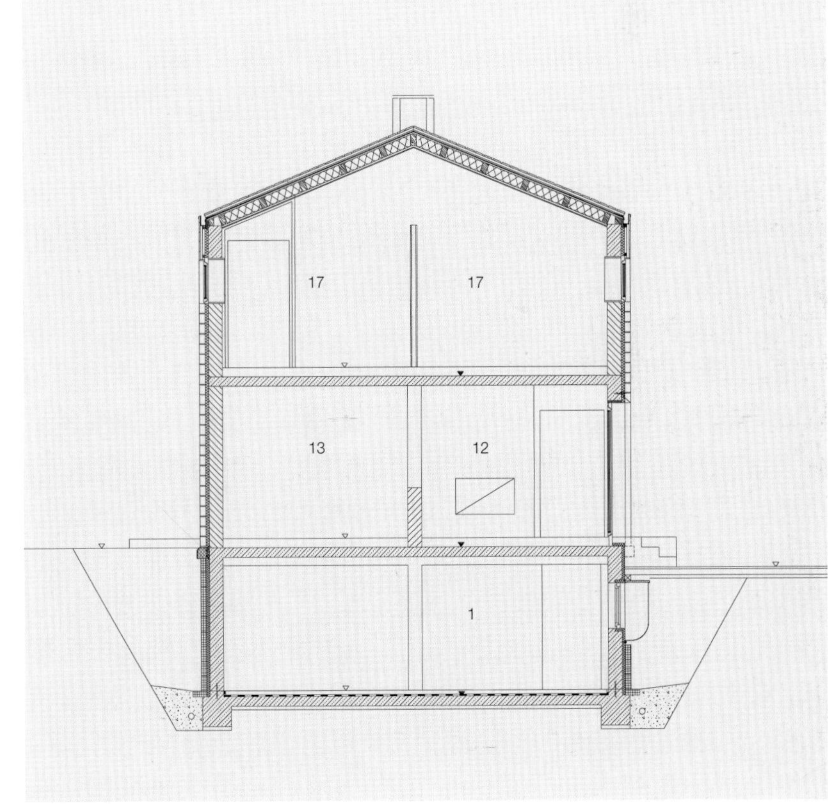

Above left: The basement, ground-floor and first-floor plans.

1. storage; 2. corridor; 3. heating; 4. washroom; 5. changing room; 6. entrance; 7. office; 8. dining room; 9. WC; 10. wardrobe; 11. kitchen; 12. living area; 13. reading area; 14. terrace; 15. cinema; 16. bathroom; 17. bedroom.

Top right and above: A long-section and a cross-section through the house.

The Lodge

Whithurst Park, West Sussex, UK 2001
James Gorst Architects

Building in the English countryside is never easy. Or rather, obtaining permission to build in the English countryside is never easy. Architect James Gorst has, during his career, been tarred with the label of a Classicist, but in fact he has a distinctly contemporary sensibility. He embraces some traditional rural forms and is fascinated by craftsmanship, but his main concern is to give his clients houses that are a pleasure to live in without harking back to earlier forms.

This has not prevented him falling foul, on almost every occasion, of the English planning system, which combines a genuine concern for preservation of what is best with a kind of pettifogging conservatism; and, all too often, a rigid application of rules by overworked and undertrained officials who have little understanding of the thinking that lies behind them.

Indeed, in 2003/04 one of Gorst's projects became something of a cause célèbre, when its failure to achieve planning permission became caught up in an outcry over the government's proposed changes to a piece of legislation that had previously allowed the construction of houses of exceptional quality in the countryside. Following sustained pressure by the architectural profession, orchestrated by *The Architects' Journal*, the government backed down over the changes, providing brighter prospects for proposals by Gorst and his contemporaries in the future.

Gorst's proposal to build the Lodge at Whithurst Park predates this turmoil, since he was seeking planning permission in 1999, but the project did not have an easy ride. Despite the fact that the building would be hidden from public view, councillors in Chichester, West Sussex, twice rejected Gorst's scheme as being too modern. But he did receive the backing of Chichester's planners, and also had some distinguished architectural supporters, and the built project won a national award.

The name 'lodge' suggests that this is not the principal dwelling, and that is the case. It is a secondary building for clients who were also constructing a main house, for which Gorst also made a proposal but which, in the end, went to another architect. His clients occupied the Lodge while the house was being built. Once that was complete, the intention was to make the lodge a rental property.

Although it is substantial, with three bedrooms and a total floor area of 363 square metres (3,910 square feet), the lodge's subsidiary role removed the need to make a grandiose statement. Gorst drew on the concept of a hay barn for its design, an idea that, since it is derived from an outbuilding, might not have been considered 'posh' enough for the main residence. He has shown, however, how elegantly this idea can be achieved. And, indeed, the design has pupped its own subsidiary in the form of an

Above: Oak-framed windows and oak cladding contribute to the pale palette that gives the building a lightweight appearance.

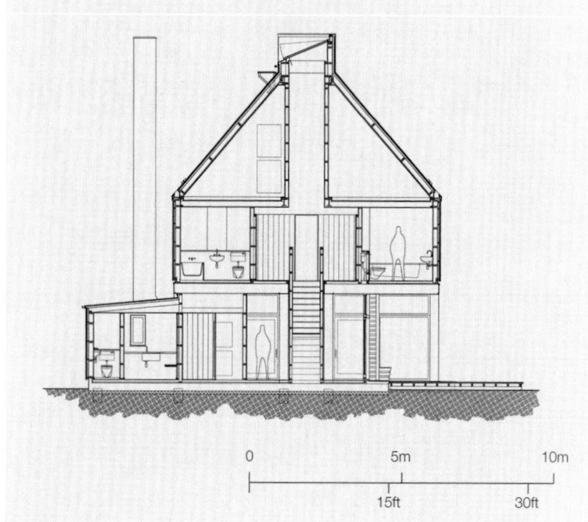

Above right: A cross-section of the Lodge, showing the central light slot.

Above: The ground floor presents an open face, whereas the first floor is much more introverted.

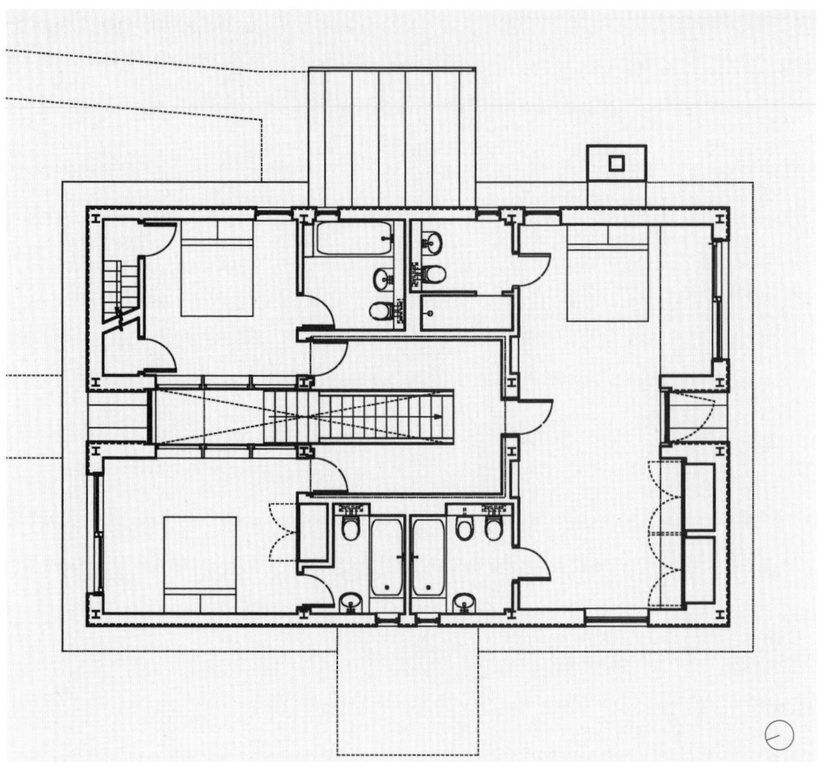

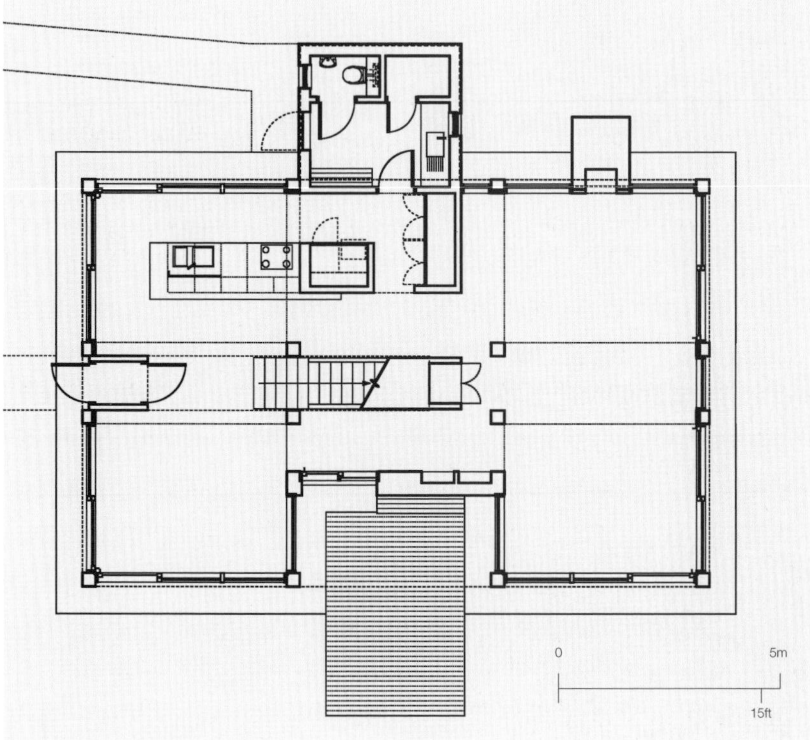

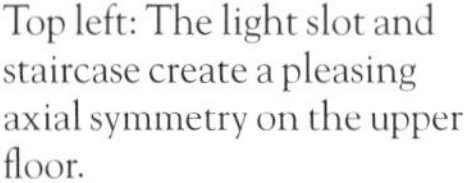
Top left: The light slot and staircase create a pleasing axial symmetry on the upper floor.

Above left: Oak-framed glazing on the ground floor makes the most of views of the Sussex countryside.

Top and above: Plans show the contrast between the open ground floor and the more compartmentalized upper floor.

adjacent single-storey garage. Turned through 90 degrees from the lodge, the garage seems to address it directly and is linked to it by a walkway.

In the Lodge, Gorst created a deliberate contrast between the openness of the ground-floor living area and the enclosure of the first-floor sleeping accommodation. Although he in fact brings a great deal of natural light into this upper floor, from the outside it offers a distinctly closed face. It is here that he uses the echoes of the barn, and the garage is like a smaller version of this upper level, lifted off, shrunk and placed on the ground.

Materials also change as you move up the building, but the consistent element is that Gorst has kept to a very pale palette – the light grey of exposed concrete, the transparency of glass, the pale beige of oak cladding and the silver of the metal roof. This gives a certain insubstantiality to what is, in fact, a very four-square, solid structure.

For the ground floor, Gorst used precast concrete framing to enclose simple but carefully considered oak-framed windows. This space is open plan and as simple as possible so as not to detract from views out. The house sits in a roughly demarcated semicircle of grassland, beyond which are surrounding trees. On the east side is the front door, set centrally and indented so that the glazed seating areas to either side of it effectively project into the landscape.

At the centre of the plan is a staircase to the upper floor, and directly above this is a glazed slot at the centre of the pitched roof. This brings light down into the heart of the house, most noticeably to the upper floor with its restricted external glazing. Here there are three bedrooms plus a generous provision of bathrooms (there is a total of five lavatories in the house). Each of the two guest bedrooms has a translucent wall facing onto the staircase, allowing them to borrow light coming down from the central slot. The main bedroom, at the north end of the house, has one large window, albeit facing north. Initially his clients wanted the addition of another large window on the western side, but Gorst's argument that this would spoil the closed nature of the design prevailed.

There is a concrete slab to the first floor, and above this the structure is steel framed, so structurally this is not a timber building at all. But timber, mainly oak, is used extensively. The upper floor is clad with air-dried oak board-on-board cladding, 100 millimetres (4 inches) wide, screwed to battens, with plywood sheathing behind it. This cladding is also around the oak front door to form an entrance that, although clearly demarcated, is not obtrusive. The staircase is oak, as is the ceiling to the ground floor, and oak has been used on some internal walls.

The roof is metal, a zinc/copper/titanium alloy, with double standing seams. Guttering is recessed into its edge, with water running into internal drainpipes so that the clean lines are not interrupted. Underfloor heating is incorporated in the floor screed, and the rooflight is operated electrically so that it can open to allow the escape of warm air drawn up by a stack effect. In this way the house should be comfortable at all seasons of the year, albeit with not the most rigid of energy-saving strategies. Gorst may not have given his clients the very greenest of houses, but he has certainly provided one that sits comfortably within its green surroundings.

Above: The central staircase is beneath the glazing slot, and brings light down to the ground floor.

Bunch Residence

Napa Valley, California, USA, 1999
Turnbull Griffin Haesloop

In many cases a house's position is predetermined: the plot is scarcely large enough and the architect's main challenge is finding a way to squeeze enough accommodation into the limited space available. But, given a large enough site, positioning can become a major issue, one that may well determine the success or otherwise of the project.

For the Bunch Residence, on a hillside above California's Napa Valley, architect Turnbull Griffin Haesloop solved this problem in a way that looks blindingly obvious – so often an indicator of original thinking. The 230-square-metre (2,500-square-foot) house sits just below the only relatively level area of the site, with a courtyard between it and the garages buried in the hillside above.

The form of the single-storey building follows the contours of the hillside, with the complex-shaped living space occupying most of the plan, and the accommodation wing off to the south. The shape of the large living room, with its sawtooth windows, offers the best possible views through the trees and down the hill. At its centre, a timber deck cantilevers outwards, with a mature oak tree thrusting through it and providing shade.

There is a definite sense of arrival and drama on reaching the house. From the somewhat bland courtyard you see a relatively modest-seeming structure, clad in vertical 2 x 6 tongue-and-groove cedar boards that have been left to weather naturally. Then you pass through an anteroom, modelled on the concept of the *tokonoma*, a small lobby in a traditional Japanese house or tea house that is used to display a calligraphic scroll or a carefully conceived arrangement of flowers.

This builds a sense of anticipation that is satisfied by progressing into the main living space. As if the shape and the views did not provide enough drama, both are enhanced by the form of the ceiling. The exposed timber rafters fan out towards the wall of windows and also rise upward towards the centre of the ceiling, drawing the eye with them. With all this overhead, it is fitting that the walls should have simple white-painted drywall finishes, with white-framed windows set into them. The floors are in warm-looking cherry, finished with clear varnish, and Douglas fir plywood has been used in the construction of cupboards.

Overall, the house offers a sense of drama to which the residents are unlikely ever to become over-accustomed.

Top: From the courtyard, the single-storey house presents a relatively closed face to the onlooker.

Above left: There is outdoor seating around the understated entrance, which is clad in tongue-and-groove boards.

Above right: The house is entered through an anteroom modelled on the Japanese *tokonoma*, a small lobby.

Above: The house perches above the Napa Valley, with the courtyard occupying the only level ground.

Top left: A section through the house, with the cantilevered terrace shaded by an oak tree.

Above left: Sawtooth windows in the main living room make the most of the spectacular view.

Top right: The unusual shape of the main living room allows intimate areas to be created.

Above right: A large expanse of cherry flooring provides warmth of colouring and unifies the living space.

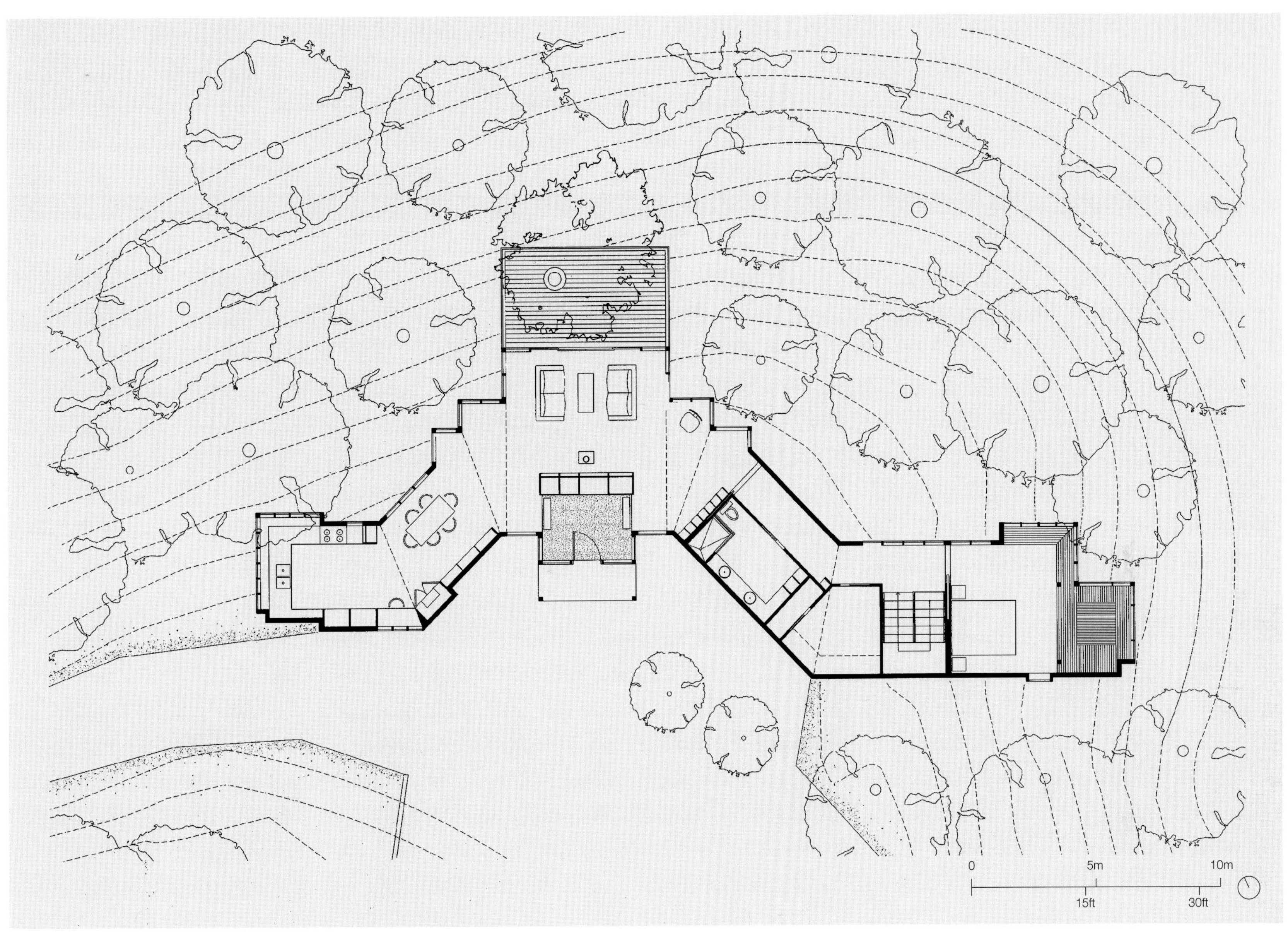

Above: The site plan shows the house's colonization of the only piece of flat land available.

Casa del Sole di Mezzanotte
Tuscany, Italy 2002
Roderick Romero

Above: Sting's tree house is in an oak tree, the sacred tree of the Druids, which stands next to a lake.

Tree houses may be seen as a vanished pleasure from a more innocent past, the preserve of middle-class children in large gardens enjoying unsupervised play. But, perhaps because of this, these houses have entered the collective nostalgia of many adults in affluent parts of the world. The effect is most extreme in the United States, where several organizations have been formed to promote their resurgence. One – Forever Young Tree Houses – has as its aim the construction of universally accessible tree houses in every state; at present it boasts 'seven down, 43 to go'.

This nostalgia is reflected in the construction at Alnwick, a stately home in north-east England, of a structure believed to be one of the largest tree houses in the world. The present incumbent of the house has spent a great deal of money transforming its garden, and the tree house is just one of the attractions. Opened at the start of 2005, it is in fact a complex of buildings, linked by suspended walkways and with a total area of about 555 square metres (6,000 square feet). Care has been taken to make it fully accessible to the disabled – a laudable intention, but one that slightly defeats the purpose. A degree of inaccessibility and a makeshift quality are key to the romance of the tree house.

This has been true throughout history. In the nineteenth century, jaded Parisians found diversion in eating at a tree-house restaurant outside the city at Le Plessis, south-west of Paris, where all the food had to be hauled up in baskets by ropes. Founded by Joseph Guesquin, who was enamoured of the tale of Robinson Crusoe, it was called Le Grand Robinson. Guesquin combined his restaurant, nestled in chestnut trees, with a dance hall below, the first of a rash of ginguettes that were constructed at Le Plessis. This was so influential that in the early twentieth century the town was renamed Le-Plessis-Robinson.

Even earlier the Florentine potentates, the Medicis, built themselves a tiny tree house of a palace. But, in that age of conspicuous consumption, it was made not of any kind of humble material but of marble.

Today it is music and film stars who combine wealth with the glamour of the Medicis and, sometimes, even their patronage of the arts. It is appropriate, then, that the musician Sting and his wife Trudie Styler, who have homes around the world, chose their Tuscan one as the site for a tree house. Sting is widely known for his environmental concerns, so a fast car or some other piece of costly technology would not have been an appropriate indulgence. How much better to return to the dreams of childhood with a house built in trees.

This particular tree house, known as the Casa del Sole di Mezzanotte (the house of the midnight sun), was designed by another, one-time rock star. Roderick Romero was a founder of the 1990s Seattle band Sky Cries Mary but, with his wife

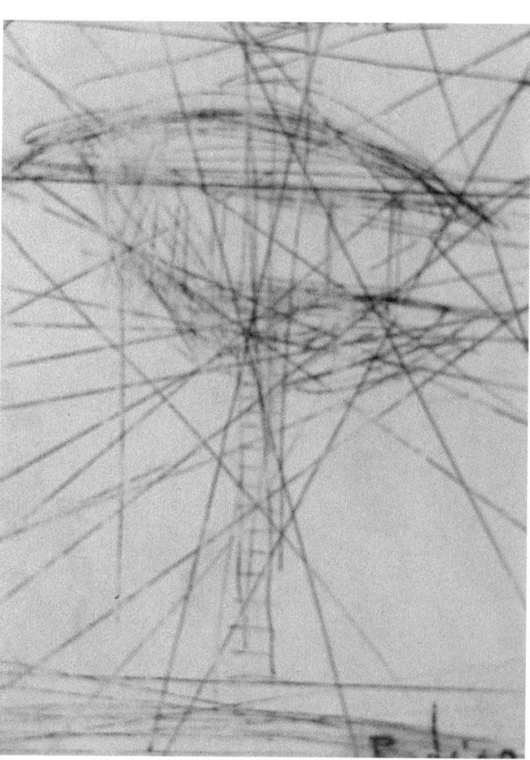

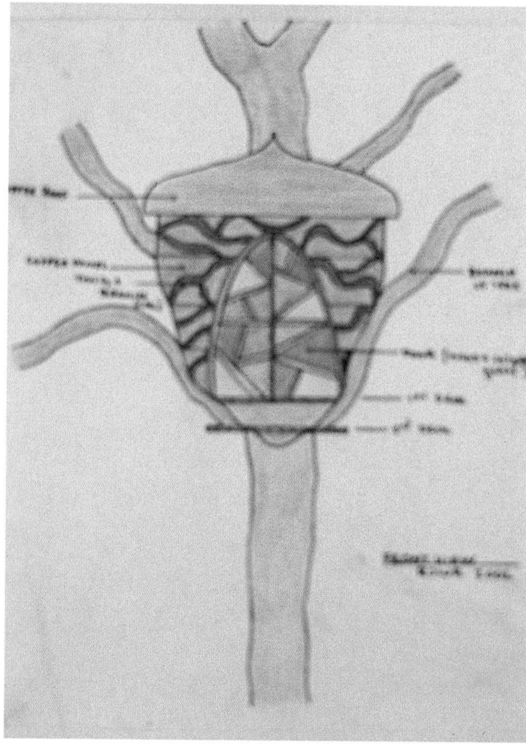

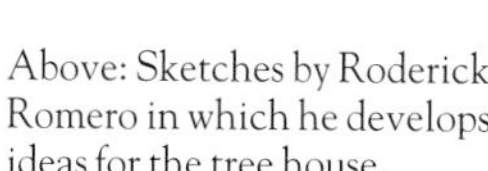
Above: Sketches by Roderick Romero in which he develops ideas for the tree house.

Anisa, has diversified into many other projects. Anisa, who has an associate degree in architectural interior design from Parsons and a masters in painting from NYU, has concentrated more on fine art, whereas Roderick, with no particularly relevant qualification, has set himself up designing tree houses through his firm Romero Studios. He has built several in the United States, including one for the fashion designer Donna Karan, but the Tuscany house is his first venture into Europe.

In an interview in the *New York Times* in October 2003 Romero described his approach: 'I try to let the tree communicate with me and I communicate with the tree. The tree tells you where to move and what your boundaries are, where you can stress things and what directions you can go.' The article goes on to say, 'Mr Romero is a tree house architect, inspired by a syncretic blend of esoteric studies, and where most people see only leaves and branches, he locates chakras and receives spiritual guidance.'

This may sound to some like so much New Age whimsy, but Romero has designed some attractive tree houses and in any case his sentiments chime with the concerns of Sting. Romero chose an oak for the house, one standing on a bluff by the edge of a lake. This means that although the tree house is only 6 metres (20 feet) above the ground, it is 10.5 metres (35 feet) above the lake. Built from fallen oakwood found on the estate, it is octagonal, with an area of about 14 square metres (150 square feet), plus another 11 square metres (120 square feet) of outdoor deck space that comes to a point above the lake. The house is clad in live oak and copper, with a copper roof. A stained-glass window represents the three suns of Druid folklore and there are bells and wind chimes.

Access is by a steep, timber stair, with a timber and rope handrail, and there is a real sense of arrival as your head pops through a small octagonal opening into the tree house itself. Sting may be one of the more mature of today's musical legends but, with his much-trumpeted healthy life, he is certainly not yet starting to worry about universal accessibility.

Above: Having climbed a timber stair, access to the tree house is through an octagonal opening in the floor.

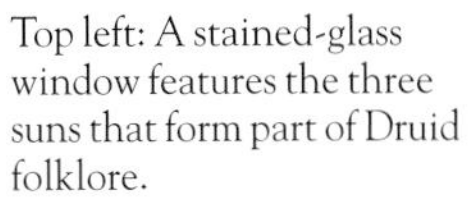

Top left: A stained-glass window features the three suns that form part of Druid folklore.

Above left: An external deck adds considerably to the overall space that can be enjoyed above ground.

Top right: The tree house cantilevers over a lake so as to provide the outdoor deck area.

Above right: Timber stairs with a timber-and-rope handrail are used for the steep access ladder.

What does 'modern' mean today? Much longer books than this could be written in response to that question, and fail to reach a conclusion. Long ago, in the 1920s and 1930s, it might have been possible to say it meant looking forward rather than back, that it meant eschewing unnecessary ornament and embracing technology.

Today nothing is so simple, and little is designed that does not draw on the past in some way, even if that past is those same heroic days of pioneering Modernism. With timber design, however, it may be a little easier to define what is modern. There is such a history and feeling of tradition associated with the material and, particularly, with wood houses that a modern approach can be described as one that does not slavishly follow any tradition. It is an approach that looks at the needs and requirements of today, and either ignores the way things have always been done in the past or draws on them only where appropriate, for very rational, logical – and modern – reasons.

Australia has many interesting examples of this, perhaps because it does not have a long indigenous tradition of building – although there is more than one might expect. In Darwin, for example, Build Up Design has built a 'love shack' that is based on two separate traditions (see opposite). One is the *dongas* or transportable buildings that were put up near ruined buildings around the city in the aftermath of Cyclone Tracey in 1974. The other is the Aboriginal platform shelters that were traditionally built in Arnhem Land. Supported on timber platforms of stringybark (a kind of eucalyptus) and clad in bark, these relatively makeshift structures were adaptable to the climate, since their occupants would simply peel back a section of the cladding for views or ventilation. Build Up has followed this design with its love shack – an extra bedroom that is structurally independent of the main house. Although it has been brought up to date with a slender steel frame, the floors and walls are of timber – the latter, in fact, a series of shutters that allows the building to open up almost completely.

The idea of a relatively primitive dwelling in the country is one that the young architect Nicholas Murcutt has embraced in his Box House and Collopy House in New South Wales (see page 84). The former, says Murcutt, is a building that 'any good bush carpenter can put together', and although the latter is more sophisticated it has a similarly rugged feel. What makes these buildings definitively modern is the fact that Murcutt, while drawing on traditional skills and approaches to living, in no way follows an aesthetic that has gone before.

On the edge of Barcelona, Tito Dalmau and BDM have designed a luxurious and spacious house that uses timber to temper what otherwise could be an excessively austere appearance (see page104).

Another hallmark of contemporary design is the fusion of ideas from different countries. Yung Ho Chang, a Chinese architect trained in the United States, has achieved this with his Split House near Beijing (see page 92), a building that draws on Chinese ideas of courtyard housing but gives them a new twist. One of Yung Ho Chang's concerns is that the architect should celebrate the still-existing beauty of a landscape that is increasingly under threat. In contrast, Korean architect Byoungsoo Cho has designed a courtyard house – his C-shaped Metal Roof House at Bockpoori – to make the most of a previously ravaged landscape that has now been restored (see opposite). There is a layering of different materials, with timber used for the cladding and roof beams, as well as for decking and flooring.

Byoungsoo Cho had to face the difficulty of dealing with a site that had been entirely flattened and lost all its personality. Fernau and Hartman, when designing the Mann Residence in California (see page 110), had the advantage of wonderful scenery, but the immediate environment had been similarly destroyed. Its solution, faced with a flattened surface, was to create not a single building but a campus of buildings, an approach more commonly used for offices or universities than for a single house.

Another approach to modernity in timber design is to draw on tradition, but on a tradition of carpentry rather than architecture. Swiss architect Peter Zumthor has done this with a family house at Graubünden in Switzerland, which is a beautifully crafted, opening box. Similar projects include a garden pavilion by BEHF Architekten at Arlsdorf in Austria, which again is a box that can close down completely or open up on both sides. A similar idea is used in the prefabricated Retreat homes, intended as an alternative to the permanently sited caravan. Like very elegant conjoined wardrobes with windows, these are designed by London-based architect Buckley Gray Yeoman and are being sold in the United Kingdom and Spain (see opposite). On a much larger scale, Fink + Jocher has created a beautifully crafted box on Lake Starnberg in Germany (see page 122).

For Damien Carnoy, with his 'house in the orchard' in Belgium (see page 118), the main aesthetic influence comes not from traditional Modernism but from the organic ideas of Rudolph Steiner. These link with a very twenty-first-century concern about the environment, which is also the driving force behind the house in Savoy designed by French practice Tectoniques (see page 100). In both cases, the intelligence behind the design has resulted in buildings that, while certainly interesting, are visually far from perfection.

This does not apply, however, to Will Bruder's Riddell Residence in Wyoming (see page 114). Built for two artists, the house itself is also an artwork, integrated with its environment and benefiting from a level of overall control that few architects today can hope to enjoy. More than any others, this house, in terms of the relationship between architect, client and surroundings, harks back to the modernist agenda of the last century – but, again, with a solution that is utterly of today.

Chapter 3
Modern Houses

Top: Buckley Gray Yeoman has redefined the idea of the holiday home with its Retreat cabins for all-year living.

Above left: Build Up Design's 'love shack' is based on the Australian tradition of the *donga* transportable building.

Above right: At Bockpoori, Korea, Byoungsoo Cho has designed a courtyard house that makes the most of a previously ravaged landscape.

Box House and Collopy House
New South Wales, Australia
2000/2001
Nicholas Murcutt

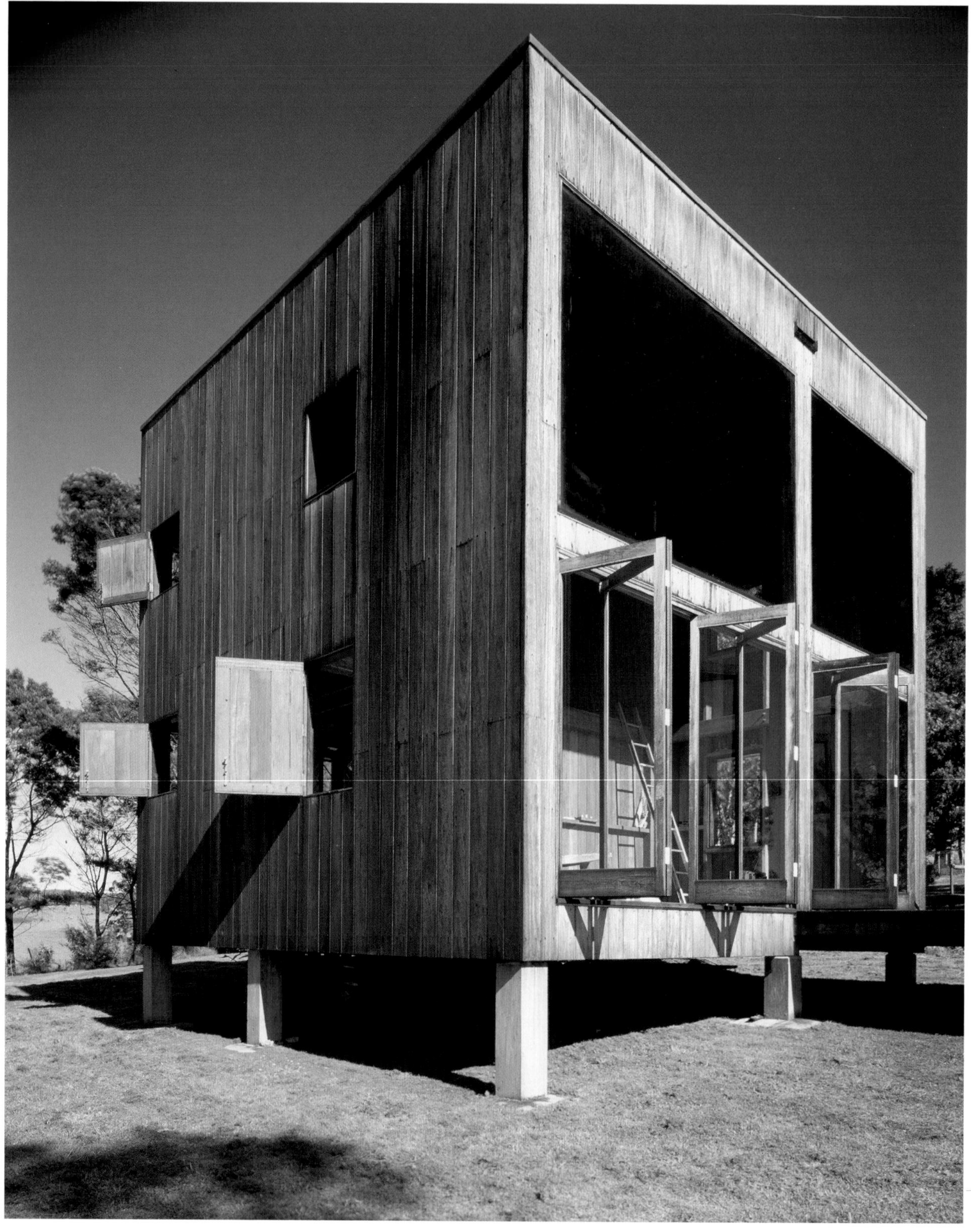

Above: As its name suggests,
the house can shut up like a box.

It is perhaps not surprising that Nicholas Murcutt should understand how to design houses. His father, Glenn Murcutt, has a small and seemingly modest practice in Australia that has won him international renown and even, in 2002, the Pritzker Prize, one of the highest honours in international architecture. And Glenn's father, Arthur, was a builder with a deep interest in architecture.

Nicholas Murcutt can design houses that are elegant and beautifully finished, in which you could live a well-appointed but not excessive life. But neither of the buildings shown here is like that. They are proper holiday houses, homes for when you want to get away from it all and live fairly roughly, with the sand between your toes. Murcutt has designed houses that have all the romance of camping but with a few (just a few) more home comforts.

Box House obviously deserves its name. A simple wooden box measuring 6.3 metres (20 feet 6 inches) in every direction, raised on a platform, it would be a joy to open it up at the start of a holiday, like getting a toy ready to work. Indeed, the clients, who are artists and had a limited budget, wanted the house to have some of the feeling of the traditional Australian shack, the most primitive and ad hoc kind of dwelling. Built at Tathra on New South Wales' Sapphire Coast, the 'shack' is in a magnificent location where most of life can be lived out of doors.

What Murcutt designed was an entirely timber-framed and -clad building on a reinforced concrete platform. Areas beyond it, which were used for cooking (a campfire) and hygiene (an open-air bath and open-air lavatory) during the construction process, have remained, although there are also some rudimentary facilities within the house itself. The clients' priorities are indicated by the fact that they saw the enclosure itself as the first phase, and planned a gas stove and hot water (heated by panels) as the second phase, and an indoor composting lavatory and a shower as the third phase. They are still happy to light the space with candles, and heat the water in their old cast-iron bathtub by lighting a fire beneath it. All the construction process is exposed internally, and Murcutt has said this is 'a building any good bush carpenter can put together'.

Entrance is via a ramp of old timbers that culminates in a similarly scruffy deck at the northern corner. Internally there is a separate area is for the planned bathroom; otherwise the only division is a wall that runs halfway across the centre of the space. A ladder propped against this provides access to the sleeping platform above.

Top left: Internally, the construction used is entirely visible.

Above left: Set in a magnificent landscape in New South Wales, Box House is designed with the intention that its residents will spend most of their time outside.

Above right: A wall of folding windows on the north-west axis can open up completely.

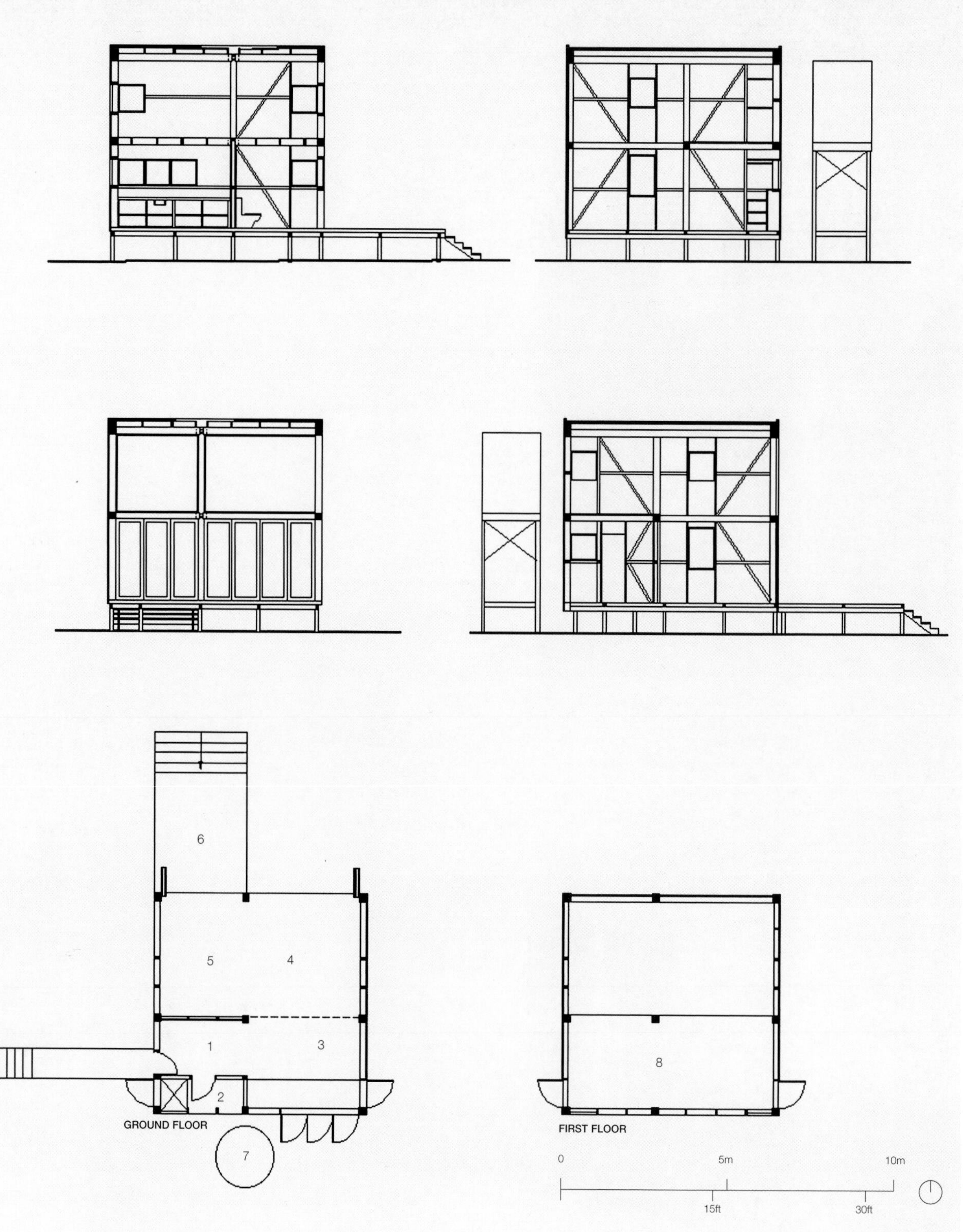

Above: Sections and plans of Box House. 1. entry; 2. bath/laundry; 3. kitchen; 4. living; 5. dining; 6. deck; 7. tank; 8. bedroom.

Opposite: On the rear of the building, the water tank provides an element of articulation.

A wall of folding windows on the north-west side can open up completely. Even the tracks in which these run are made of timber. Windows on other façades have hinged shutters that are effectively openings in the external cladding. The only other elements are the galvanized metal roof and the utilitarian water tank that sits on a workaday platform next to the house.

Murcutt hopes the building could become a prototype for anybody who wants to create an inexpensive house. But those with just slightly more luxurious tastes may prefer his Collopy House.

Also in New South Wales, in Tea Gardens an hour's journey from Newcastle, Collopy House looks luxurious only when it is compared to Box House, for it too embraces the concept of outdoor living and the simplest construction. It is in two parts, out of step with each other on either side of an 80-metre (260-foot) boardwalk that runs north to south. To the north, the boardwalk leads to the road; to the south, to the sea. Both parts are raised 1 metre (3 feet 4 inches) above ground level to cope with high tides, and have been constructed entirely from recycled timber. The effect is rather of a casual agglomeration of buildings although in fact it has been carefully planned.

To the west of the boardwalk is the 'night pavilion', comprising three bedrooms, a laundry and bathroom, and a semi-open shower. The 'day pavilion' is to the east of the boardwalk, and pushed slightly south. Its main element is a single large space that comprises kitchen and dining room, with a side that can open up entirely. To anchor this area and provide a service zone there is a long masonry 'working wall' made from a series of alcoves. The boardwalk broadens between the two pavilions, and it is possible to put a canvas shade between the buildings to colonize this space.

As with Box House the concept is simple and, again, construction is almost exclusively of timber, apart from the spine wall. But there is an increased level of sophistication, reflected not least in the client's selection of a number of twentieth-century design classics. These include Marcel Breuer and Alvar Aalto tables, and Eames and Arne Jacobsen chairs. They all have an elegant austerity that matches their surroundings, but the fact that they do not look out of place is an indication of how much clever architectural thinking has gone into this seemingly unsophisticated home.

Above left: A boardwalk runs between the two elements of Collopy House.

Above right: Despite the simplicity of the house, classic furniture sits comfortably.

Top: It is as if the two elements of the house have been slid away from each other laterally.

Above: The house is separated into a 'night pavilion' (left) and a 'day pavilion' (right).

Above left: The boardwalk leads to the sea in one direction and the road in the other.

Above right: As at Box House, Collopy House has a wall that can open entirely to the external environment.

Opposite top: At night in particular, the boardwalk between the two pavilions becomes part of the living space.

Opposite bottom left: Plan. 1. entry; 2. platform/boardwalk; 3. bedroom; 4. bath; 5. outdoor shower; 6. kitchen; 7. living/dining; 8. storage wall; 9. water tanks.

Opposite bottom right: east elevation and cross-section.

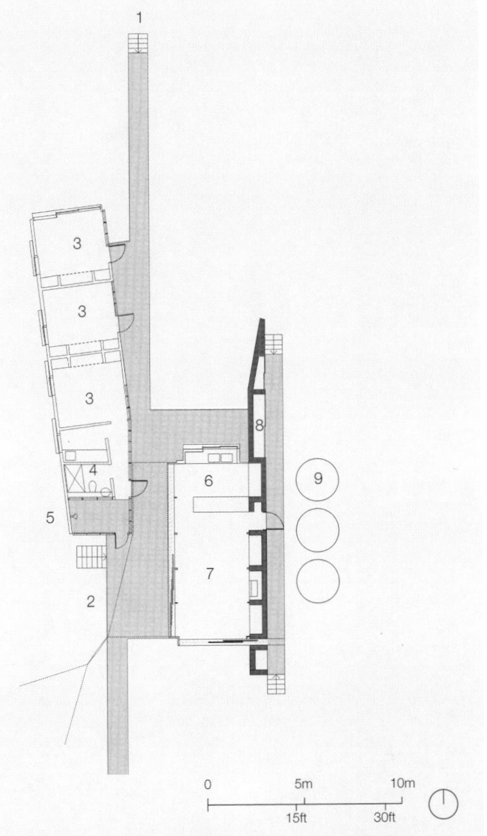
1
3
3
3
8
4
6
9
5
7
2
0
5m
10m
15ft
30ft

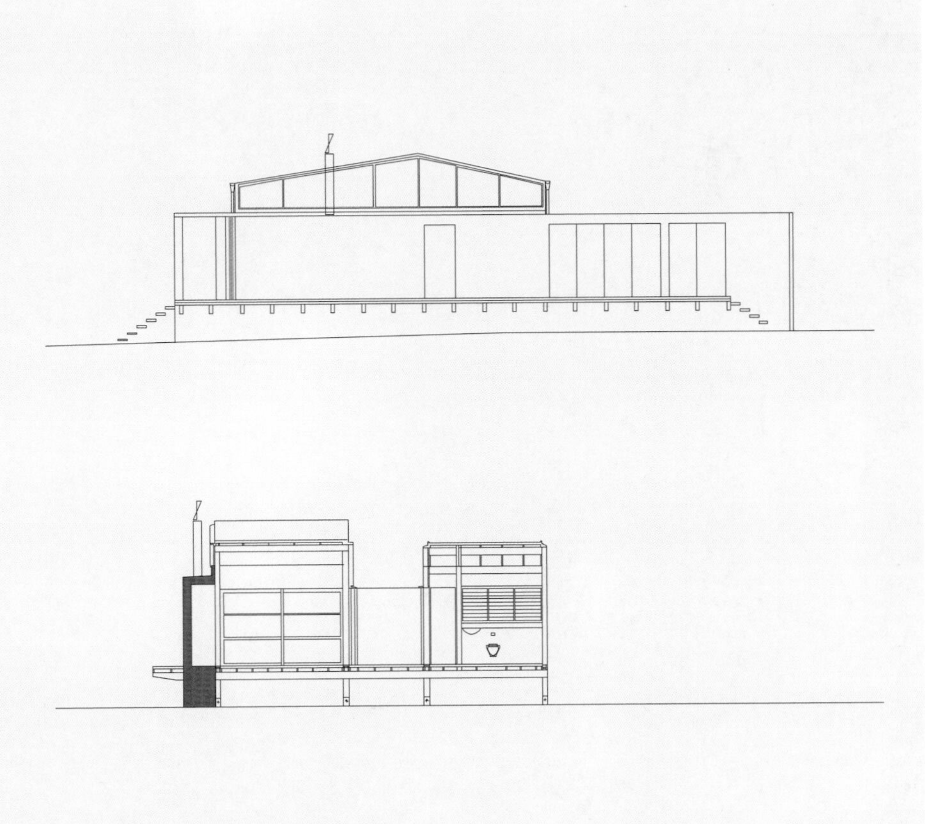

Split House

Yanqing, Beijing, China 2002
Atelier Feichang Jianzhu

Top: Entrance is through a glazed box bridge above a stream rerouted through the courtyard.

Above: Pine framing is augmented by slender steel cross-bracing for the wider elements of the structure.

If China is to win its place on the contemporary architectural scene, a project like the Split House in Yanqing will play an important role in achieving this. It may seem odd that anything as small as a house could be significant in such a big country – and especially so when it forms part of a project that has a strong streak of the ridiculous. But the building designed by Atelier Feichang Jianzhu, the practice of architect Yung Ho Chang, is a perfect embodiment of contemporary architecture as understood in many sophisticated countries.

This means that it combines an international aesthetic sensibility (Yung Ho Chang trained in the United States) with an embrace of traditional typologies and materials. Yung Ho Chang, who set up the practice in 1993 on his return from the US (his was the first private architectural practice in China), has an interest not only in traditional forms but also in environmental issues, putting him ahead of his time in a country that still seems to be more interested in subduing the natural environment than in working with it.

If this seems like a large ideological load for a single house to carry, it is even more surprising when you realize that the building is in some ways one of the most self-effacing houses in a development that is certainly bold but is also eccentric, and that, for those not enamoured of conspicuous consumption, borders on the distasteful.

Split House is one of 12 'residences' that form part of the Commune by the Great Wall, a development by the innovative property company SOHO China. An hour's journey from Beijing, on the Shuigian section of the wall, the complex is effectively more a hotel than a true collection of houses. Each house is designed by a different architect, most of them Chinese although Japanese superstars Shigeru Ban and Kengo Kuma have also made contributions. The houses are gathered around a clubhouse that provides central hotel facilities. Those seeking luxury and the unusual, usually corporate visitors from international companies, can book the entire complex or parts of it for a visit, achieving a level of comfort and environmental peace not available in Beijing itself.

Most of the houses have a 'look at me' character, either a kind of clichéd bright white Modernism or through the use of tricksy solutions, such as the Suitcase House which unfolds to reveal its full range of facilities. In the clubhouse itself the men's lavatories are decked out with pink chiffon.

In contrast, Split House is the most private of the houses. It is in the highest position, looking down towards all the others, and the marketing material describes it as suitable for 'small meetings and private functions'. Yung Ho Chang based it on the traditional courtyard houses in Beijing, which are fast disappearing in the rush to build third-rate high-rise developments. But whereas these are usually inward-looking Split House, in its magnificent natural setting, makes the most of the view of hills and woods. The courtyard is therefore triangular, with the two halves of the house joined at the narrow end by a glass bridge that forms the entrance, and with the two arms opening out to embrace the view at the wider end. This geometry made it possible to preserve a group of existing trees on the site and, to make the relationship with nature even closer, the architect rerouted a stream

Above: A partially enclosed courtyard sits between the two wings, private to the left and public to the right.

so that it runs through the courtyard. There are four bedrooms, two with en-suite bathrooms, on the partial upper level. With each of the wings only one room wide there was no need for hallways, so the building makes the most effective use possible of its 450 square metres (4,840 square feet) of space.

The building has a framework of laminated timber elements, using pine from north-east China, with some slender steel rods providing cross-bracing for the wider elements. Two solid L-shaped walls on each half of the house are made of rammed earth, a traditional technique in this part of China, with some timber cladding. There is extensive glazing to take advantage of the views. Most dramatic is the entrance foyer, reached by a steel staircase with cantilevered timber treads. This is a real 'glass box', with not only a glazed roof and walls but also a glazed floor which allows views down past the timber beams to the stream as it runs out from the courtyard. Elsewhere internal materials are simple, with dark stone floors and little decoration, appropriate in a building that is intended to be outward- not inward-looking.

But while this shape is particularly suited to the orientation and surroundings of Split House, Yung Ho Chang sees it as having a more universal application. He has produced block models showing that the two halves could be combined at right angles, in parallel or in other configurations to suit the requirements of different sites. He is keen that the house can be seen not only as one part of a collection of architectural ideas, but also as a prototype that can be reproduced elsewhere. Although he has not yet been able to do so, he is still looking for opportunities to build it in other parts of China.

Despite some criticisms of the level of workmanship at the Commune by the Great Wall, the development won a prize at the Venice Biennale in 2002. China is waking up to the importance of international architecture, staging its own biennale for the first time in 2004, and employing international superstars for its Olympic structures and other cultural buildings. But if it is to really raise its game architecturally it must have some quieter, yet considered and architecturally valuable, buildings to go with the big set pieces. And this is a role that Split House and its descendants seem ideally placed to fill.

Above left: The understated simplicity of the upper floor's furniture focuses attention on the proportions of the interior.

Above right: Terraces on the ground-floor roofs offer much opportunity for enjoying the views.

Above: Visitors step from the glazed entrance onto the dark stone of the ground-floor accommodation.

Overleaf: The house is set against the dramatic backdrop of the scenery by the Great Wall. The orientation was determined in order to protect the existing trees on the site.

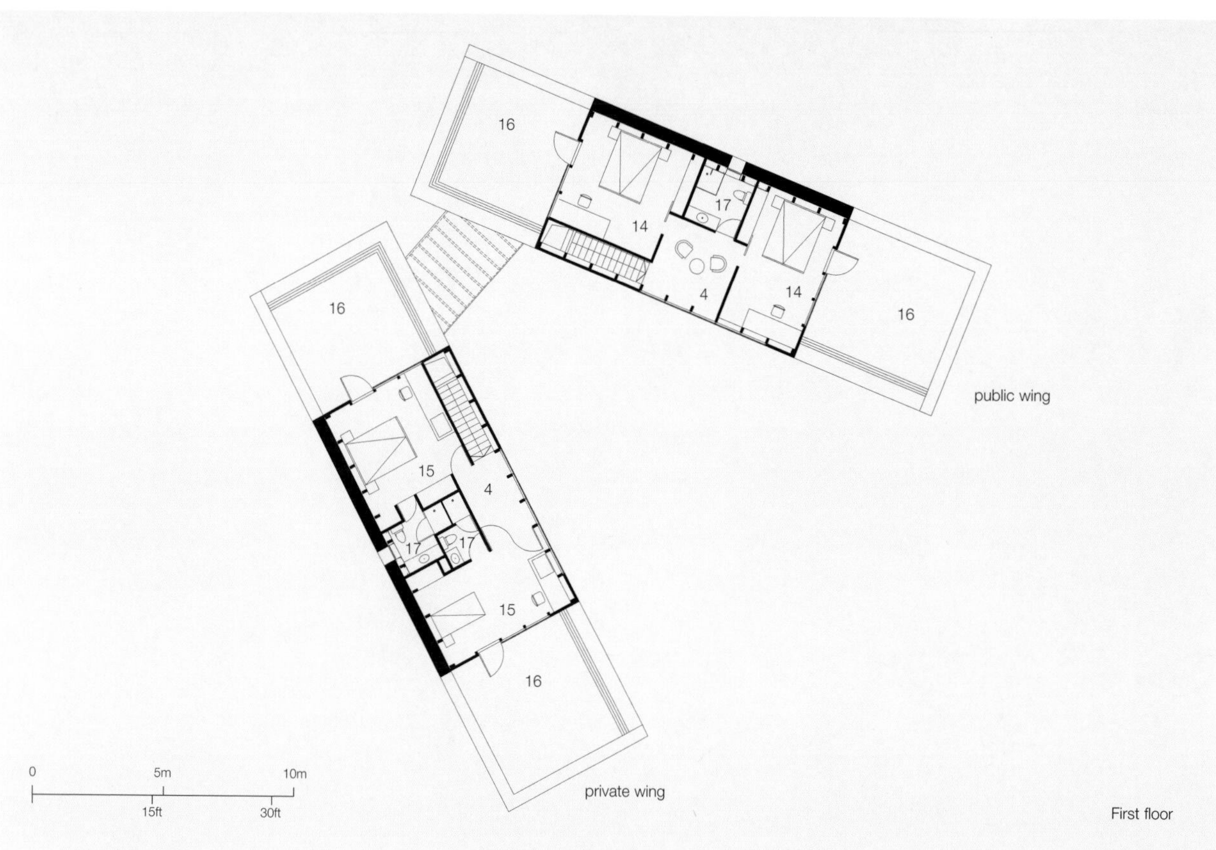

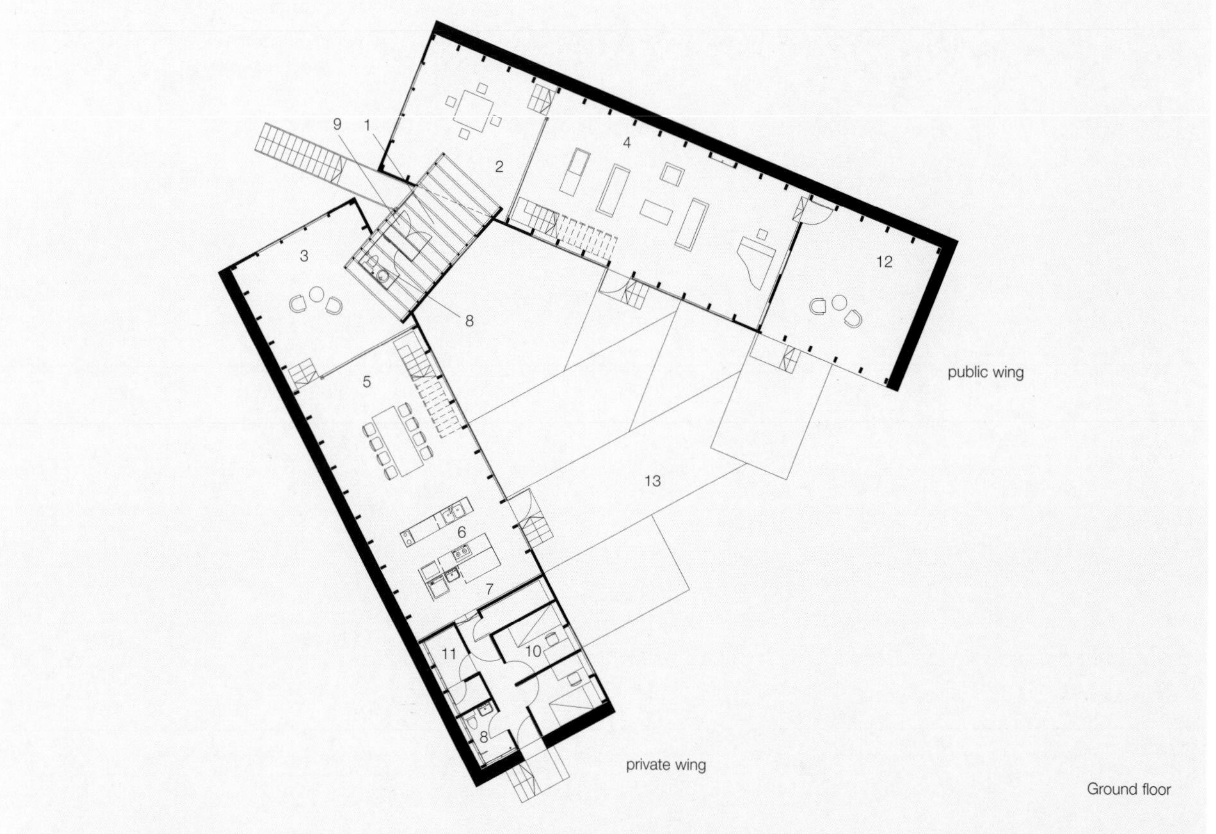

Top right and right: First-floor and ground-floor plans showing the private and public wings.
1. vestibule; 2. mah-jong;
3. sitting; 4. living; 5. dining;
6. kitchen; 7. laundry; 8. WC;
9. storage; 10. servant's room;
11. machine room;
12. semi-outdoor room;
13. courtyard; 14. guest bedroom; 15. master bed;
16. roof terrace; 17. bathroom.

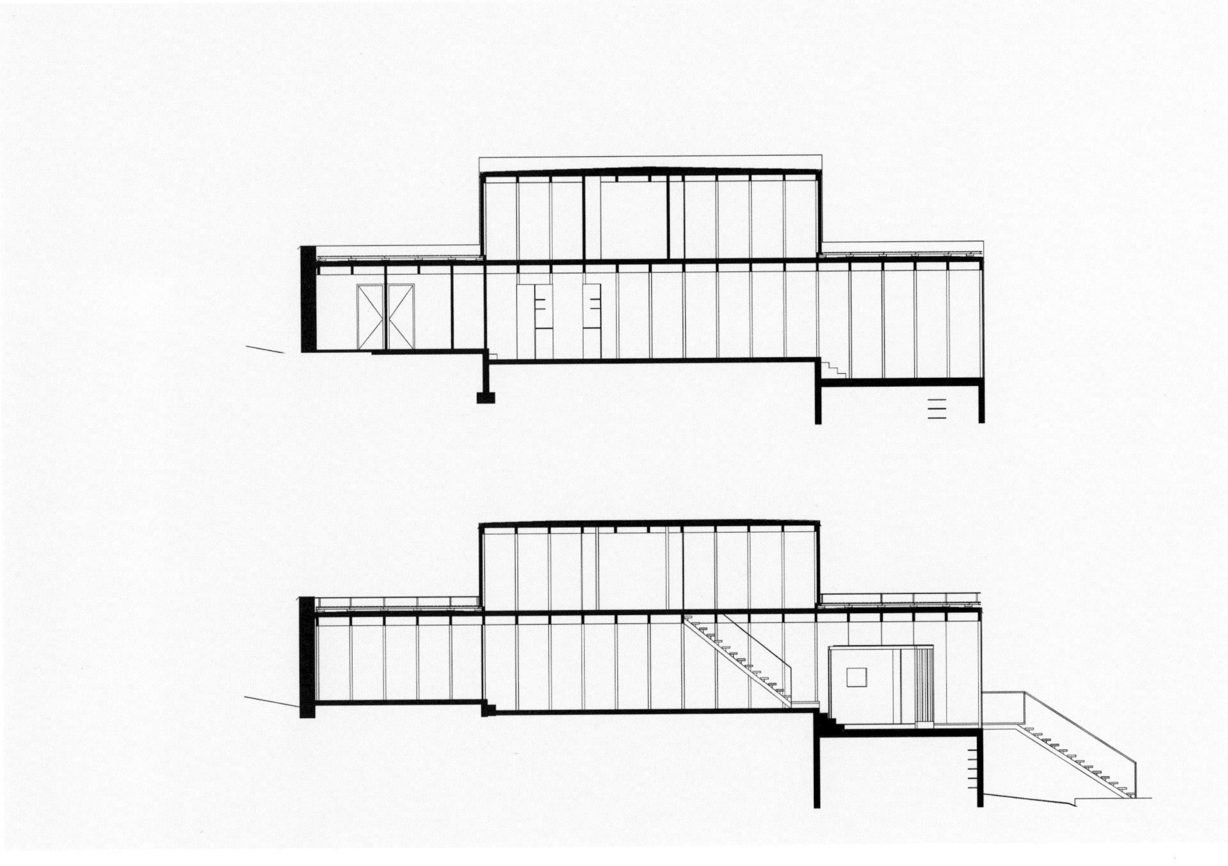

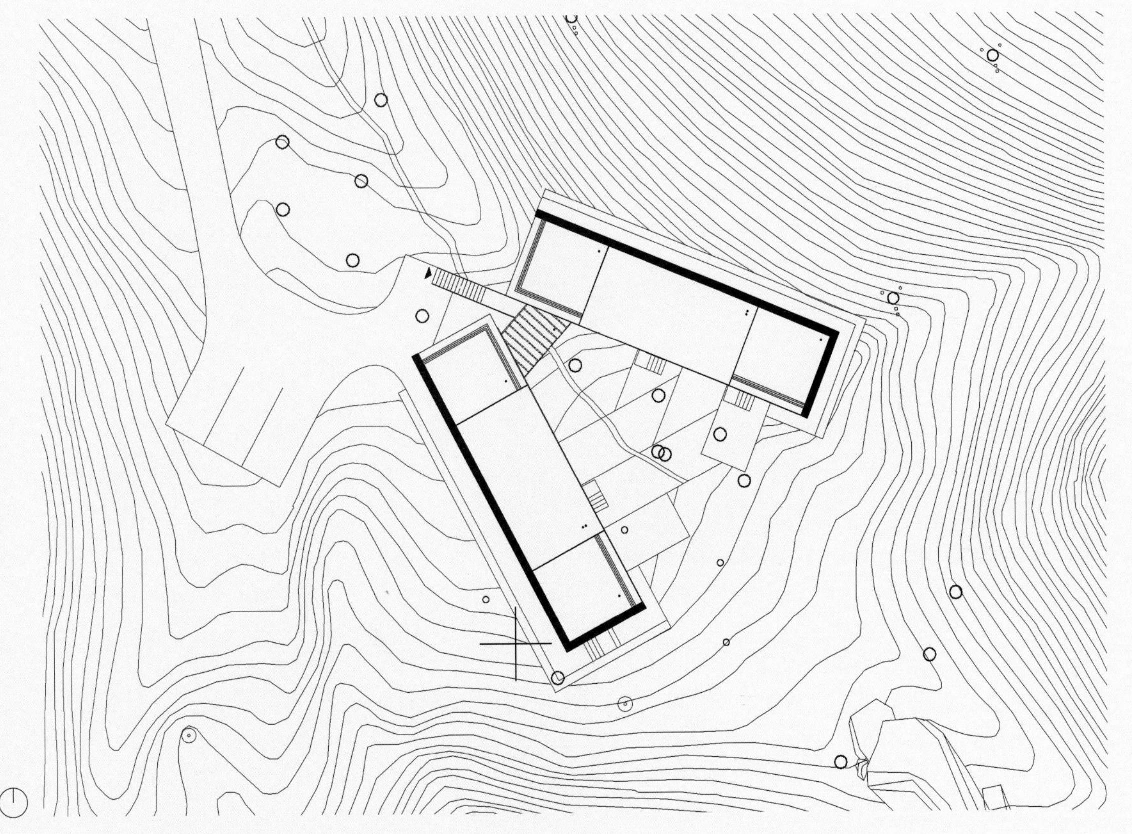

Top: Sections through the private wing (above) and public wing (below) of the house.

Left: A site plan shows the careful positioning of the building within the landscape.

House in Savoy

Novalaise, France 2002

Tectoniques

The achievement of Lyons-based co-operative Tectoniques in this house in France's Savoy region is to have designed a building that ticks all the correct environmental boxes while maintaining an uncompromisingly modern look that makes no concessions to any kind of folksy architecture.

Placed among woods at the top of a slope, above its steepest part so that it can benefit from the best views over a lake, the house has been positioned to touch the ground as lightly as possible. But this is not a self-effacing structure that looks as if it could have been put up by a slightly more sophisticated than usual vernacular builder. In terms of colour it may blend into its surroundings, with its larch cladding and blue-green panels almost the colour of a mountain lake, but it owes its origins in terms of form more to the urban villa than to a peasant hut.

Framed in pine, with elements 140 millimetres (5.5 inches) thick, the house is uncompromisingly square in form, with a gently sloping roof that kicks up again on the south side to provide a large shading overhang. This forms one part of the environmental strategy, reducing the ingress of direct sunlight in the summer. The larch cladding is in open horizontal blades, allowing air to circulate in the 30-centimetre (12-inch) gap between it and the watertight enclosure of wood-cement panels. Again this helps with summer cooling, whereas winter temperatures are kept up by the 14 centimetres (5½ inches) of insulation contained within the timber framework.

Folding, sliding louvred larch panels, flush with the cladding, can cover the windows to provide shade. When covering the windows in this way, they reveal the blue-green panels beneath them, so changing the appearance of the building according to the way it is being used.

The structure allows an open ground floor, arranged around a central island comprising the kitchen and the staircase. Simple and open, the staircase is made from folded dark-coloured timber that matches a couple of timber screens to either side of it. The effect is of sophisticated elegance; although the building has been positioned, and the windows placed, to make the most of the views there is nothing rustic about this interior. On the upper floor there are four bedrooms and two bathrooms. In summer ventilation is improved by the circulation of air within the plenum of the roof space. In winter there is radiant heating in the ceiling.

The four members of Tectoniques (Jocelyne Duvert, Pierre-Yves Lebouc, Max Rolland and Alain Vargas) are dedicated to the use of renewable and recyclable materials, and to efficient and rapid methods of construction. They like to explain their principles and ideas in a somewhat obscurantist fashion, but there is nothing pretentious about this house or about their other projects, many of which are on a larger scale. Instead, they demonstrate that it is possible to have strong environmental principles and a fondness for timber as a material without in any way embracing a homespun aesthetic.

Above left: When the larch shutters slide across the windows, they reveal blue-green coloured panels beneath.

Above right: The open ground floor is effectively arranged around a central island.

Above: A large overhang on the roof is an ingenious means of providing shade to the south façade.

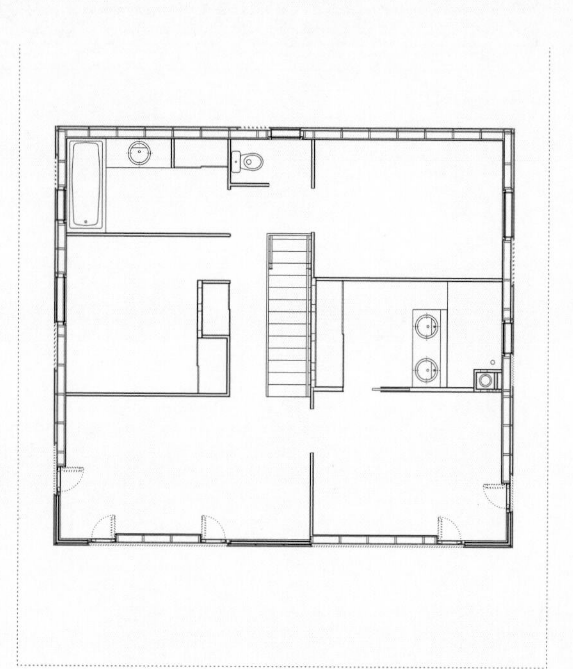

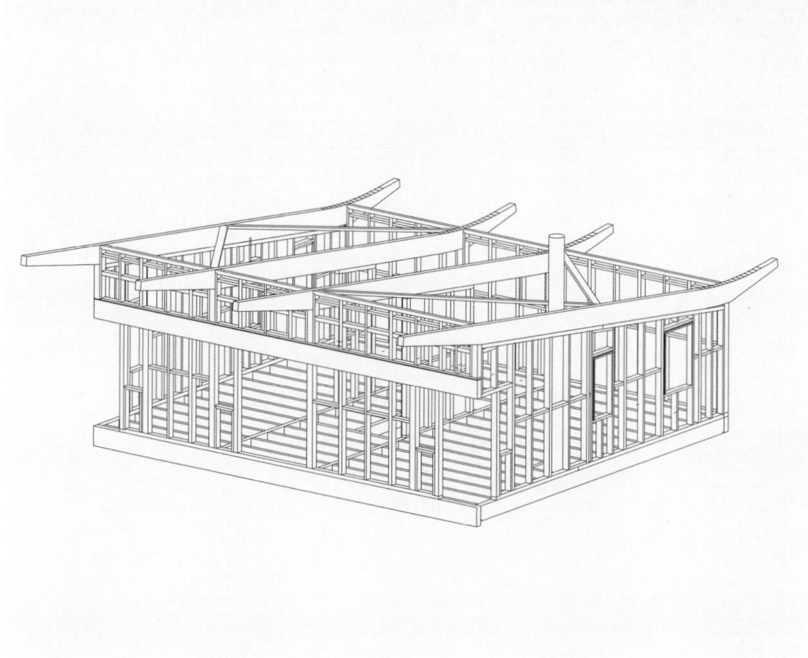

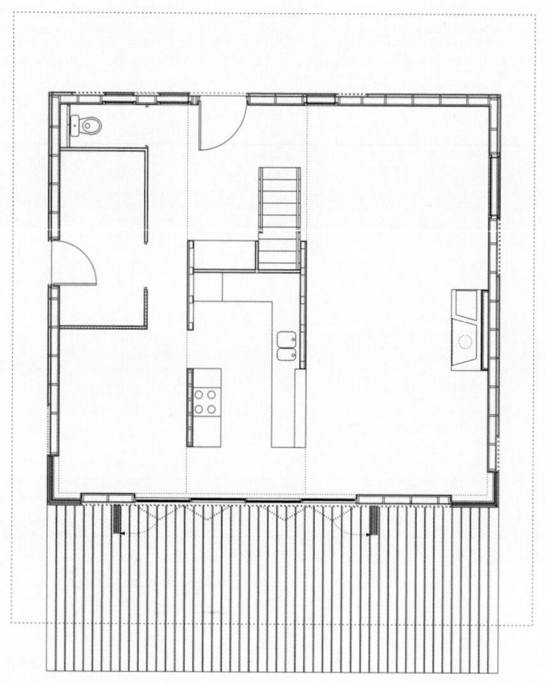

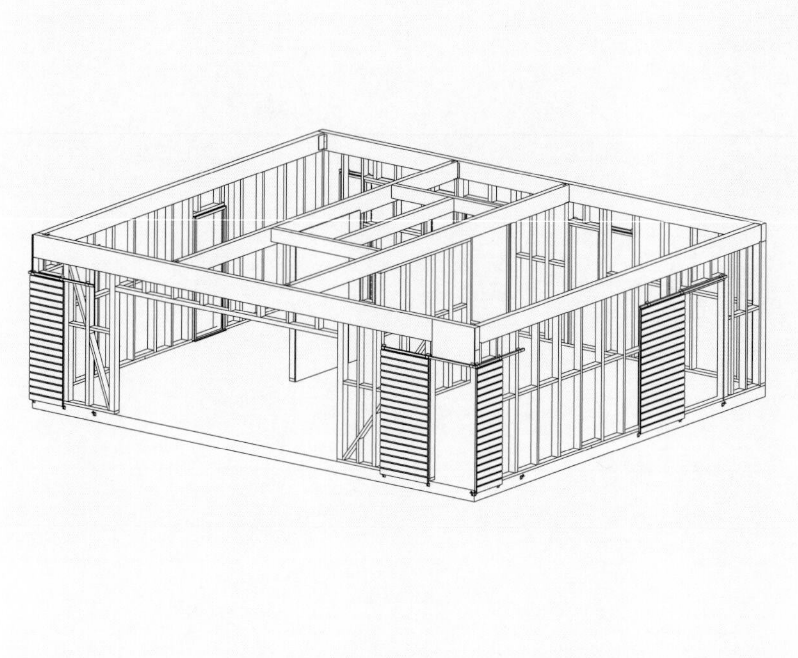

Top and above left: Ground-floor and first-floor plans of the house.

Top and above right: Drawings show the structure of the ground floor and the upper floor with its distinctive roof form.

Above left: The folded wood staircase forms an elegant centrepiece to the interior.

Above right: The house sits on top of a hill, allowing its occupant to enjoy superb views of the area.

House in Pedralbes

Barcelona, Spain 2002
Tito Dalmau,
BDM Arquitectos

Above: Timber terraces and an overhanging roof provide essential shade to the glazed southern façade.

Barcelona is one of the most vibrant cities in Europe, but sometimes the hustle and bustle can become overwhelming. What a joy it must be, therefore, to have a house that allows you to get away from it all, while still being in easy reach of the city and enjoying magnificent views. That is the lucky situation of the clients of Tito Dalmau of BDM Arquitectos, who have a site of 4,700 square metres (50,600 square feet) in the elegant hillside suburb of Pedralbes. Dalmau has extended their fortune by giving them a house with a massive total floor area of 1,200 square metres (12, 900 square feet) that can open up entirely to the views over the city and the sea beyond. The house, which he has described as like an aeroplane ready to take off, is poised on the highest part of the site, so that the garden falls away beneath it.

The southern façade is almost entirely glazed, but evidently needs considerable shading. This is supplied partly by Venetian blinds, and also by having large overhangs above each level. Those at first- and second-storey level double as balconies, in super-hard ipe timber, effectively extending the bedrooms into the garden. The top-floor master bedroom is particularly dramatically placed, with a high, glazed roof above exposed aluminium trusses, and with effectively another timber deck above, although this one is not reachable and is purely there to provide shade. A final timber deck forms a terrace at ground level and incorporates a pool.

The lowest floor of the house is organized around two main axes. One runs from the entrance, a timber-and-glass porch at the back of the house, through to the projecting double-height living room at the front. This is the only space to use full-length curtains rather than venetian blinds. The other axis goes from one side of the house to the other, passing through the principle spaces of library, living rooms and dining room. Spaces at this level are not rigidly defined; instead they are divided by sliding birch screen walls, allowing considerable reconfiguration.

This use of wood, although very crisply detailed, prevents the building having an over-harsh aesthetic and is reinforced by the presence of a third timber element – the oak floors, used everywhere but in the kitchen and bathrooms.

The primary purpose of this house is to allow its inhabitants to look outwards, but on occasions, when they direct their gaze inwards – when it is either too cold or too hot to engage fully with the external world – the generous use of timber will have a significant effect on their experience of the building.

Above left: With such large gardens, space can be afforded for cooling pools.

Above right: The house sits symmetrically around the double-height living room.

Top left: A shaded walkway leads to the main entrance.

Above: Extremely hard ipe timber is used for walkways and balconies.

Top right: The garden falls away to allow magnificent views over Barcelona.

Above: Oak flooring is found through almost all of the house.

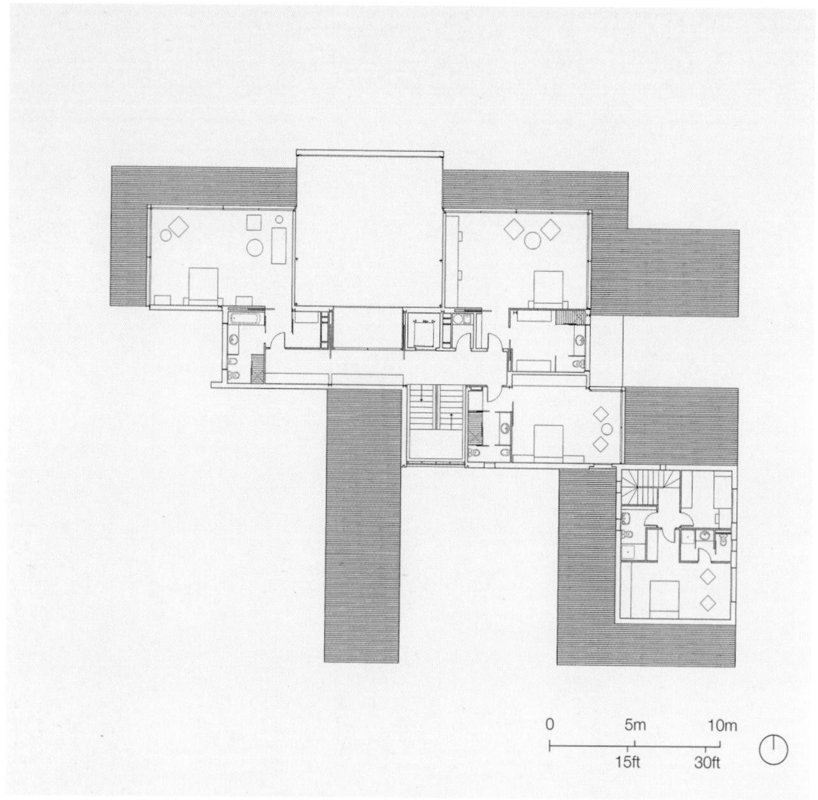

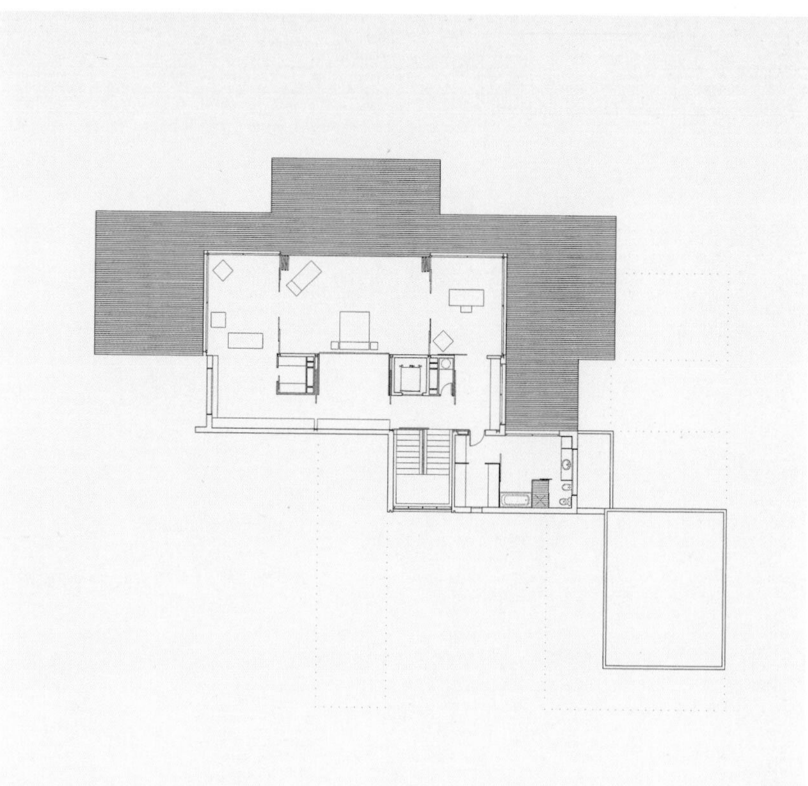

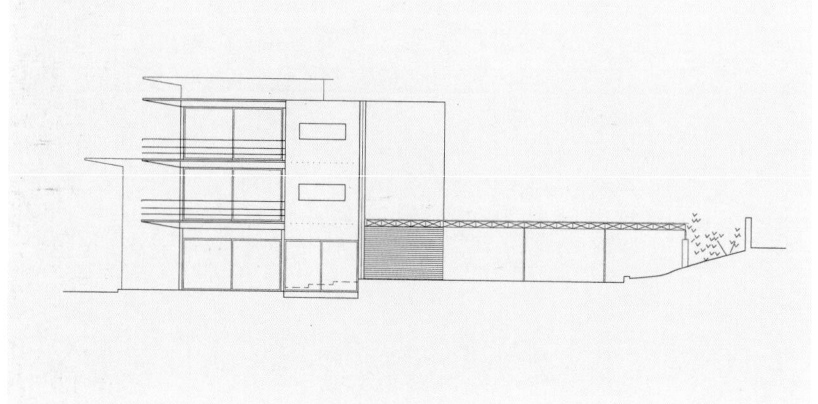

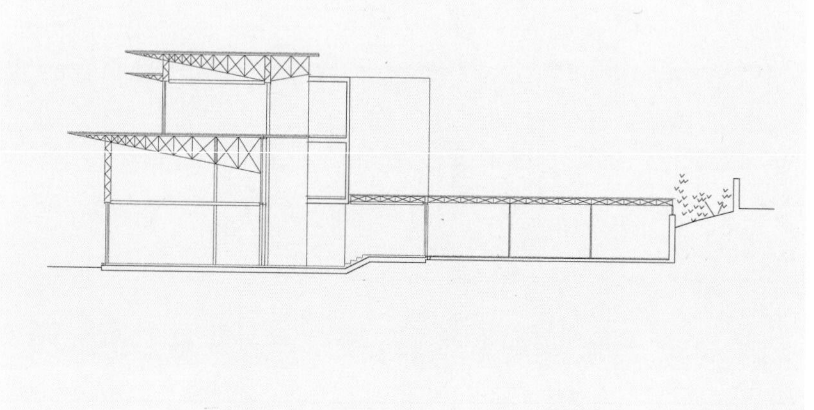

Top left and right: Plans of the first and second floors, showing the terraced balconies that provide shading to the levels below.

Above left: East elevation.

Above right: Section through the house showing the north-south axis.

Above: master bedroom, with a timber screen, shaded roof, and the very best terrace and view.

Mann Residence

Sonoma County, California, USA 2003
Fernau and Hartman Architects

Put a house in a fantastic setting and the last thing you want is to have to stay indoors all the time – especially if it doubles as your workspace and you spend a considerable amount of time there anyway. The traditional solution is to provide plenty of outdoor space, with shelter that allows it to be used as much as possible. But Fernau and Hartman Architects has gone a step further with a house it designed in Sonoma County, California. It has taken the concept of the campus and scaled it down, so that the 'house' is in fact more of a collection of buildings, relating to each other and each one enhancing the experience of the user by its relationship to its neighbours and the way in which it exploits the views.

Sonoma County is an important wine-growing area and there are vineyards to the east of the Mann Residence, which is two hours' drive north of San Francisco. But the site itself is on a knoll that forms part of a chain of hills running roughly north–south, with the coastal range of mountains rising to the west. The clients, Frederic and Kitty Mann, wanted a home where they could both live and carry on their work as artists. Fernau and Hartman is a practice that prides itself on a pragmatic approach and on responding to its environment. But in this case, although the environment was in many ways unbeatable, in the most immediate sense it had been destroyed – the developer had scraped down the topology of the knoll to create a flat surface.

Faced with this tabula rasa, albeit in a magnificent setting, the architect decided to take a different approach. 'We thought of the site as an acropolis,' says partner Richard Fernau. Although the cluster of buildings gives the impression of a studied informality, the effect is achieved only by following a much more formal approach. In this way, despite the relatively isolated nature of the site, you are given a sense of moving from the public to the private realm. A dead-straight granite walkway runs north–south. At its southern end are an observation point and a pool. Going north, it then crosses the carport before coming to the courtyard prescribed by the buildings of the house. Kinked and set at an angle to the walkway, the courtyard is not fully visible until you enter it, both preserving privacy and giving a sense of arrival.

The buildings themselves have a simplicity of form and structure that belies the care with which they were designed. Although they are obviously all the work of one hand, the use of a range of bright colours and of different heights and forms could lead the casual visitor to see them as an accretion over time. Structurally they are timber framed, although some auxiliary steel has been used. Cladding is in a mixture of shiplap western red cedar, used as horizontal boards, and integrally coloured ochre cement-plaster walls. With the cladding stained a greenish brown or painted a strong red, this is not a house that shrinks into its environment. But, because of the way it is broken up, it is less of a presence on its vantage point than a single monolith could be.

Internally there is a similar mixture of effects and colours, as one volume projects into another or there are views between different rooms. Again, a catholic mix of materials has been used, including bamboo – an attractive material that is both more dimensionally stable and harder than many timbers – for flooring. With windows placed to make the best of views rather than for any purely formalistic reason, there is again a sense of a house that has 'just happened' – an effect that could be achieved only by the very clear and rigorous thinking of its designers.

Above and top: There is a studied informality in the clever arrangement of the different structural elements.

Right: The cladding is a combination of shiplap western red cedar and ochre-coloured cement render.

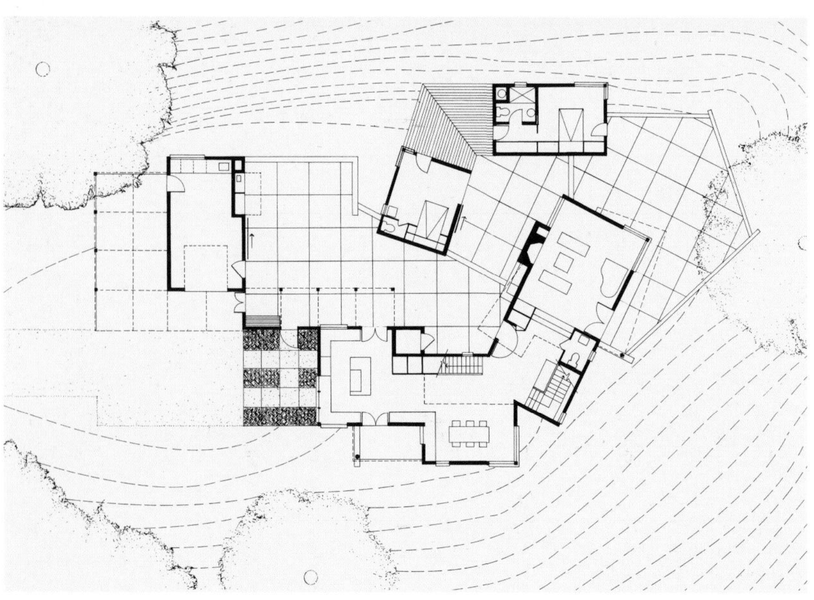

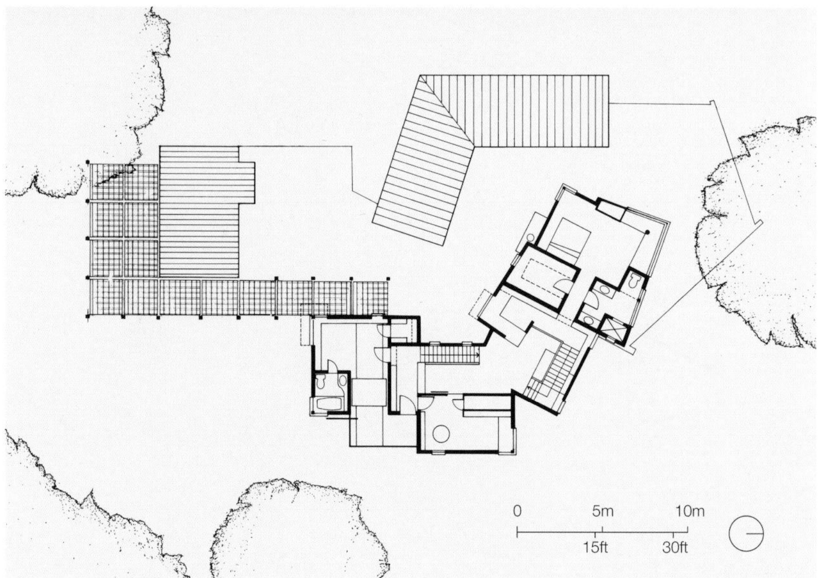
0
5m
10m
15ft
30ft

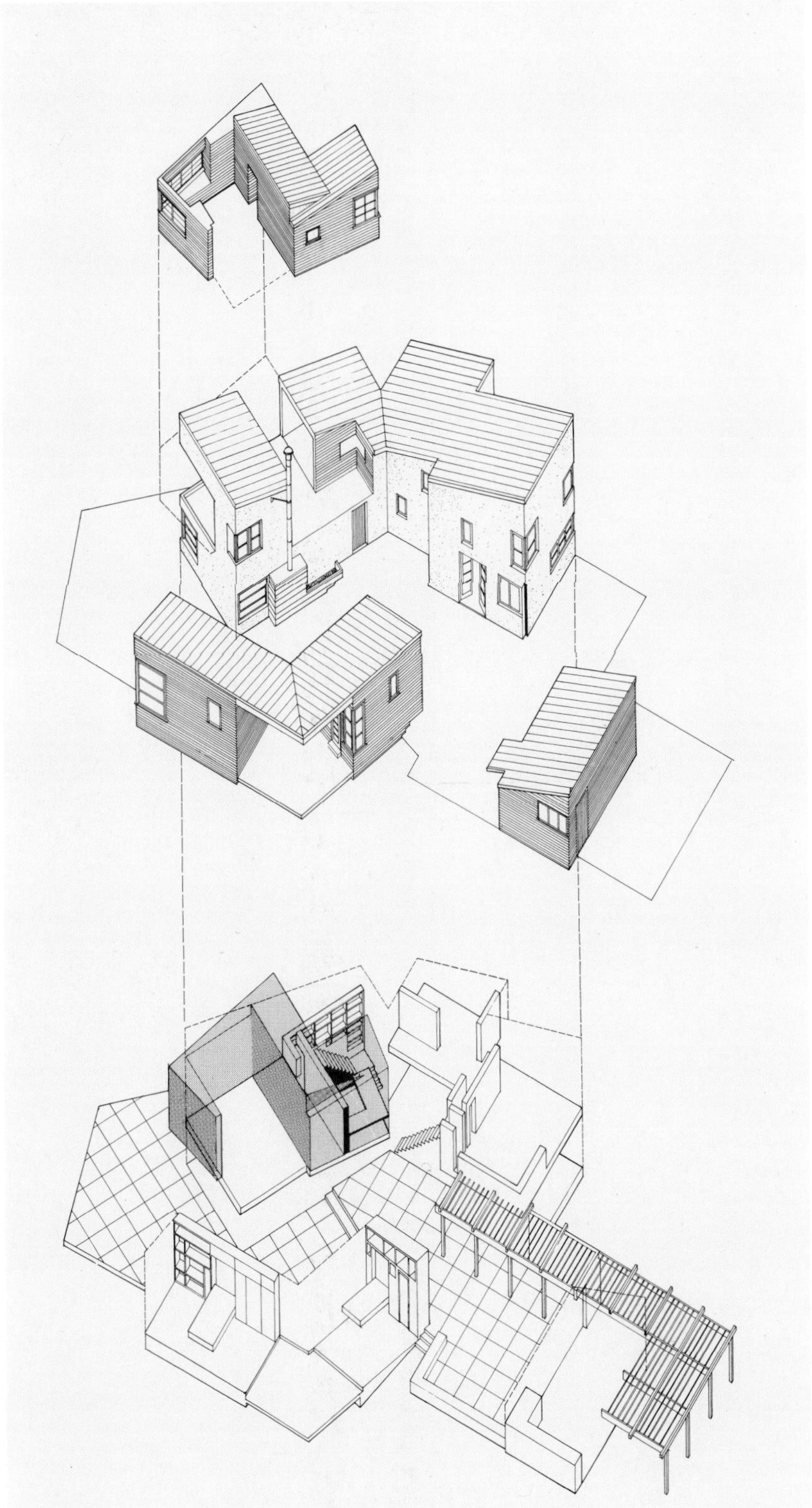

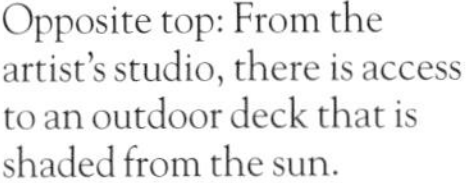

Opposite top: From the artist's studio, there is access to an outdoor deck that is shaded from the sun.

Opposite bottom: Ground-floor and first-floor plans of the building.

Above left: The arrangement of elements provides a campus-like feeling to the structure.

Top right: Framing to the glazing is minimal so that attention does not become focused on it.

Above right: Colourful treatments extend from the exterior to the interior, serving as a visual link.

Riddell Residence
Wilson, Wyoming, USA 2002
Will Bruder Architects

Right: A shady grove of aspen trees provided a serene setting in which to build the house.

Top: Iron nails create a deliberate pattern of staining that adds interest to the vertical cedar cladding.

Above: The entrance to the Riddell Residence is situated on one of the building's long sides.

What would you miss if you gave up work? The money, the friends, the intellectual stimulation? Few people would say they would miss the office itself, but this was the case with Ed and Lee Riddell when they sold their advertising and design business in Jackson, Wyoming, to concentrate, respectively, on photography and painting. Their office had been designed by Will Bruder of Phoenix-based Will Bruder Architects, and the couple missed it so much that they commissioned him to design their house.

Bruder, who is an individualist and a determinedly non-theoretical architect, is convinced of the value of having the right clients. 'I believe architects work because of clients, not in spite of clients,' he has said; and he could not have had better clients than the Riddells.

The connection was close. As well as employing Bruder to design their office, Lee Riddell was on the board of Teton County Library, which gave Bruder one of his larger commissions. And the architect stayed frequently with the couple. In return, they were prepared to put themselves entirely in his hands. Whereas on large projects, United States architects frequently have to concede almost all control of the interior to interior designers, here Bruder had total control – right down to specifying that the clients should have a particular lime-green cushion on their sofa. Although they were sceptical they went along with this, and now find that it reflects and anticipates the colour of their environment.

This environment is a grove of aspen trees, which was the reason for the Riddells choosing the site. They would have liked an entirely transparent house, but there was not enough seclusion to allow this, so Bruder created a compromise, providing privacy for the studio and bedrooms, with a much more open, and open-plan, feeling for the living room, dining room and kitchen.

The single-storey building, with an area of 232 square metres (2,500 square feet), is on land that slopes away in two directions. Although it is broadly rectangular, the plan is far more imaginative than this might at first suggest. The entrance is on one of the long sides, past two sculptural rocks and via a timber deck. The near-diagonal hallway, with a change in level of four steps halfway along its length, allows spaces of differing sizes and shapes for the bedroom, exercise room and studio, and opens out to the open-plan space at one end of the building. At the other end are the garage and storage areas.

The house uses standard platform framing, with glulam beams at the ridge and eaves, and trusses acting as rafters for a vaulted ceiling in the living room. There is an asymmetric pitched roof, adding interest to the gable ends which are clad with vertical cedar planks in which iron nails create a deliberate grid of staining. The long elevations use a combination of zinc siding, horizontal cedar and flush-detailed glazed openings, designed to mirror the landscape format Ed Riddell uses in his photographs. Internally, Bruder has used maple extensively, both on floors and in custom-made joinery, giving a warm and elegantly detailed feeling to the spaces.

Originally trained as a sculptor, Bruder is dismissive of work such as Gehry's that is too self-consciously 'sculptural'. 'I like to look for the extraordinary in the ordinary,' he has said. 'I like to create the extraordinary with the ordinary.' At the Riddell Residence he has achieved this, allowing his clients to enjoy the interaction with nature that they desire, in a house that is itself a self-effacing artwork.

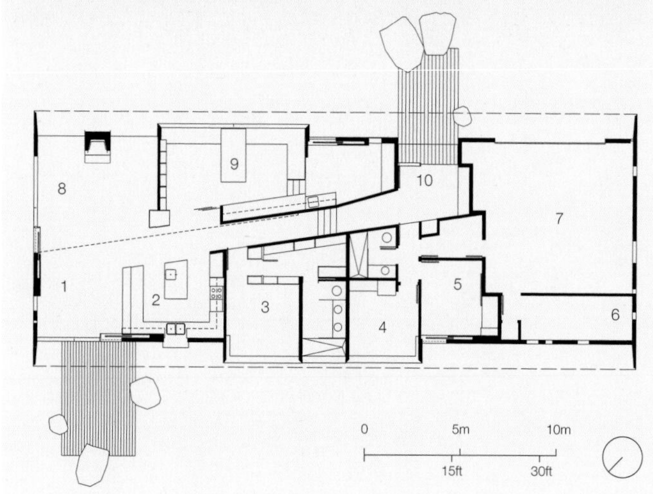

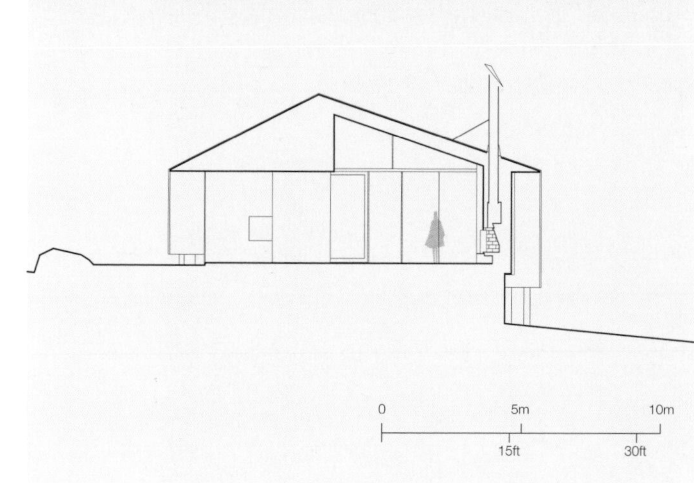

Top left: The living room forms part of an expansive, but still interesting, open-plan space.

Above left: By running the hallway diagonally, unusual spaces are created within a rectangular box. 1. dining; 2. kitchen; 3. master bedroom; 4. guest bedroom; 5. exercise room; 6. storage; 7. garage; 8. living; 9. studio; 10. entry.

Top right: Maple is used for both flooring and custom-made joinery, adding warm tones to the interior.

Above right: A section through the house that shows its asymmetrical pitched roof.

Above right: An intriguing combination of privacy and openness is successfully provided by the façades.

House in the Orchard
Corroy-le-Grand, Belgium 2002
Damien Carnoy

Above left: The glazed enclosure to the entrance doors is reminiscent of a tree of life.

Right: Brick cladding to the lower floor gives a sense of heaviness and solidity to the building.

Belgian architect Damien Carnoy is a romantic, but also a technically capable architect. His buildings embrace organic forms in a manner that is almost a throwback to Rudolph Steiner, while garnering prizes for top-rate thermal performance through both their conceptual design and an execution that takes care to eliminate cold bridges entirely.

The house he designed at Corroy-le-Grand in Brabant-Wallon demonstrates this thinking. It consists of a main elliptical volume, with a curved turret to one side. At the other extreme the end of the oval is intersected by a rectangular form containing a compact, separate two-level apartment with a very tight spiral staircase, and a carport at its end. Carnoy describes this combination of shapes as, 'The result of my analysis of my client's (informal) desires and the will to create a mini built-up area in the landscape. This multiple shape was the best solution to encounter all these elements: the complementarities of a circle – not really round – featuring the ideal or the dream and a square – not perfectly square – for the link with reality.'

The result is a building where, with the exception of a small laundry room, not a single space has walls that are all straight. The use of curves is accentuated by the roof, which is a saddle shape like an ellipse that has been folded down the middle, a form that Carnoy has used before on a crèche in Louvain-la-Neuve, completed in 1998.

The main entrance is through conventionally rectangular doors, but they are set in a larger, two-storey, leaf-shaped glazed enclosure. On the upper storey the glass has curved timber glazing bars coming out from a timber stem, like the ribs of a leaf or even a tree of life. Some of the timber-framed windows are also curved to echo the form of the walls, and the canopy over the carport has a curving upward sweep that terminates the butterfly roof of the rectangular element.

Photographs of the construction process reveal that the timber framework is surprisingly slender – it looks almost as if it could be blown away. But the end result is not a lightweight house. The building is anchored by the fact that some of the cladding to the lower floor is red brickwork. There are also heavy internal rammed-earth walls to provide thermal mass that can modulate variations in temperature. The rest of the cladding is timber boarding, with the whole held down visually by the dark grey of the fibre-cement slates on the roof. Inside there are timber floors, and timber boarding on the underside of the roof. In summer the setting of the house, in an orchard, allows the leaves of the trees to add to the shading of the structure.

This is very much a building that acts as an object in the landscape, and one that must have represented a considerable challenge in its construction. If it is more intriguing than beautiful to many eyes, it is certainly a demonstration that a determined architect can ensure that even the most complex domestic design can be executed effectively to give the home-owner an unusual structure that performs to the highest standards.

Left: The curved form of the main house crashes into a rectangular form containing a separate two-storey apartment.

Above: During its construction, the building's very delicate-seeming timbers were particularly evident.

Top left: Timber floors are used throughout the main house, linking one space to another.

Above left: Heavy internal construction gives an almost subterranean feel to the living room.

Above right: A spiral stair provides an elegant link between the two levels of the independent apartment.

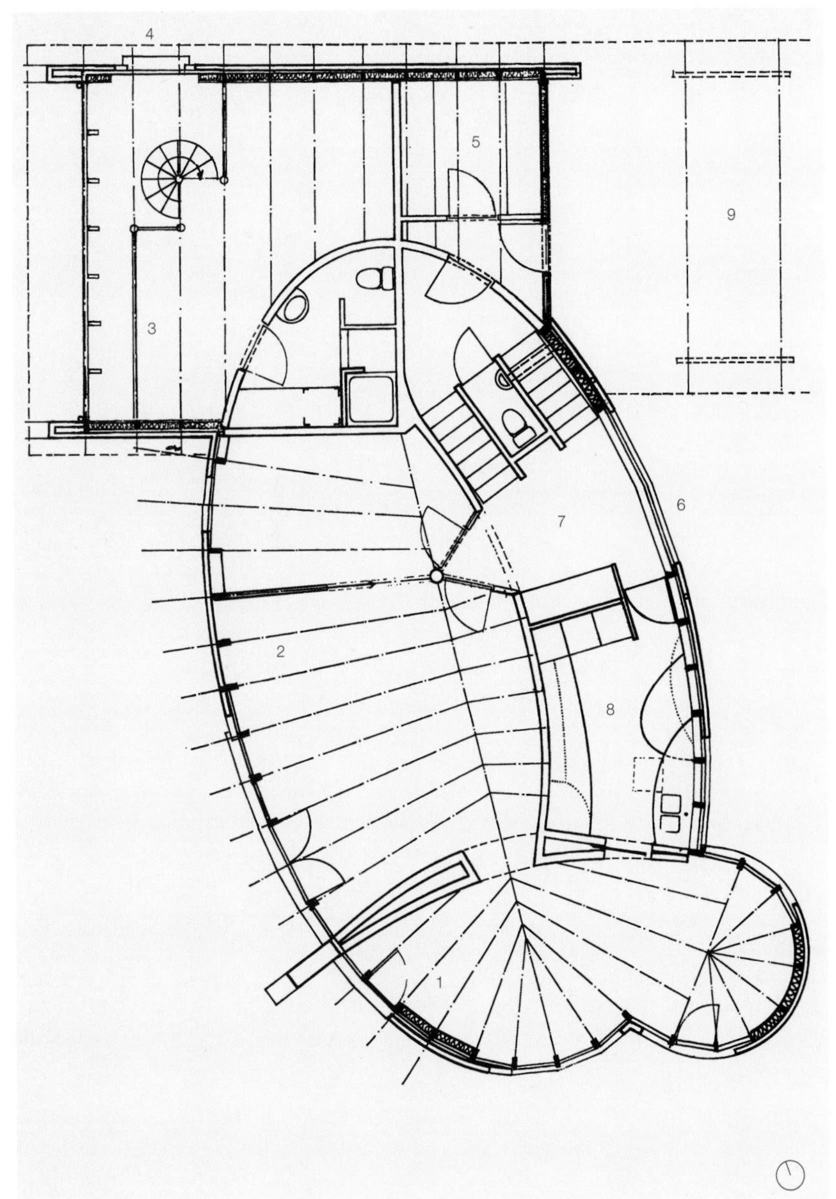

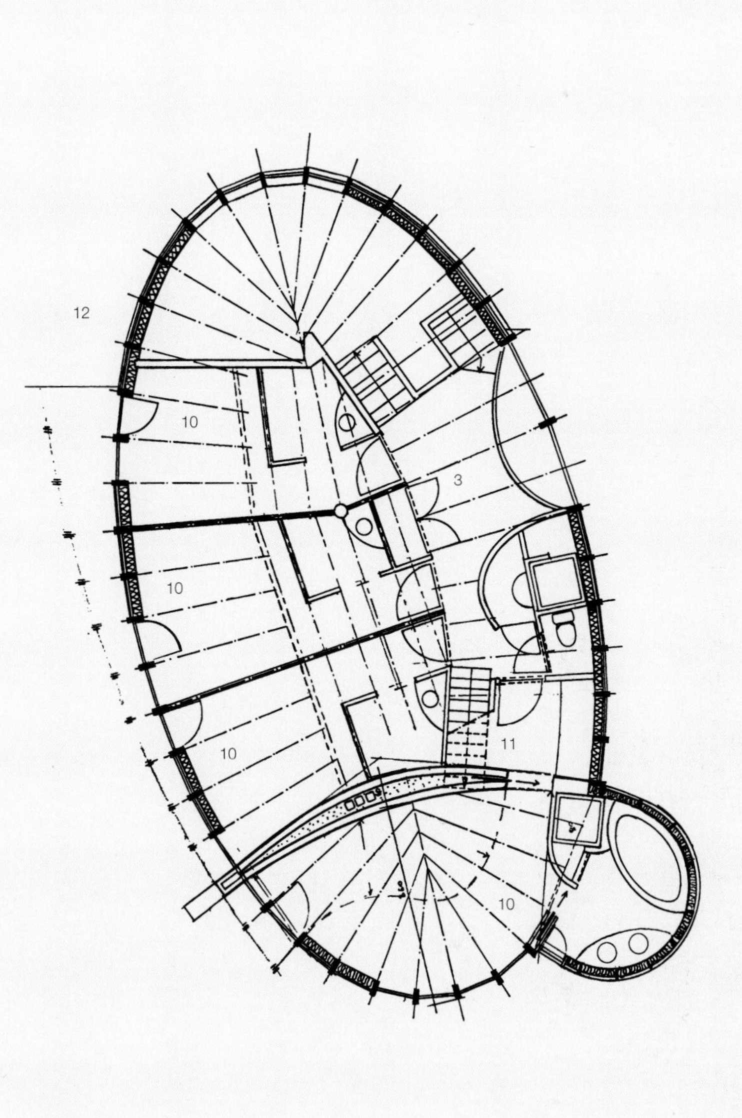

Above left and right: Ground and first-floor plans. 1. dining room; 2. living room; 3. apartment; 4. apartment entrance; 5. laundry; 6. house entrance; 7. hall; 8. kitchen; 9. carport; 10. bedroom; 11. dressing room; 12. balcony

Villa B

Lake Starnberg, Germany 2001
Fink + Jocher

Lake Starnberg in Germany is a well-known beauty spot and an area of high-cost housing. Not surprisingly, anybody building there will want to make maximum use of the views. So when Fink + Jocher designed a house to suit multiple members of a family, it was not surprising that it wanted as much accommodation as possible on the upper layer. It has achieved this with a design that is slightly reminiscent of *geta*, those traditional Japanese sandals that support a dark platform of wood on two rectangular wooden blocks.

The house is on a plot near the centre of a village, separated from the lake by a road and a narrow strip of land. Existing trees give the site a park-like feel. The organization of the building, although at first seeming slightly wilful, solves a number of problems. It provides views from the main living areas and also enhances the privacy of these spaces by lifting them above ground level. With all access to the upper area contained in the forward 'block', which also has two study rooms and stores, the rear supporting block can function as an entirely self-contained flat. Since part of the brief was that the house should accommodate an extended family, this was a major achievement.

Given this arrangement, the architect had then only to solve a couple of trivial problems – how to support the cantilevered structure of the upper volume, and ensure high levels of sound insulation, without which all efforts at segregation would have been wasted. The structural problem was solved by the use of a relatively compact timber frame. Beams 220 millimetres (8½ inches) deep and 120 millimetres (4¾ inches) wide support the cantilevered structure. By using impact-sound insulation on the floors above inhabited areas, coupled with the use of elastic bearing strips, the architect has reduced the transmission of sound between floors. A similar approach has been taken for occupied rooms, where the walls are made from the following: 12.5-millimetre (½-inch) plasterboard; 27-millimetre (1-inch) sound-insulating elastic strips; 12-millimetre (⅖-inch) plywood; 120-millimetre (4½-inch) cellulose-fibre insulation between 60 or 120-millimetre (2⅓ or 4½-inch) timber studding; two layers of 12.5-millimetre (½-inch) plasterboard.

Larch is used extensively on the building. Cladding is with three-layer larch lam, stained black, and the entrance door is set flush into the front face, with minimal ironmongery. This, combined with the use of dark blinds on some of the ground-floor windows, creates the impression of almost uninterruptedly dark supporting volumes. These contrast with the much lighter, brighter upper area, with its large windows framed in unstained larch. This near-transparent volume, which glows at night if curtains are not drawn, therefore seems to float above its supports.

Internally, there are oak parquet floors, and custom-designed white-varnished oak shelves and built-in furniture. The furniture tends to be long and shallow with minimal detailing, cleverly echoing the form of the house itself. The effect is not quite of today; somehow there is a whiff of 1960s corporate design about both the interiors and the building. Nothing about it is soft or whimsical, and it is easy to imagine it being used for an informal office meeting in beautiful surroundings.

But while not to everybody's taste, it is definitely a house that makes the most of its surroundings, and carries the concept of its design through to the smallest details.

Far left: At night, Villa B is an intriguing structure as it glows within its parkland setting.

Left: A rear view shows the self-contained apartment, which is situated on the ground floor.

Above: Unstained larch windows form an effective contrast to the black-stained larch lam cladding.

Above: White-varnished oak shelves and furniture accentuate the horizontal nature of the design.

Above: The living space is on the upper floor to take maximum advantage of the views.

Left: Oak parquet floors add subtle pattern and texture to the interior of Villa B.

Opposite top right: The long, narrow kitchen runs across the entire width of the building.

Opposite bottom right: The elegant interiors would work equally well for private and for business entertaining.

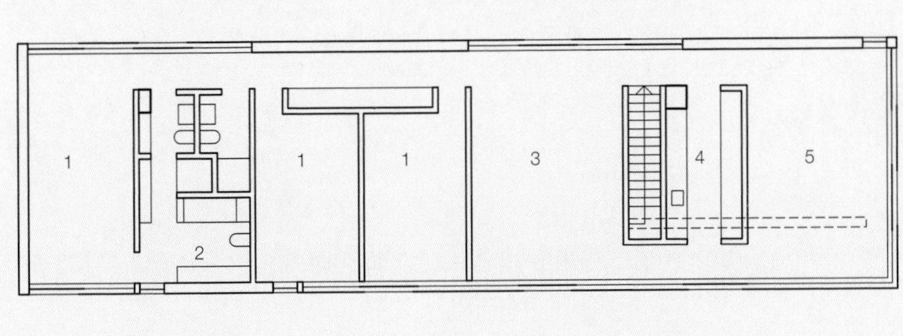

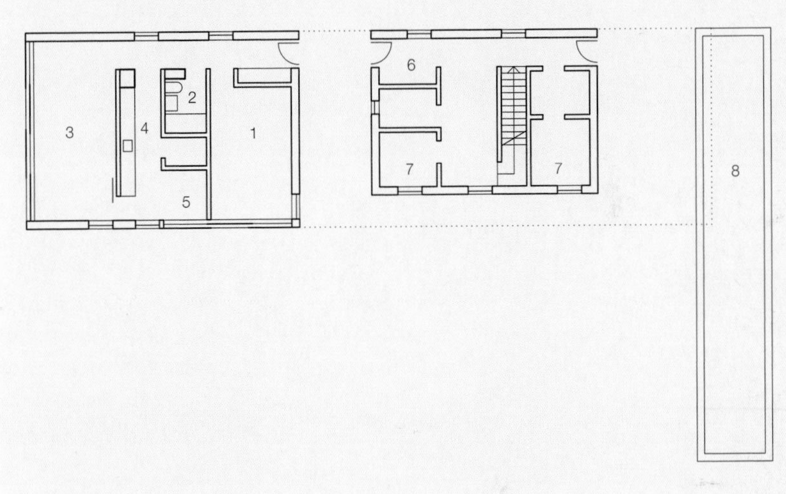

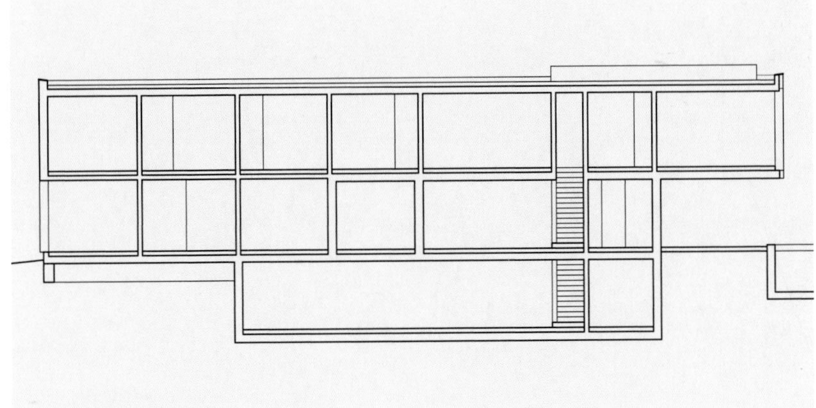

Above right: A long section through Villa B.

Top right: The ground-floor and first-floor plans of the building. 1. bedroom; 2. bathroom; 3. living area; 4. kitchen; 5. dining area; 6. storage; 7. study; 8. swimming pool.

There is a sense in which all wood buildings are prefabricated. For the timber elements at least, there is no concrete to pour on site, no units as tiny as bricks to stick together with anything as messy as mortar. The simplest kind of construction may involve just cutting down trees, letting them season a bit and nailing them together to make an elementary log cabin. And the log cabin is a form that has not disappeared. The sophisticated may see it as merely an upmarket garden shed, but plenty of companies make good livings selling prefabricated log cabins for retirement or holiday living. They are, perhaps, a more attractive version of the caravan, that 'mobile home' that often spends its entire life in one place.

But what of more contemporary approaches to prefabrication? One method is to use timber elements to make the walls, like building blocks. An example is Steko, a block system developed in Switzerland that fits together almost like Lego, and allows very rapid construction. It has been used for a project in the United Kingdom designed by architect de Rijke Marsh Morgan, and, ironically, because it is self-build it is taking a very long time to reach completion!

A block developed recently by the French company Kallisté Eco Forêt has won industrial prizes and is patented in several countries. Described as a sawn-timber breeze block, it is intended to be a lighter and more environmentally responsible alternative to this near-universal building material, offering advantages to the small builder and self-builder alike. The blocks can be made from a variety of sustainably sourced timbers, allowing local production.

Probably next to these simple units in terms of complexity is the use of prefabricated cladding panels, as, for example, on the house by Sinikka Ropponen and Atelier Brunel in Fontainebleau in France described in this chapter (see page 134). A sensible and rapid way to build, it is an approach embraced by architects interested in achieving good buildings in a relatively simple manner, but does not offer the combination of romance and technology that some designers find so appealing in more thorough-going prefabrication solutions.

One can sense this thinking, for instance, behind Holzbox Tirol and Anton Höss' creation of prefabricated housing in Merano, Italy (see page 142), where there is a sheer delight in showing that things can be done in a different way, almost a holding up of two fingers to those who are wedded to tradition. At this level there is always a hope that the new approach will eventually prove to be less expensive than the traditional one, but this usually involves reproducing it on such a large scale that by the time this happens the original architect is likely to have lost interest.

Italian architect Matteo Thun, for example, admits that the HEIDIS prefabricated house he first designed for timber company Rubner in 1999, is about 15 per cent more expensive than a more conventional rival (see opposite). About ten of these houses have since been built, using prefabricated walls, windows, floors and ceilings. Thun describes them as a contemporary reinterpretation of classic Tyrolean architecture and they are certainly handsome buildings, filled with light. The cost is justified not only by their attractive nature, but also by their intelligent use of daylight and high insulation levels to drive down their energy consumption, and their relatively short construction times. Thun claims there is no need for a heating system. And neither does prefabrication mean that only one version is available. A HEIDIS House can be anything from the 74-square-metre (795-square-foot) 'weekend' model right up to the generous 258-square-metre (2,780-square-foot) 'luxury' version.

Nevertheless, a HEIDIS House is easily recognizable, and so is another prefabricated home that has found widespread acceptance – the German Huf Haus (see opposite). This distinctive A-frame house again offers relatively rapid construction and a high environmental performance, coupled with a distinctive appearance, albeit one that can be customized to the buyer's specific needs. With no loadbearing internal walls, the houses allow a lot more open space and light than is normal with traditional masonry construction. They are relatively expensive, but engender such affection that in the United Kingdom, for example, a Huf Haus Owners Group was formed at the start of 2005, rather in the way that owners of certain types of classic car choose to band together.

Another such upmarket solution is the Haiku House, a form of pole-and-beam construction that reinterprets the Japanese country house for today, nodding along the way to the ideals of Frank Lloyd Wright and Greene & Greene (see opposite). Aimed at the relatively affluent, these houses have been built in the United States, the United Kingdom, the Netherlands, France and the Caribbean.

At the University of Kansas, students are given the design and build of a modular home as a course exercise. The most recent result, Modular2, has recently been completed in Kansas City (see page 154). It aims to be an affordable solution, but is still a relatively expensive structure.

The architects of the Hangar House in Nantes, France (see page 130) could not afford such an expensive structure. Instead, faced with clients who wanted a lot of space at relatively low cost, and who had no preconceptions about appearance, they went for an agricultural framing system.

This is not the only type of pragmatism that works with wood. Over the centuries people have built and rebuilt houses, using the same materials over and over again, a tradition that Arturo Frediani Sarfatí continued when he built a house on a site packed with history in a village in north-west Spain (see page 146). And so did Bone/Levine Architects when designing a house in Milanville, Pennsylvania for one of the practice's partners. With an existing barn on the site, the architect decided to reuse this structure, despite the enormous amount of work involved (see page 136).

One thing all the projects described above share is that they were designed; their architects used drawings. But Nick Fisher and Jo Jordan, building their own house in Tanzania, scorned such planning altogether (see page 150). Scavenging materials or buying them cheaply, they built their house using no more than what they describe as a 'day plan', a decision on what to do at the start of each day. Their house, a mix of serendipity and personal prejudices, looks back to a time before the invention of planning, or even of the architect as we understand the role today.

Such an approach would not work in most cities, and instead some architects have been toying with the idea of bringing in whole buildings that could be added onto existing ones. For example, in 2003 German architect Werner Aisslinger came up with the idea of the Loftcube, a self-contained unit that could simply be craned onto the flat roof of a building and used either as a home or an office. This attractive box, constructed from timber but edged in curved white Corian, has windows covered with timber shutters on all four sides. It measures 6.6 x 6.6 metres (21.5 x 21.5 feet) and weighs 2.5 tonnes. After receiving a lot of publicity for his concept, Aisslinger claimed he was ready to put it into commercial production, but there has been little sign of this so far.

A similarly appealing, but also improbable, idea is the Parasite LP2 house, which Korteknie & Stuhlmacher Architecten built in Rotterdam when the city was European Capital of Culture in 2001. Violent green, and attached to the top of an existing building by clinging to a concrete upstand, the LP2 was made from the German product Dickholz (thick, solidly glued sheets of pine) and from Kerto LVL (laminated veneer lumber). The idea is that it taps into the services of its host in a relationship that, while not really symbiotic, is more benign than parasitic.

Projects like this may be fanciful – Parasite in fact stands for Prototypes for Advanced Ready-made Amphibious Small-scale Individual Temporary Ecological houses – but it is the very versatility of timber that allows them to be made so easily. And, as with all crazy ideas, the best of them are likely to seem remarkably mainstream in the future.

Top: The German Huf Haus is adaptable, but always retains its distinctive outline.

Above left: The HEIDIS House, designed by Italian architect Matteo Thun, exploits intelligent use of daylight and high levels of insulation to drive down energy consumption.

Above right: Haiku Houses, based on a Japanese concept, have found favour in the United States and Europe.

Hangar House

Nantes, France 2002
Sylvain Gasté/ Michel Bazantay

Appearances aren't everything. When two friends approached architects Sylvain Gasté and Michel Bazantay about the design of a house they were very specific about their needs, but these did not include any concern about its external appearance. They had a plot of land at Le Pallet, a small community in wine-growing country 20 kilometres (12 miles) south of Nantes, on which they wanted to build a house for themselves and their child that they could later sell to build their real dream home.

Money was tight, but they were eager to have as much space as possible. Currently they were renting a place where the living room was spacious and filled with light, and they stipulated that the new house must offer 'at least that'. But as far as what it looked like from outside went, they didn't care. Nor were they concerned about the materials used or the method of construction. They had been looking at off-the-peg solutions from construction companies, none of which really satisfied them, when they approached their architect friends.

Gasté and Bazantay saw the brief as a challenge. If they designed the building, it would be their first completely new house. Previously they had only built extensions or remodelled existing houses. They knew that others before them had created large spaces very cheaply, and set about finding a way of doing it themselves.

They were looking for an off-the-peg method of construction that would allow them to build a self-effacing space, in the manner of the deliberately non-stylistic Bordeaux architects Lacaton and Vassal. They started by looking at systems for building conservatories, but found the experience frustrating. The systems were not as cheap as they had hoped, particularly for a one-off project, and the builders of the systems had little understanding of the architects' requirements.

In the end, the solution came as a result of a conversation with the mother of one of the practitioners, who exclaimed at the magnificence of a neighbour's new cattle shed, a single, simple timber structure that housed a hundred cows. This was the solution Gasté and Bazantay had been looking for. They approached the manufacturer, who made 15 hectares (37 acres) of these 'hangars' a month and, not surprisingly, was not interested in becoming involved with the bother of designing a house. So the architects then asked for a standard enclosure, settling for one that measured 20 metres (66 feet) long, 10 metres (33 feet) wide and 5 metres (16½ feet) high – about the smallest the company would make, but certainly substantial for a house.

There were planning issues to overcome, especially as Le Pallet's main claim to fame is as the birthplace of the famous romantic theologian Pierre Abelard, and the Abelard chapel is within sight of the new house. But the planners were satisfied once the architects agreed to have a tiled roof and produced a Photoshopped representation of the house, showing how it would look when the surrounding trees had grown up.

Above left: Corrugated glazing to the upper floor on the south-east side allows views over the winter garden.

Above right: The unheated two-storey winter garden has glazed sliding doors that open to the garden.

Above: Vertical pine boarding clads the north-west façade, which is punctuated by only minimal openings.

The result is a robust, unsentimental building. Not surprisingly, it looks more agricultural than residential, but it sits comfortably in a field near neighbours that are more domestic but of no great architectural distinction. Constructed in four bays, the hangar house has oak columns and pine trusses. On the south-east side, facing the garden, there is a two-storey winter garden, an unheated space. Single-glazed aluminium sliding doors open from here to the garden, and similar sliding doors, but double-glazed for thermal insulation, separate the space from the living room. On warm days both sets of doors can be opened, to create the uninterrupted volume that was one of the clients' primary requirements. Corrugated polycarbonate provides the glazing to the upper level on this façade, and to a section of the roof above the winter garden.

In contrast, the other long façade, facing north-west, is much more enclosed, even forbidding. It is clad in treated vertical pine boarding, punctured only by the front door, by a garage door at one end, and by small windows to bedrooms and bathrooms. This uncompromising cladding continues around the sides of the building.

To add to the translucency of the southern side of the house and effectively 'lift' the ceiling of the living room, the ceiling is constructed of honeycombed cellulose which allows considerable light transmission.

To keep costs down still further the clients played an active part in the construction of the house, despite a previous lack of building skills. Just before they moved in their second child was born, and they plan to have more. As a result they are looking at making changes to the spaces within the building. This they will certainly be able to do without ruining the concept of the house. Almost anything would be acceptable within its uncompromising framework, where the accretions of daily living provide the only decoration that is needed.

Above left: On warm days the ground floor can open into a continuous space, and also onto the garden.

Above right: A honeycombed cellulose ceiling allows a great deal of light into the main living space.

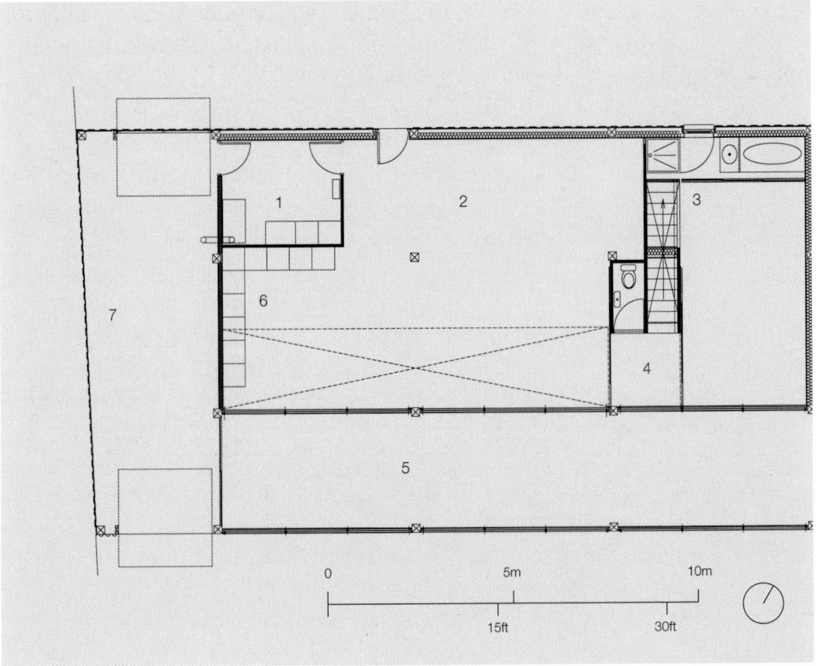

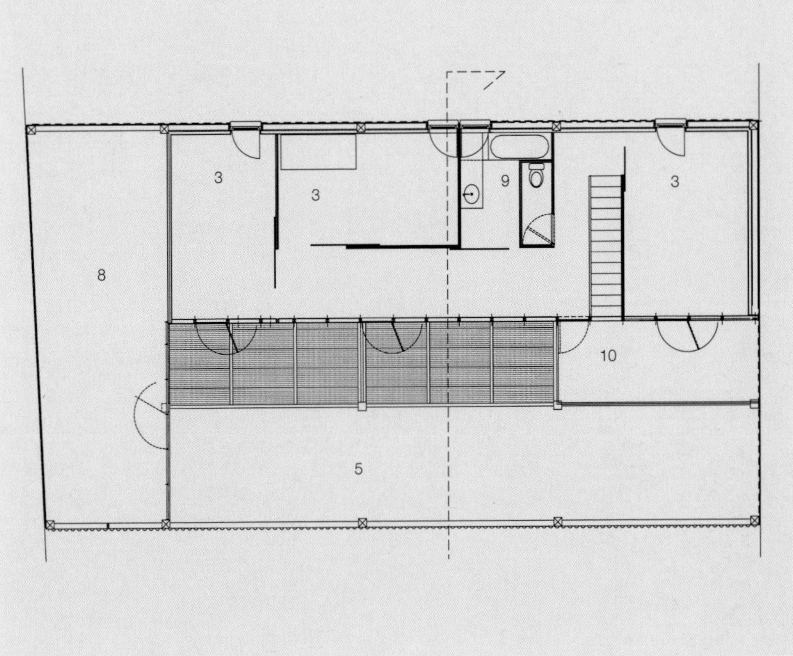

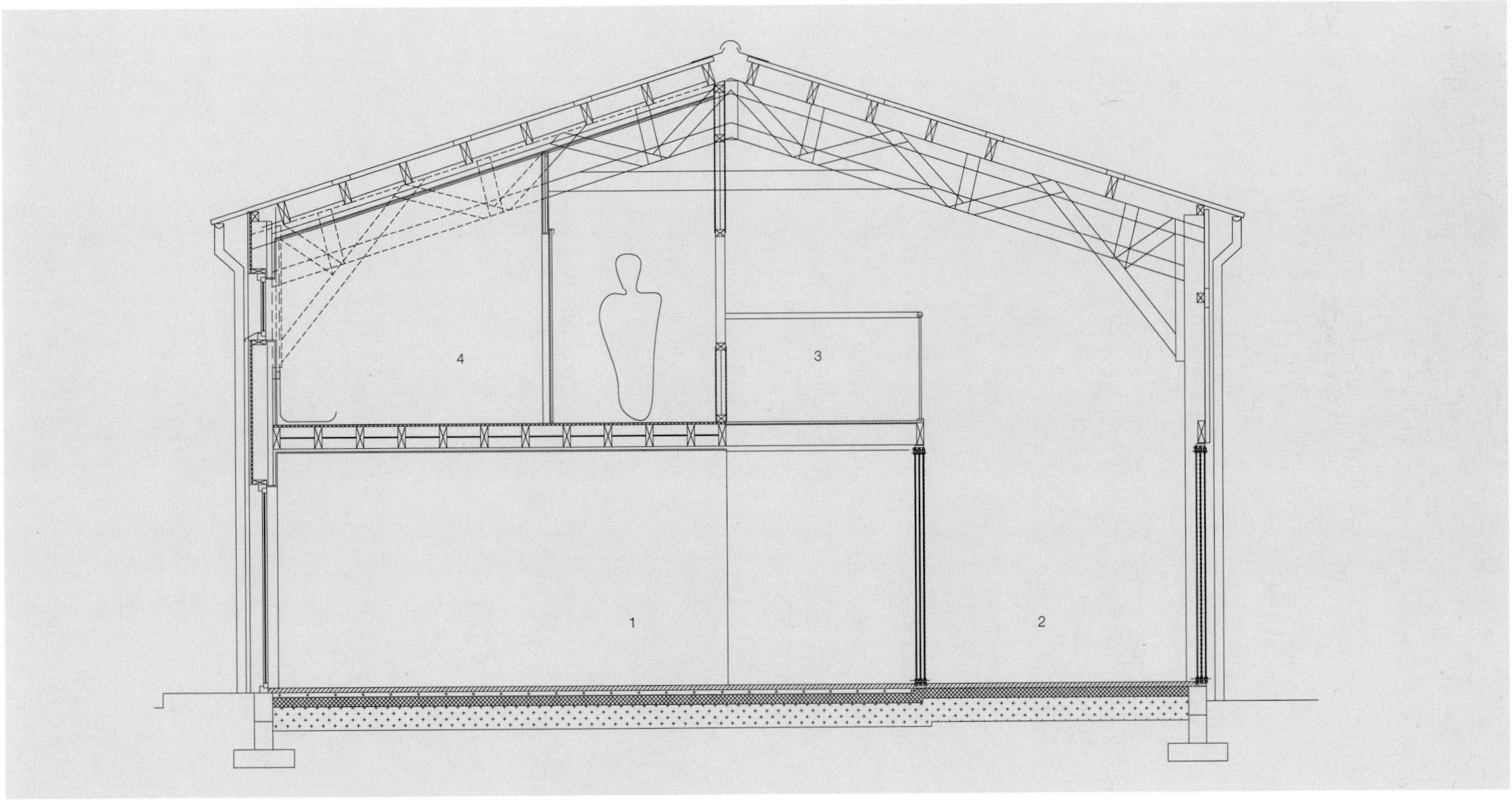

Top left and top right: Ground- and first-floor plans. 1. laundry; 2. living; 3. bedroom; 4. hall; 5. winter garden; 6. kitchen; 7. garage; 8. attic; 9. bathroom; 10. terrace.

Above: A section through the house. 1. living; 2. wintergarden; 3. terrace; 4. bedroom.

House in Fontainebleau

France 2002

Sinikka Ropponen-Brunel, Atelier Brunel

In some senses Fontainebleau is just a small town less than an hour's train journey from the south of Paris, but several factors make it more important than its size and position would suggest. It has a magnificent chateau, embellished under Francis I in the sixteenth century, and by Napoleon and Louis-Philippe in the nineteenth. It sits in the middle of wonderful woods, the reason for its existence because of the hunting they offered, and later the home of early experiments in plein air painting. It has continued this rather grand, rather outdoor association by dubbing itself the 'home of the horse', and was the intended site for the equestrian events in Paris' unsuccessful bid to stage the 2012 Olympic Games.

This is, then, a town that holds itself in high esteem, which has plenty of visitors and much to live up to. So when architect Sinikka Ropponen-Brunel of Atelier Brunel was commissioned to design an eco-friendly house in Fontainebleau it was important that the building should have a distinctly urban nature. In France, as in many countries, timber is primarily a material for use in the countryside, and therefore Ropponen-Brunel had to ensure that her design would not look out of place in its sophisticated surroundings.

This she has achieved through a taut use of materials, and by creating a house that, while offering generous spaces, still presents a fairly constrained face to the street. Indeed, it sits behind a rough stone wall that somehow offsets the extensive use of timber cladding to dispel any possible feeling of rustic whimsy.

The house is oriented so that the south-east side faces a garden. It is here that Ropponen-Brunel has allowed herself to be generous with the glazing. This façade is in fact three stepped faces, the central one of which has glazing rising the full two storeys and onward into the roof, giving the generous living room a triple-height space and a little of the feeling of a contemporary conservatory. This is made possible by the use of two beams of laminated timber, and the glazing allows considerable solar gain which cuts down on winter heating bills. Beyond the living room, and the adjacent dining area, is a generous curved timber deck that provides a good transition between the discipline of the interior and the quasi-natural wooded garden.

In contrast to the open south-east face, the north-west side, which acts as a service zone, is much more closed, and here the cladding in chestnut wood and western red cedar has a far larger part to play visually. It is crisp, with prefabricated panels of boards, 10 metres (33 feet) high, nailed to a pine skeleton.

Insulation is to a high level, consisting of blown cellulose and also sheep's wool, and internally all materials are free of artificial chemicals – paints, for example, are all water-based.

On the ground floor very low-temperature underfloor heating is embedded in a concrete slab, and the floors are of massive oak. The overall effect is of a relaxed and well-lit house that fulfils its client's environmental requirements, while not upsetting the pretensions of the citizens of Fontainebleau.

Above left: There is a triple-height, glazed space in the living area that faces south onto the garden.

Above right: Stepped decking echoes the form of the garden façade, and provides a transitional area between house and garden.

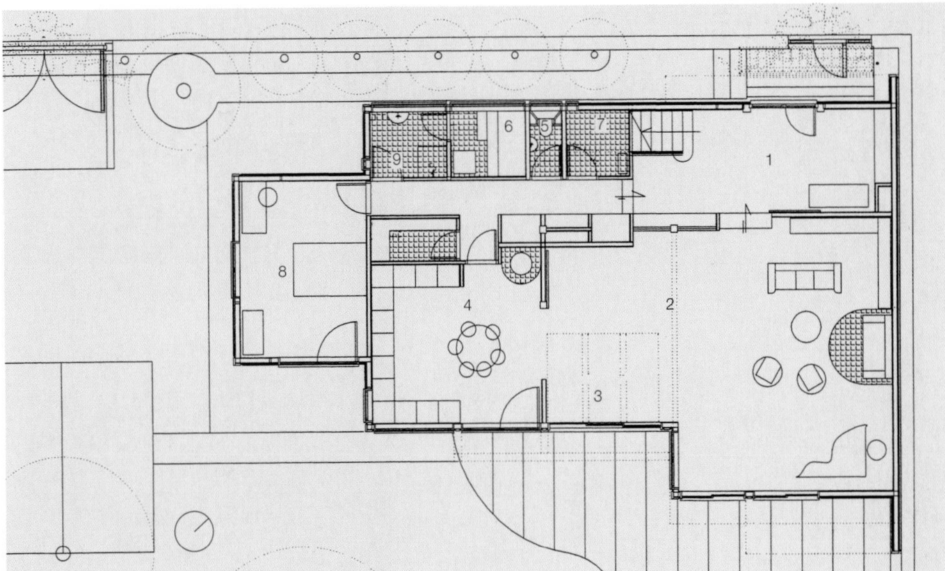

Top left: The south-facing glazed façade is stepped, with the central face rising two-storeys high.

Top right: Ground- and first-floor plans. 1. entrance; 2. living; 3. wintergarden; 4. kitchen; 5. WC; 6. sauna; 7. shower; 8. bedroom; 9. bathroom.

Above: Prefabricated cladding panels in chestnut and red cedar are fixed to a pine skeleton.

Milanville House
Milanville, Pennsylvania, USA 2002
Bone/Levine Architects

Top: With the windows open, one can see through the house to the trees behind. Reclaimed boards provide shading.

Above: At night, the contrast between the transparency of the upper floor and the opacity of the lower level becomes clear.

There are many reasons for refurbishing an existing structure rather than building from scratch, but simplicity and cost saving are rarely among them. This is exemplified in the transformation by Bone/Levine Architects of a barn dating from 1850 in Milanville, Pennsylvania. Fortunately the New York-based practice is skilled in working with old structures, so when Joe Levine and his wife, Jane Cyphers, decided to transform this building overlooking the Delaware River, about 160 kilometres (100 miles) north-west of New York, he had some idea of what he was letting himself in for. Nevertheless, it was a formidable task.

In addition to the barn's setting, Levine fell in love with its handsome frame, the sense of space and the way light filtered through between the planks of the cladding. But this was not a building that needed only a little attention; it was a building in trouble, no longer weathertight and with its frame twisted and distorted. Furthermore, Levine was not looking merely to refurbish it, but to transform it from a barn into a light and contemporary house.

He also needed to lift the whole structure to a new permanent position, and to excavate foundations beneath it. To facilitate this, the entire building had to be propped up by about 3.5 metres (12 feet) while excavation took place below.

All the cladding was stripped off and the architect, working with structural engineer Edy Zingher of ETNA Consulting in New York, had to contrive a way to get the frame back into shape. This was done by attaching a pair of Y-shaped steel braces to the columns at the centre of the barn, which in turn supported a new aluminium I-beam that was slipped under the ceiling rafters. Every day for a month, workmen cranked the braces until the frame returned to its right-angled form. This system remains in place and, along with diagonal tensioned steel cables that provide lateral resistance, adds an intriguing element to the interior.

Levine would have liked to do all the detailed work himself. However, he realized that he did not have the time. Instead, he was fortunate to find a local cabinetmaker and carpenter, Larry Braverman, who shared his approach. Braverman

Above left: A charming, circular bath house on the property was constructed from New York water tanks in 2004.

Above right: Raised to its new level the frame, which had become distorted, underwent substantial repairs.

Above: The steel braces that pulled the frame back into shape remain in place.

executed most of the work, including all the doors and windows, milling them from recycled local timbers. Windows on the north and south façades punch outwards, allowing them to be seen from the interior as entirely frameless.

Externally, the north and south ends of the building are clad in stained cedar. The west-facing wall is clad in corrugated fibreglass, with a pair of glass barn doors set into it as a main entrance. The cladding on this side is divided into panels, which echo the ones that frame the glazing in the doors. The most important – east – façade faces down the slope to the river and is almost entirely glazed, with a top row of fixed windows. Below are eight sliding doors that can roll away to open it up. Reclaimed boards from the old barn can slide across this face to provide some privacy and shading, allowing the sunlight to penetrate in the same striped patterns that it did in the original structure. Looking at the east face of the house, you can see right through the open living space, and through the large glazed doors on the west façade, to the trees beyond – a degree of transparency that undermines the solidity of the building, making it very much an object within a landscape.

At a lower level, however, there is no such porosity. The building has been raised on a plinth, which is beautifully clad in long narrow strips of a grey local stone. On the west side, there is a stone deck leading up to the front door. On the east doors lead to the servant space below the main house.

The internal arrangements are extremely open. The only enclosed space is the bathroom, a self-supporting pod of fibreglass walls and timber cabinets. The ground floor has a kitchen and dining space to one side, with a steeply twisted, metal spiral staircase leading to the sleeping loft above. On the other side there is another metal stair, more like a loft ladder than a conventional staircase.

All the carpentry is detailed exquisitely, in maple-veneer ply. The kitchen stands on a steel floor. Otherwise all the floors are in highly polished cherry – there is a strict policy forbidding the wearing of shoes indoors, but underfloor heating is provided as a compensation/temptation!

Although the house is welcoming and not severe, it imposes certain disciplines on the residents, not least the requirement to do away with almost all vestiges of privacy. But for this visually attuned family it is doubtless worthwhile. The hard work and complexity of the project's achievement are more than justified by an end result that provides a wonderful contrast to the hustle and bustle of New York City.

Above left: Floors are of highly polished cherry and heated from underneath.

Above right: The open plan allows the structure to be enjoyed.

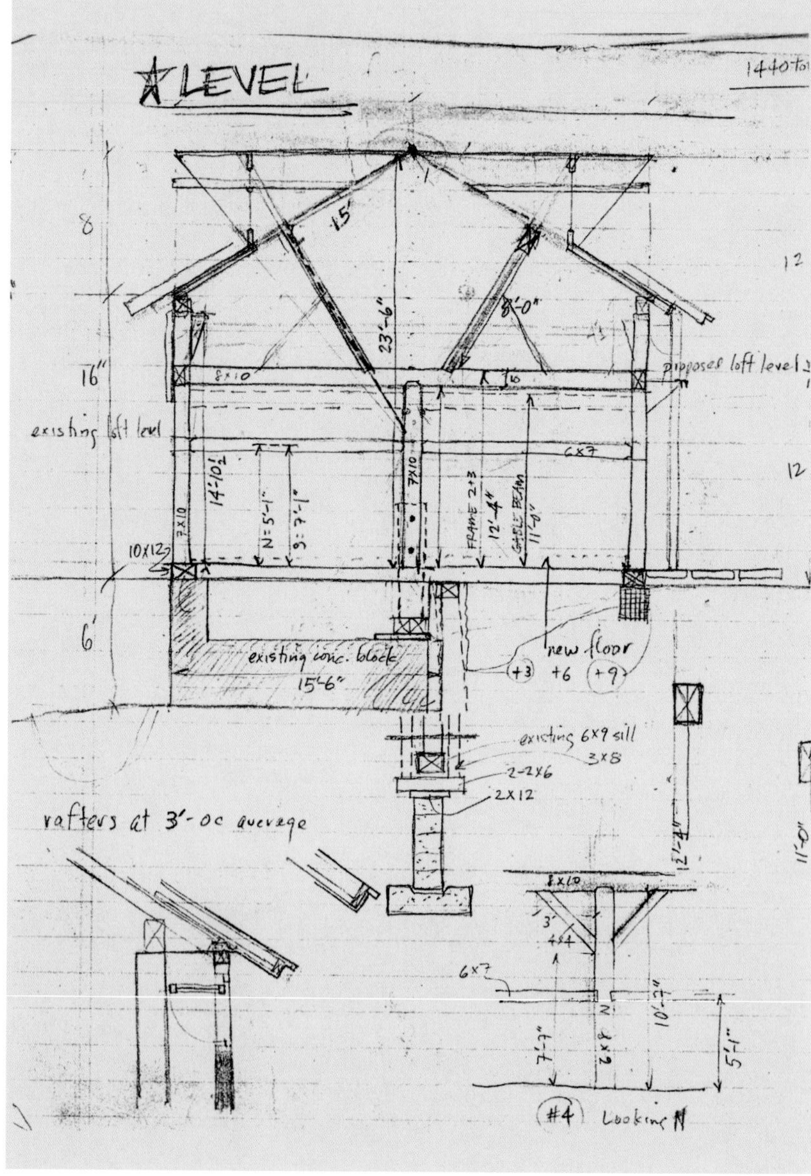

Above left: A stair leads up to the sleeping loft, from which the old structure and the new interventions are easily seen.

Above right: A sketch shows the architect's ideas for adapting the original structure to create a home.

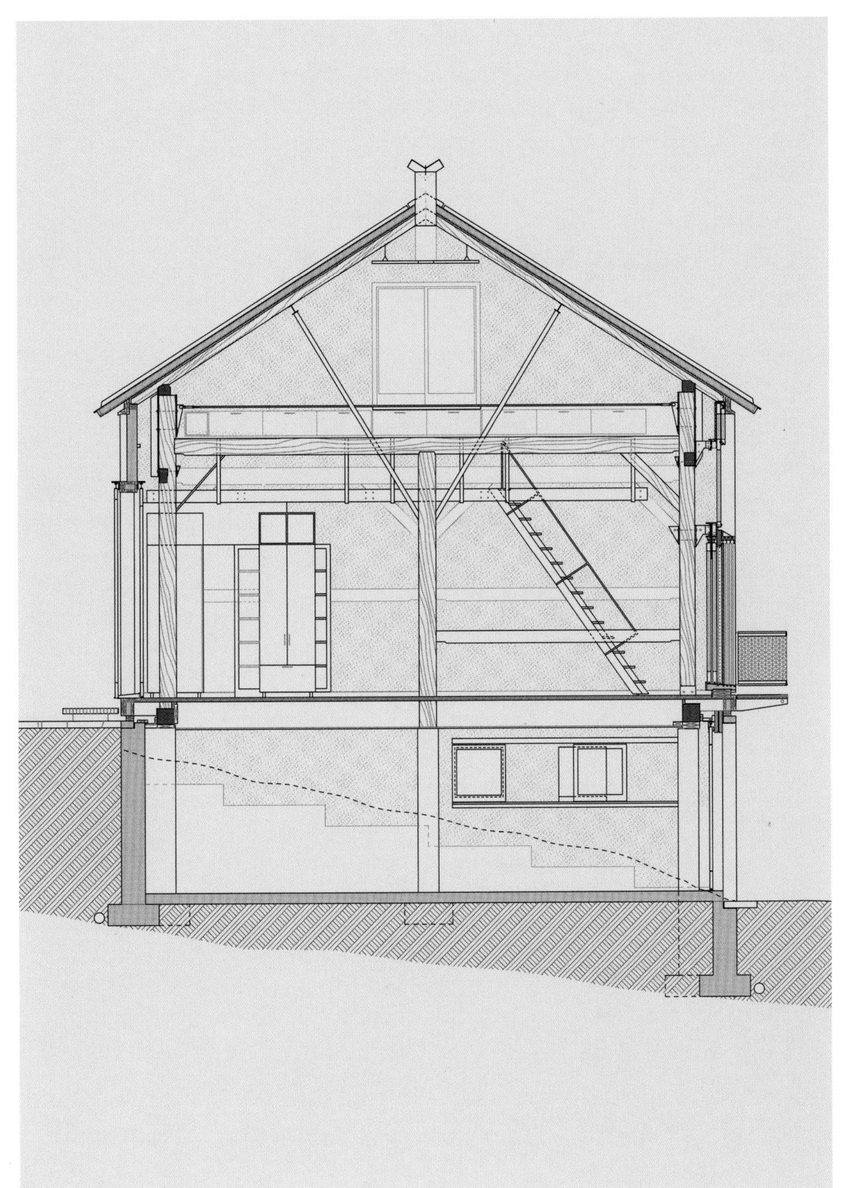

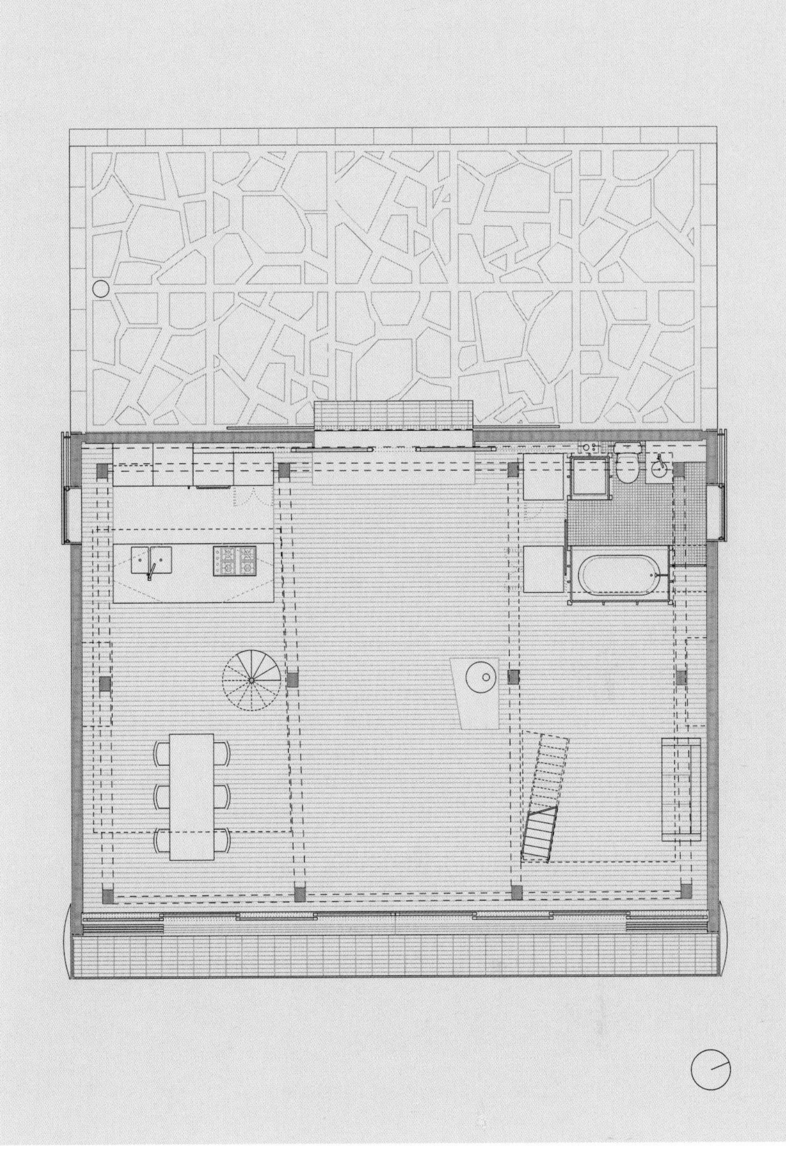

Above left: A section through the house that was created within the old structure of the barn.

Above right: The ground-floor plan of the house.

Prefabricated Housing
Merano, Italy 2003
Holzbox Tirol and Anton Höss

There is an almost childlike simplicity to this housing block in Merano, in Italy's south Tyrol region. At four storeys high it is of the size and scale of neighbouring developments, but takes an entirely different approach to construction. There are three apartments on each floor, with their handedness reversed from one floor to the next. The building is made from large prefabricated solid timber panels that impart so much rigidity the architect believes this construction method could be extended up to ten storeys. The panels also provide both thermal mass and acoustic insulation.

Access is from the south-east side of the building, where there is a lift and straight flights of larch stairs, or from the opposing end, which also has stairs. All the decks are in larch.

The front doors to the 50-square-metre (538-square-foot) apartments are on the north-east façade. This and the south-eastern sides are wrapped in a metal mesh which also extends round to the extremities of the south-west façade. Supported on a slender metal framework, the mesh looked slightly brutal and provisional directly after completion of construction in 2003, but the intention is that climbing plants will be trained up it, softening the outside and offering both shade and privacy.

On the south-west façade these two essential elements are provided in a more dramatic and less natural manner. The cross walls of the apartments extend beyond the end walls to create private balconies. And each balcony has half its opening shaded by a brightly coloured stretched-fabric panel. The panels swap positions from one level to the next, reflecting the change in handedness of the apartments themselves, and providing a striking chequerboard effect that makes the building stand out among its more conservative neighbours.

A spiral staircase offers access from the top floor to the roof, where there is a central roofed walkway (more timber) and, to one side, a row of solar panels angled to the south. Palms are planted on each side of the walkway. The effect of all this rooftop activity is to add weight equivalent to another two floors to the structure.

For Holzbox Tirol, which is based in Innsbruck in Austria, this is one of the latest developments in a long series of buildings with large, prefabricated timber elements, often used in conjunction with other materials. Frequently there is a quirky twist, as with the sunshading at Merano, indicating that prefabrication can be a flexible and sensible solution that does not preclude the exercise of the imagination.

Top left: A covered timber walkway on the roof passes between palm trees and an array of solar panels.

Above left: The appearance of the metal mesh enclosing the entrance façade will be softened once clothed in plants.

Above right: From the top floor, a spiral staircase leads up to roof level where there is a central walkway.

Opposite: Brightly coloured fabric panels shade balconies, with their positioning creating a chequerboard effect.

Left: The north-west façade of the building has prefabricated timber cladding, creating thermal and acoustic insulation.

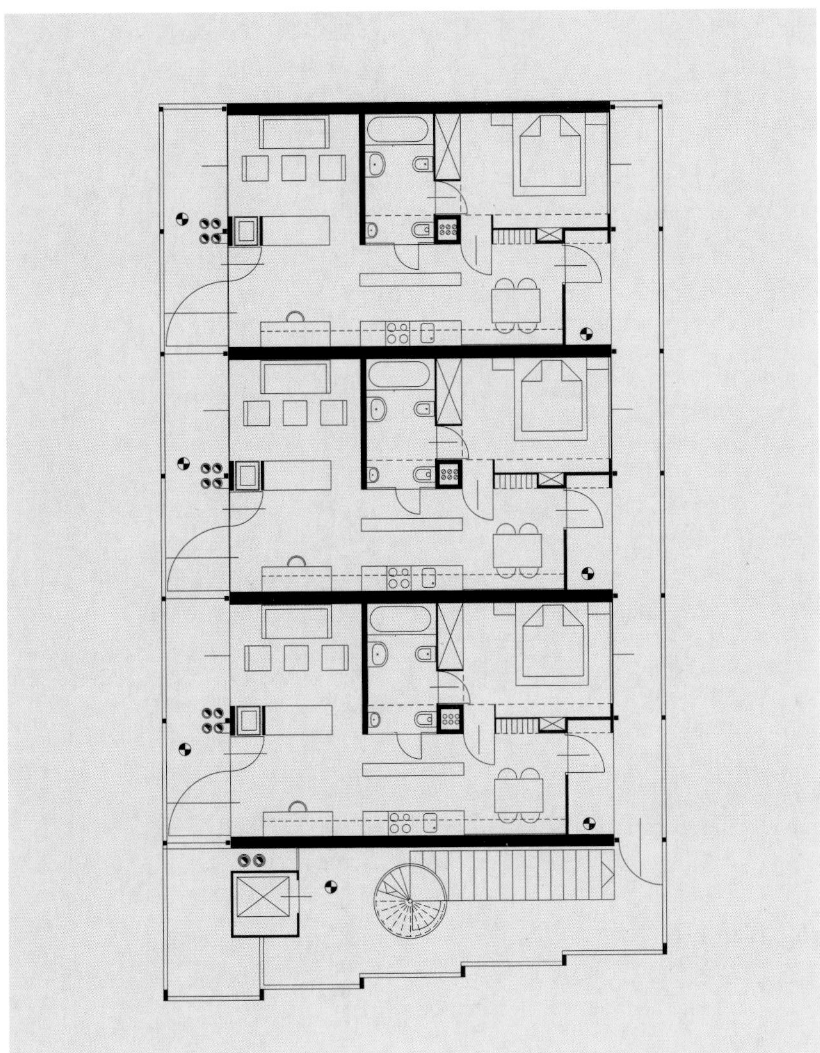

Above left: The top-floor plan of the building.

Above right: A section through the apartment building shows how the individual dwellings are arranged.

Garriga-Poch House
Lles de Cerdanya, Spain 2002
Arturo Frediani Sarfatí

How should you design a second home in a remote agricultural village? This was the problem that faced Barcelona-based architect Arturo Frediani Sarfatí when he designed a house in Lles de Cerdanya. While planners were evidently keen to preserve the traditional appearance of this tiny Pyrenean village as much as possible, the architect felt it would be inappropriate to reproduce the style of subsistence farmers for a couple who would be using their house in such a different manner.

In Lles de Cerdanya more than half the population of 291 is still employed in agriculture. And at an altitude of 1,471 metres (4,826 feet) this is a relatively tough environment, a fact that is reflected in the design of buildings.

Sarfatí's clients had chosen for their site an old forge building with a picturesque history. Although it and its accompanying house were started in 1796, they had been built with stones from an older building. This had been the home of an escapee from the military prison in Valencia, who had turned up in Lles de Cerdanya in 1701 and lived in a ruined hayloft. Once settled in the village and free from discovery, he turned the ruin into a house for himself. After he died in 1711 it fell into disrepair, and nearly a century later the blacksmith appropriated the stones for his workplace and dwelling.

By reusing these stones in his own design, Sarfatí is employing them in at least their fourth incarnation in the village. Coincidentally, he felt a strong connection with the place since he had stumbled on it accidentally some three years before his clients, Xavier Garriga and Conxita Poch, commissioned him, and he had heard the romantic story of the convict's hideaway. He therefore had a feeling of sympathy for Lles de Cerdanya and its history. Nevertheless, despite his willingness to use traditional materials – timber and Arabic tiles in addition to the stone – he was determined to do so in a non-traditional manner.

The result is a building with an undulating, timber-clad façade which can operate as either one dwelling or two independent ones. Sarfatí has used steel for the external framing, in a manner that he compares to the iron used in a Steinway piano. Internally, however, much of the structure is created by a balloon frame of Finnish pine. The two elements of the house are offset from each other, joined by a connection 2 metres (6½ feet) wide, and the larger of the two has a cantilevered first-floor pod. The feeling of liveliness engendered by this most unconventional plan is accentuated by Douglas fir cladding on the exterior. In addition to defining a wide range of window openings, the cladding is not in one plane but has projecting elements that add to the articulation. And neither is this an entirely passive exterior, since many of these projections are in fact large, metal-framed shutters that can slide across to shut up the house entirely when it is not occupied.

Internally, finishes are predominantly white-painted walls and hardwood floors. But the effect is not one of classical austerity, since the shapes and angles of the rooms all veer away from the traditional rectangular box.

The stones that form part of the house may have played a part in several dwellings before this one, but they have never been subject to the invention of an architect. Sarfatí has ensured that this time they are incorporated in a dwelling like none that the village has seen before.

Above left: When the Douglas fir shutters are pulled across, the house presents an entirely closed face.

Above right: Opening the shutters reveals an intriguing fenestration pattern.

Opposite: The shutters give a three-dimensional quality to the timber façade.

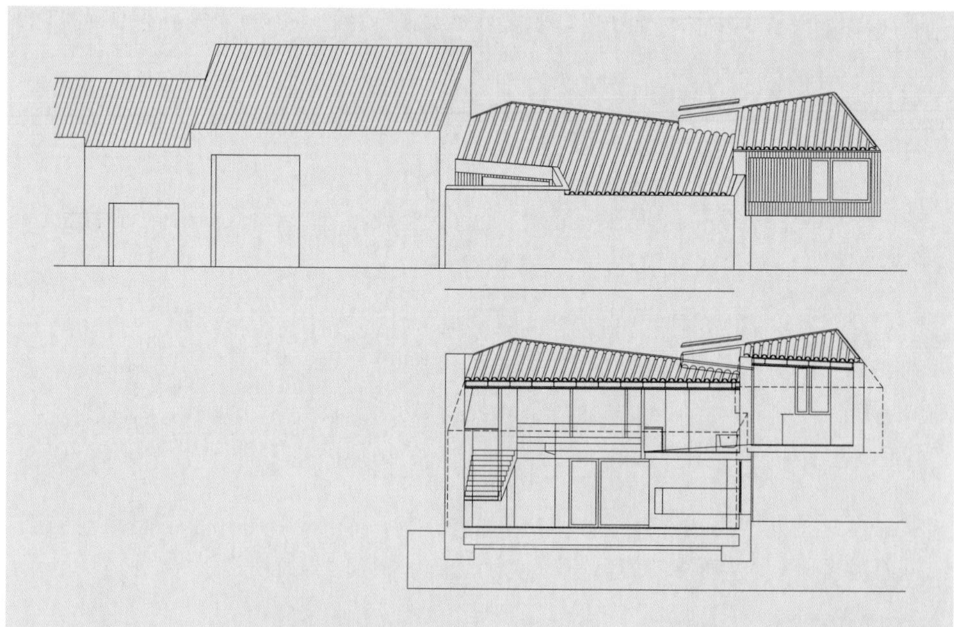

Top left: Re-using old stones allows the house to fit comfortably into the texture of the village.

Above left: Internally, there are frequent changes of direction in both the horizontal and the vertical plane.

Top right: Façade and section showing the changing roofline and cantilevered pod (right).

Above right: Despite the use of simple, modern finishes internally, occupants remain aware of the tough nature of the reclaimed historic fabric.

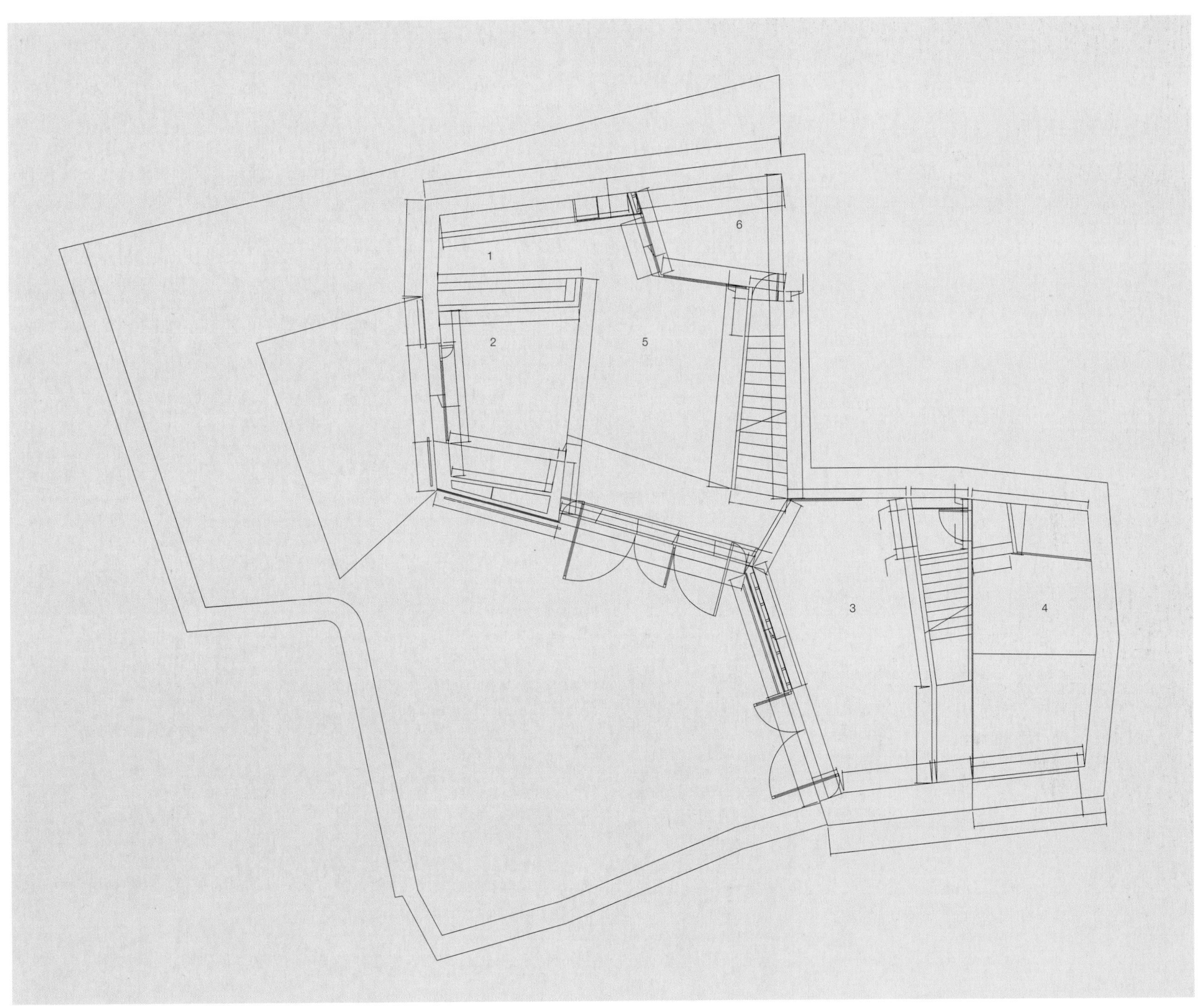

Above: The upper-level plan shows how easily the house can be divided into two dwellings. 1. kitchen; 2. winter room; 3. living; 4. garage; 5. living/dining; 6. courtyard.

Self-build House
Arusha, Tanzania 2005
Jo Jordan and Nick Fisher

There are some who like to plan ahead – and then there are the others. British couple Jo Jordan and Nick Fisher certainly fit the second category. The pair, who for 30 years used to run trans-Africa safaris, bought a plot of land in Tanzania almost on impulse and have spent five years building a house there, even though they intend to spend no more than three weeks a year in it.

They designed the house as they went along, starting at one end, using the materials that were available and changing their minds as they went. 'It is nice to be able to build how you want, with no building inspectors and no planners,' says Nick Fisher. 'The only requirement was my wife's – that we had a long veranda on which she could drink gin and tonic.'

Even the position of the house was chosen pragmatically. The site is on a hill overlooking the town of Arusha, with magnificent views of mountains. The first thing to arrive was a container. 'If you are going to build a house in Africa,' says Fisher, 'you need protection against weather and theft.' But the container could only make it a certain distance across the site. Where it stopped, the house was built – above and around it. Building materials were locked away in it, and it is now used to store precious or fragile items when Jordan and Fisher are not there.

The next piece of serendipity was the opportunity to buy, very cheaply, a set of timber tree-trunks from a match factory that had gone bust. These poles, which form the structural framework of the house, had been lying in the open for several years and were therefore fully seasoned. The disadvantage is that they are pine which, says Fisher, 'the termites love'. He initially dealt with this by sticking the uprights into post holes filled with concrete, rather than straight into the ground. But this could only be a temporary defence against the determined termites. So Jordan and Fisher infilled their structure with rock (again, they proved lucky – they had believed there was some on the site, but there turned out to be much more than they anticipated) and cut away the lower parts of the posts, putting in rocks to plug the gap. Now they are crossing their fingers that they acted soon enough, and that the termites have not already penetrated the higher parts of the structure.

Because of the slope of the site, the house has two storeys at the front and one at the rear. The main, ground floor measures 18 x 12 metres (60 x 40 feet) and includes the veranda, which stretches

Above: The veranda, more than 12 metres (40 feet) long, is designed for sipping gin and tonics.

Opposite: Both the pitch-roofed porch and the lookout tower were added as afterthoughts when construction was fairly well advanced.

slightly beyond the full 12-metre (40-foot) length of the sitting room. There are also three bedrooms on this floor, and another one below, along with the storage container and secure parking spaces. Steps connecting the two levels are hewn from stone.

Originally the building was to have a roof with a single low pitch, but the couple decided it would be nice to have a more formal porch to the entrance hall, so they built a steeply pitched one. Even more dramatic was the decision to add a lookout tower – when standing on a ladder on the roof they discovered how good the view was from there. One, exceptionally long, timber post forms the basis of its structure, and the tower is wood panelled internally, with a timber spiral staircase.

Some flooring and cladding is in cypress, a timber, says Fisher, to which 'the termites are not so partial'. The floor to the master bedroom is painted red, although other floors have been given a thin screed of pink-tinted concrete. Internally walls are plastered directly against the timber frame, against stone or against concrete blocks. Like the surrounding houses, this one has a tin roof, supported on timber battens and with a timber lining. There is no insulation, in keeping with other local homes, although these tend to be wooden huts with tin roofs. At 1,830 metres (6,000 feet) the climate, says Fisher, is rather like that of an English spring – warm and sunny at Christmas when the pair usually visit. Around August it can be cold and wet, conditions that the locals put up with stoically and Jo and he simply avoid.

Jordan and Fisher are great aficionados of salvage yards and auction houses. So, whereas the windows at the front of the house were made in the area using a local hardwood, those at the rear are second-hand English softwood ones, brought out as a partial load on the truck of a friend who travelled frequently between the United Kingdom and Africa. Similarly, the doors, including some magnificent panelled ones, 2.4 metres (8 feet) high, and an undersized 'rice door' originally from Indonesia, plus furniture and bathroom fittings, have come from either the UK or Dubai.

The most original item, however, is the sturdy kitchen table. In the days when the Fishers were running safaris across Africa they carried with them thick planks of Nigerian hardwood which they placed on the supports of derelict Bailey bridges. These planks, complete with the original chainsaw marks, now form the table top. The posts of the four-poster bed in the master bedroom come from the Tanzanian coast and are carved with highly figurative Makonde motifs, a speciality of that part of the country.

By Christmas 2004 the house was finally, says Nick Fisher, '99 per cent complete'. But it may be a project that can never be truly finished. It was built by local labour, using little more than a chainsaw and a hammer, and the subsistence farmers in the area have come to rely on working there as their only source of cash. Maintenance and small improvements may keep them going in the future. But for Jordan and Fisher, with the house now nearly as they wish it to be, the creative effort is turning to rebuilding their farmhouse in Suffolk, England. They have equally imaginative ideas for this, but a little more negotiation with the planners may be needed.

Opposite: Tall, panelled doors form a magnificent entrance to the house.

Above left: An undersized rice door, originally from Indonesia, was used as the door to the bathroom.

Above centre: Timber framing is left exposed in the kitchen, where the table displays chainsaw marks from its earlier use.

Above right: Most floors have a thin screed of pink-tinged concrete.

Modular2

Kansas City, Kansas, USA 2005
Studio 804

Building a house from start to finish in twenty weeks seems in itself a pretty impressive achievement. How much more so, then, when this also involves the design process, and when the people doing the work have no previous experience.

In the case of the Modular2 house, built in the Shawnee Road district to the south of Kansas City, there was, however, a secret ingredient. The house was a product of Studio 804, a unit at the University of Kansas. And although all the students involved were new to the work, the studio itself has an impressive ten-year pedigree, under the supervision of local architect Dan Rockhill. Aimed mainly at third-year graduate students, it provides experience in design and building, giving them just five months to create a building. Since its instigation in 1995, Studio 804 has focused on the problem of providing affordable housing for those with low incomes, and the emphasis has moved increasingly towards the use of prefabrication.

In 2004, the students on the course produced Modular1, the first instance of offsite prefabrication of an entire building. Students in the following year learnt from the experience of their predecessors, and created Modular2.

Built in a warehouse in the town of Lawrence, Modular2 consisted of five units that were then taken to the site in Kansas City and erected. These units were two bedrooms, a bathroom/utility unit, a kitchen and a living area. The building is long and thin, so the units sit alongside each other, with a corridor running past the bedroom and bathroom units to afford some privacy. Although this eats into the total dimensions, spaces are still relatively generous, with each bedroom measuring 3.35 x 4.5 metres (11 x 15 feet). The total area of the house is 111 square metres (1,200 square feet).

The building is timber-framed and of shear-wall construction. Overall dimensions were determined by the need to be able to transport the structure by truck from Lawrence to its final location on a ridge of land in Kansas City.

The base design does not include a garage. Detailed costings included a number of ways of producing one. In the case of the particular site that was used, it was necessary to build a concrete platform on which the building would stand, and, because of the slope of the land, it was possible to incorporate an underground garage within this structure. In addition, this basement contained the utilities and a further 39 square metres (420 square feet) of space that could be finished for use at a later date. A staircase was installed to give access from the basement to the main building.

Above: Computer visualiz.ation of the modular house.

Above: The final result is a sleek, modern-looking house.

There were some elements of salvage involved in the project. Chief among these was the use of recycled maple gym flooring to provide attractive warm floors. But although the aim of the project is to cut the costs and uncertainty involved with conventional house design and construction, it is not architecture on a shoestring. In contrast to the famous Rural Studio in Alabama, where students beg and borrow materials to produce structures of an unconventional audacity that is probably only accepted so easily because of the desperate poverty of their users, Studio 804 produces work that satisfies bourgeois aspirations.

Modular2 does not look like a student project but like a slick and light-filled piece of work that most people would be proud to inhabit. Cladding is primarily with cypress, and there are generous windows in channel glass, a structural glazing system that allows large areas to be given over to glazing. Its U-shaped profile makes it translucent rather than transparent, providing privacy. The same material was used on the internal walls to the bedrooms and bathrooms, allowing light to pass through to them. To contrast with the horizontal nature of the channel glass, the cypress cladding was installed vertically. At the edge of the deck that surrounds the building, however, cypress was used again, but in a horizontal manner, as slats supported on a steel framework, to provide shading and an additional layer of privacy.

Internally, storage runs along one side of the corridor, with custom-made maple sliding doors. These have translucent Polygal polycarbonate panels, which are backlit to create the impression of a glowing wall in the corridor.

With prefabrication, the gains always come with production in large numbers. By definition, this student project could not achieve that. But it is an impressive demonstration of the ability to produce something that is elegant and practical to a tight timescale. The students that have passed through the course will leave with some important practical knowledge. And Kansas City can, doubtless, look forward to Modular3, 4 and 5.

Above: Modular units were constructed in a warehouse in Lawrence, Kansas.

Top left: This was a hands-on project, teaching students as much about construction as about design.

Above left: Modules were designed so that they could resist the loads involved in lifting.

Top right: A module coming out of the warehouse.

Above right: Transport restrictions determined the size of the modules.

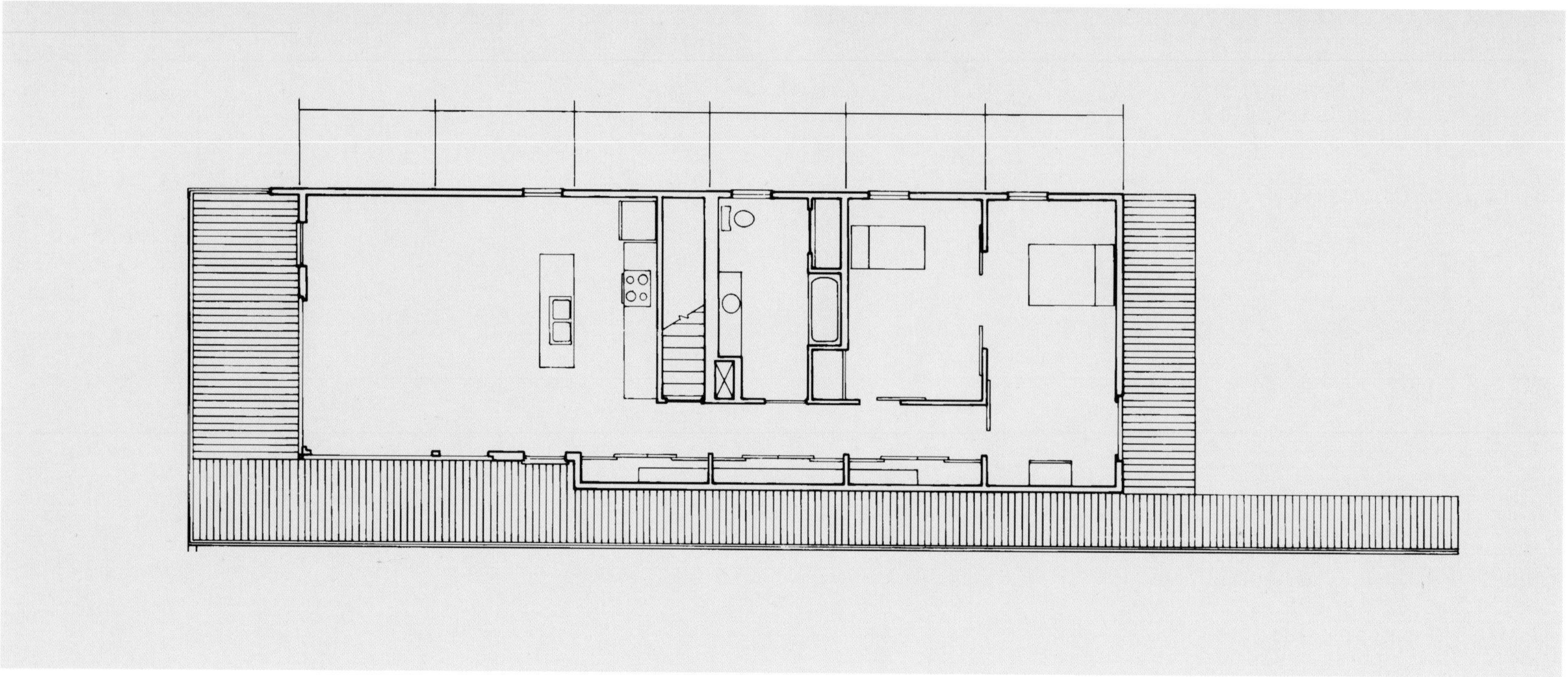

Top left: Two units are combined to provide the open-plan kitchen and living space.

Top right: Maple-framed sliding doors to cupboards line the corridor.

Above: Floor plan, showing the generous deck that surrounds the building.

Above: Because of the sloping site, it was possible to create extra space below for a garage and further accommodation.

There are several reasons for the dominance of one-off, stand-alone houses in books about domestic architecture. Firstly, the architect may be proudest of a building that can be conceived as a sculptural object, where he or she can have control over the appearance of all four façades. Secondly, the constraints are likely to be less than with groups of houses, allowing free rein to the imagination. And thirdly, all too often groups of houses are produced by commercial developers, who either dispense with architects altogether or use them as lapdogs to produce a few random flourishes or some elementary plans.

When it comes to wood, there is an additional consideration. Other chapters in this book suggest there is a natural affinity between timber and a certain type of rustic living, that its use in a house shows a link between the building and its environment where, doubtless, trees are growing. Does this make wood unsuitable for use in towns?

In one sense this is a ridiculous question, given the dominance of timber frame in new housing, and particularly in the type of insensitive developer housing described above. However, in many countries, at least in a European context, the timber frame rarely feeds through to an outward expression with the use of timber cladding. The exceptions occur where there is a great tradition of forestry, where wood is still the material of choice for everything except the densest and tallest urban construction.

For example, in Finland, where until a century ago little was built that was not timber, there is now a reaction against high-rise living coupled with an eagerness to create inexpensive and highly populated communities . Almost invariably, these houses are in timber. What is encouraging is that organizations such as the Tuikkupuisto Real Estate Company and developer Rantapuisto are keen not only to use timber construction and cladding, but also to be creative about the layout of the houses and the relationship between them (see opposite).

Of course, not all cluster housing is in urban environments. In Sardinia, Marco Petreschi has designed a group of houses for affluent vacationers in an idyllic setting (see page 168). This draws on two traditions: use of local wood and stone; and arranging the buildings in a social environment known as a *stazzu*. Yet he has paid this homage to the past while cleverly avoiding pastiche.

But if many of us yearn to spend our holidays in such environments, the reality is that for much of the year most of us are living in suburbia. In Belgium, Groupe Gamma has designed a group of houses both framed and clad in wood that take a fresh look at the much maligned suburban 'semi' (see page 186). In Dortmund, Germany, ArchiFactory.de has created an extension, the Ebeling house, that is a deliberately alien intrusion into suburban surroundings, challenging rather than embracing the prevailing aesthetic (see page 182). This could initiate a dialogue about the future direction of such areas, although its uncompromising nature means that the Ebeling house is unlikely to be rolled out as a blueprint for entire streets.

At Marine on St Croix in Minnesota, USA, architect David Salmela and landscape architect Coen + Partners had to create a sense of community on the edge of a historic town, which they achieved by instituting a strict but flexible set of design rules (see page 194).

Timber's environmental credentials mean it is likely to be the material of choice for architects who care about sustainability. So, when German practice Thomas Spiegelhalter Studio designed solar-powered town houses in Freiburg in the late 1990s, it was natural to do so in timber (see opposite). More recently, in Lewes, England, architect and academic Duncan Baker-Brown built Sparrow House for his family in that most reviled of suburban elements, the cul-de-sac (see opposite). Deliberately unpretentious externally, it was intended to demonstrate that sustainable living was attainable. This includes the use of locally coppiced sweet-chestnut wood for external cladding, and the recycling of the scaffolding boards used during construction as the sitting-room floor.

In France, the Garden City movement is taking a belated hold with one of the latest, and most interesting, examples built on a former industrial site near Reims (see page 162). There are two distinct house types, one earth-sheltered and the other opening to south-facing gardens, but both use prefabricated timber panels.

Once you get into the heart of a city, things become even more interesting. On a neglected site in London Chance de Silva built a house, Cargo Fleet, that uses timber as part of a palette of materials that flirts with a romantic notion of industrial dereliction (see page 178). But equally important is the way the building is designed to accommodate different ways of living, acting as a single unit, as two linked homes or as a combination of living and working space.

The site of Cargo Fleet is far less glamorous than that occupied by the extension designed by Christian Pottgiesser and Florian Hertwerck in Paris (see page 172). Only on a piece of prime real estate could a client justify putting in so much effort for such a relatively small increase in liveable space. The result, though, is a jewel box of clever ideas, with timber elements providing some of the most imaginative interventions.

In cities that are expanding much faster than either London or Paris, development may be high-rise, dense and frankly unattractive. This is the case in Beijing, as in many other Chinese cities. California-based architect Michele Saee has tackled the problem by designing an apartment interior called Template House (see page 190). This uses prefabricated plywood elements to create a curvaceous space that deliberately turns away from the environment outside, a solution that Saee believes is easily reproducible. It may seem defeatist to cocoon ourselves from an unpleasant external world, but in many places it is the only workable alternative. If timber cannot always be used to improve our public realm, it can at least ameliorate the private one.

Chapter 5
Clustered Houses

Top: Thomas Spiegelhalter Studio used timber construction as part of the environmental agenda for its solar housing in Freiburg, Germany.

Above left: At Sparrow House in the south of England, Duncan Baker-Brown used locally coppiced chestnut for cladding.

Above right: Tuikkupuisto Real Estate Company in Finland uses timber in its low-rise approach to dense urban living.

Garden City

Reims, France 2002/2004
BCDE Architecture

The concept of the garden city was first developed by Ebenezer Howard in the United Kingdom at the very end of the nineteenth century, and saw its first fruition in the town of Letchworth in south-east England. An idea that has waxed and waned in popularity, it is currently enjoying a renaissance in France. Although the countries are close neighbours, France is much less densely populated than the UK. This may be why, as the British are falling in love with the idea of regenerating their city centres and in increasing densification to avoid losing the last scraps of countryside, the French are flirting with the concept of the garden city. One place where this is happening is at Petit Bétheny, to the north-east of Reims.

Petit Bétheny is at the heart of champagne country, but it is not a place of viticulture and smart wine-tastings. Rather, it is an old industrial zone in need of rehabilitation. In this project the ideals of the two countries divided by the English Channel coalesce: the need to redevelop brownfield sites, and to replace the dereliction caused by industry with a new way of living.

Laurent Debrix and Anne Reychman of BCDE Architecture won the task of both masterplanning the entire site and designing the first tranche of housing. They have taken the notion of 'garden' very literally, trying to achieve an almost English informality by dividing the area into zones. In some of these scented plants will dominate, in others there will be plants to create a certain mood, or plants for touching or even tasting. The idea is that the houses will sit in a sea of green, that this will be a place where residents can be in touch with nature.

Some communal facilities are planned but the main emphasis is on housing, of which there should eventually be 230 units. As with other new garden cities defined in France, Petit Bétheny is to be relatively inexpensive, with the houses costing only around 100,000 euros each to build. An additional aspect of the brief was that their environmental performance should be exemplary.

So far, one-tenth of the units have been built – 23 four-room houses, on either side of an access avenue running east–west. Because this is an old industrial site, certain constraints affect the design, notably the presence of a noisy railway line. This lies to the south of the site, so the architects faced the challenge of providing protection from noise while still trying to make maximum use of sunlight.

This has resulted in two distinctive house types. The maisons soleil or sun houses lie to the north of the access road, and are open to the gardens in front of them. Separate garages sit at the bottom of the gardens. On the southern side, and therefore even nearer the railway line, are the maisons talus, the earth-sheltered houses. These have integral garages at the front to offer an acoustic barrier, with their sloping roofs coming down to merge with a protective sloping earth berm. The garages have 'green' planted roofs, with ferns and other shade-loving plants. This is in contrast to the suntrap gardens of the other house type. Entrance to the houses is at the side.

However, in construction terms the types are similar, and the method used means that building can be very rapid, with the main structure for a pair of units going up in only about a week. The houses are built from large timber panels, factory finished with all internal finishes. The timber is pine from the Vosges, a mountainous area in the east of France. Highly insulated with 120 millimetres (4⅘ inches) of glass wool, and a design that takes care to eliminate thermal bridges, the panels contribute to the excellent thermal performance of the buildings. Coupled with the fact that the houses

Far left: The maisons soleil are on the north side of the access road.

Left: To the south of the road are the maisons talus.

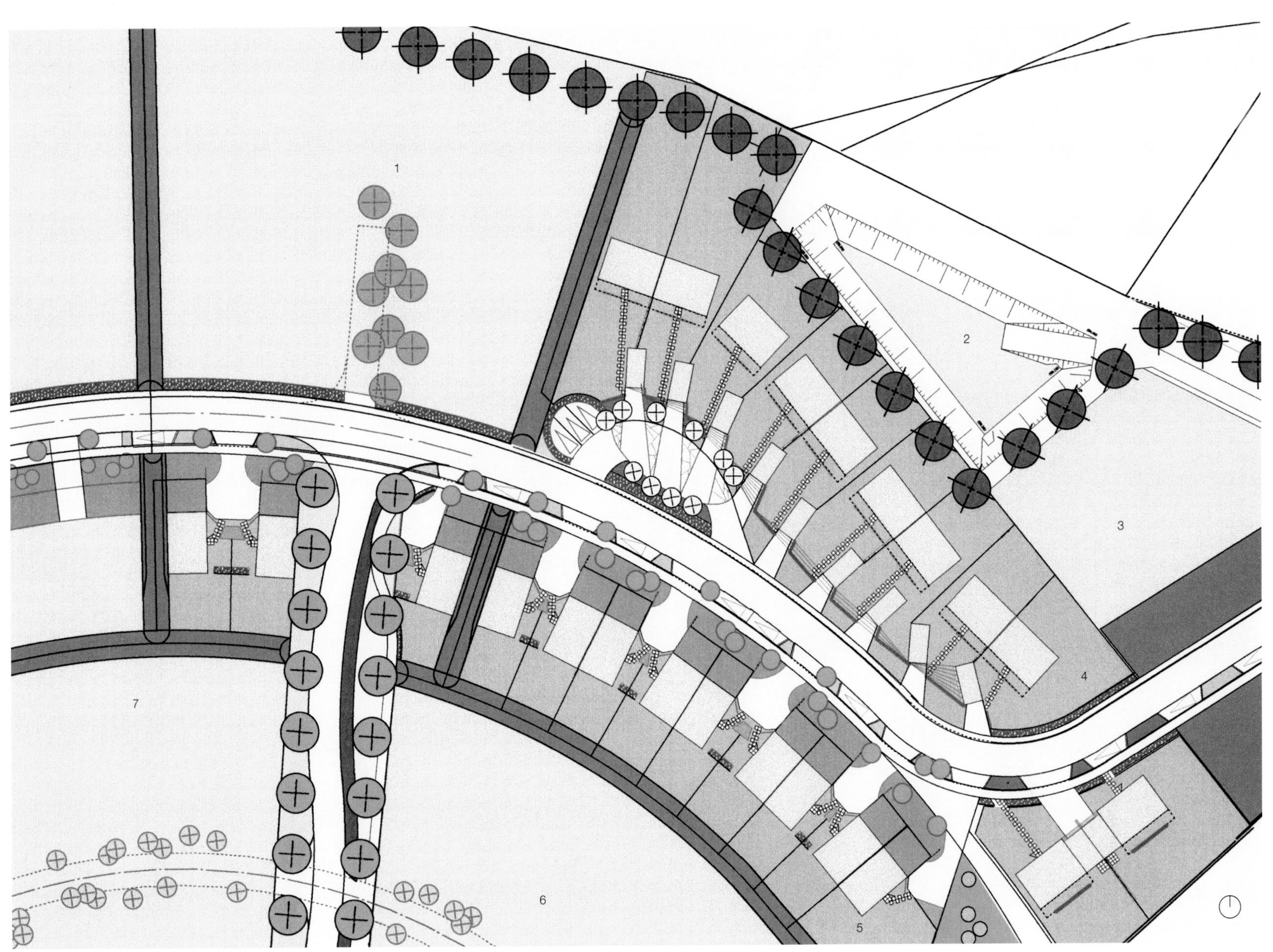

Above: Plan of part of the garden-city site, showing the range of gardens in which the housing will be set. 1. flavour garden (10 houses planned); 2. reservoir; 3. five houses in the trees; 4. perfumed garden (11 maisons soleil); 5. 12 maisons talus; 6. the groves (15 houses planned); 7. the groves (15 houses planned).

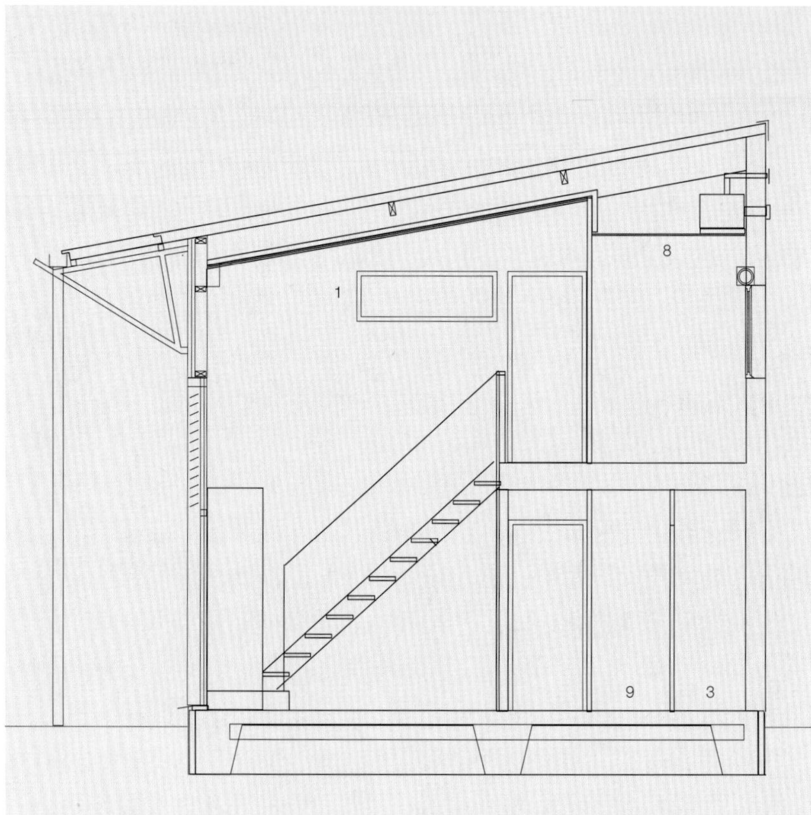

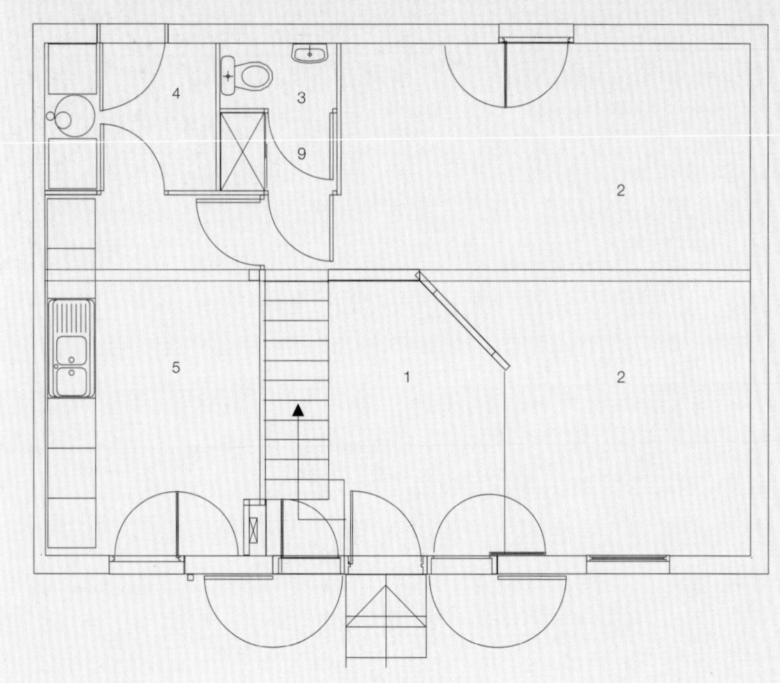

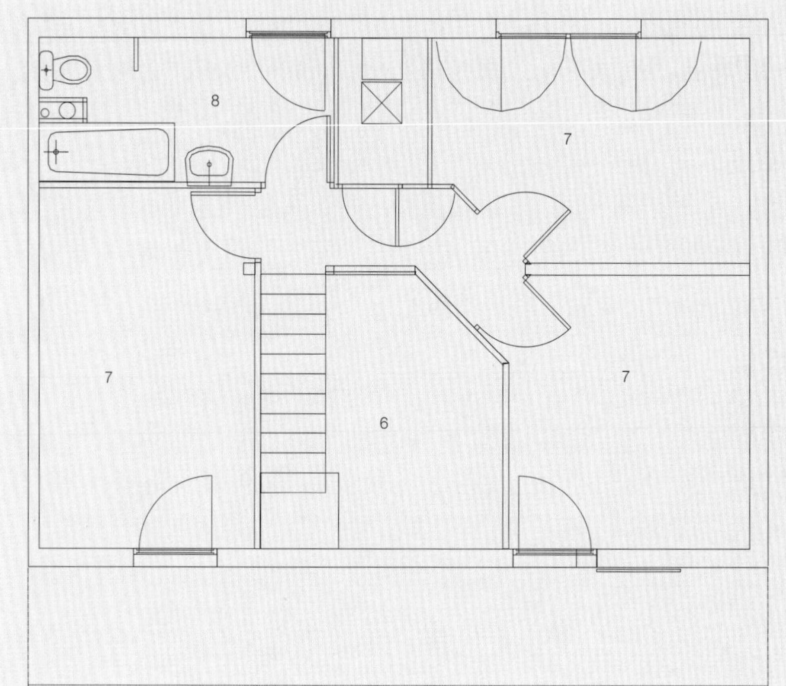

Top left: The maisons soleil with a garage in front, clad in unpainted timber boards.

Above left and right: Ground-floor and first-floor plans of a maison soleil. 1. entrance; 2. living; 3. WC; 4. store; 5. kitchen; 6: void; 7. bedroom; 8. bathroom; 9. cloakroom.

Top right: Section through a maison soleil.

are relatively compact, this results in an annual energy consumption for heating that is about 40 per cent less than the average for the region. To add to their environmental credentials, some houses recycle rain water from their roofs, and others have solar panels.

Other elements of design also contribute to the good environmental performance of the buildings. For instance, enclosed porches on the maisons talus act as barriers between the external and internal environment, offering some free heat on sunny winter days and providing additional living space in the intermediate seasons.

Neither have the architects ignored the potential problems of overheating. The open southern façades of the maisons soleil have integral shutters and blinds, and a large overhanging canopy. The poles that support this have been designed to encourage plants to climb up and colonize the canopy, adding to the shading effect.

The garages to the maisons soleil are clad in unpainted timber boards. And, at first glance, you might imagine that the houses themselves are clad in white-painted timber boards. This would be a charming conceit but, unfortunately, one that would be too demanding in terms of maintenance. Instead the material used is fibre-cement, chosen specifically for its low maintenance requirements. Accents of colour, for instance around the front doors, are provided by red-coloured sheets of Prodema, a Spanish product that first came to the awareness of the world through its use at the Seville Expo in 1992. It is a high-pressure laminate made from cellulose fibres bound with a resin. A facing veneer of real wood, also impregnated with resin, can be coloured and is protected by an acrylic coat. Again, this is a material that is extremely durable with no maintenance requirements.

France may have been behind the UK in picking up on the idea of garden cities, but it has embraced the concept with enthusiasm. Similarly, it is now waking up belatedly to the potential for constructing in wood. Whereas the UK had a highly funded campaign called 'Wood for Good' running from the start of the millennium, its French equivalent, 'Le bois c'est essentiel', was not launched until December 2004. One of the first exemplar projects on which it picked up was, not surprisingly, the garden city housing at Petit Bétheny.

Top left: Entrances to the maisons soleil have overhanging canopies to provide shade, supported on timber poles up which plants will be encouraged to climb.

Above left: Cladding of the houses is in white fibre-cement boarding, with Prodema panels providing a touch of colour around the doors.

Above right: The architectural concept of houses embedded in the landscape will not be fully realized until the landscape is mature.

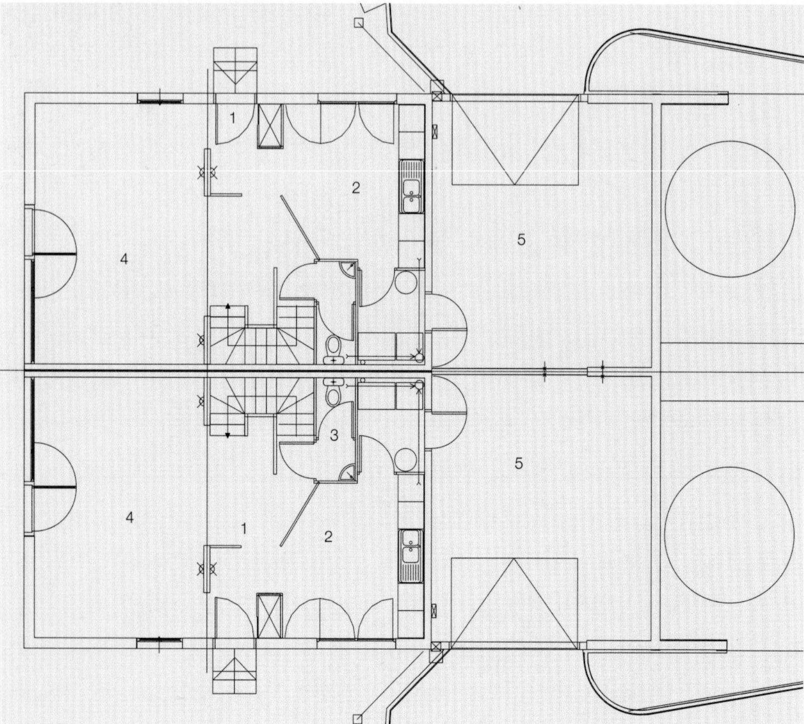

Top left: The maisons talus have their garages fronting the street, with both entrances at the side of the house.

Top right: In addition to the large areas of common planting, private external spaces are also defined.

Above left and right: Ground- and first-floor plans of two maisons talus. 1. entrance; 2. kitchen; 3. WC; 4. living room; 5. garage; 6. bedroom; 7. bath.

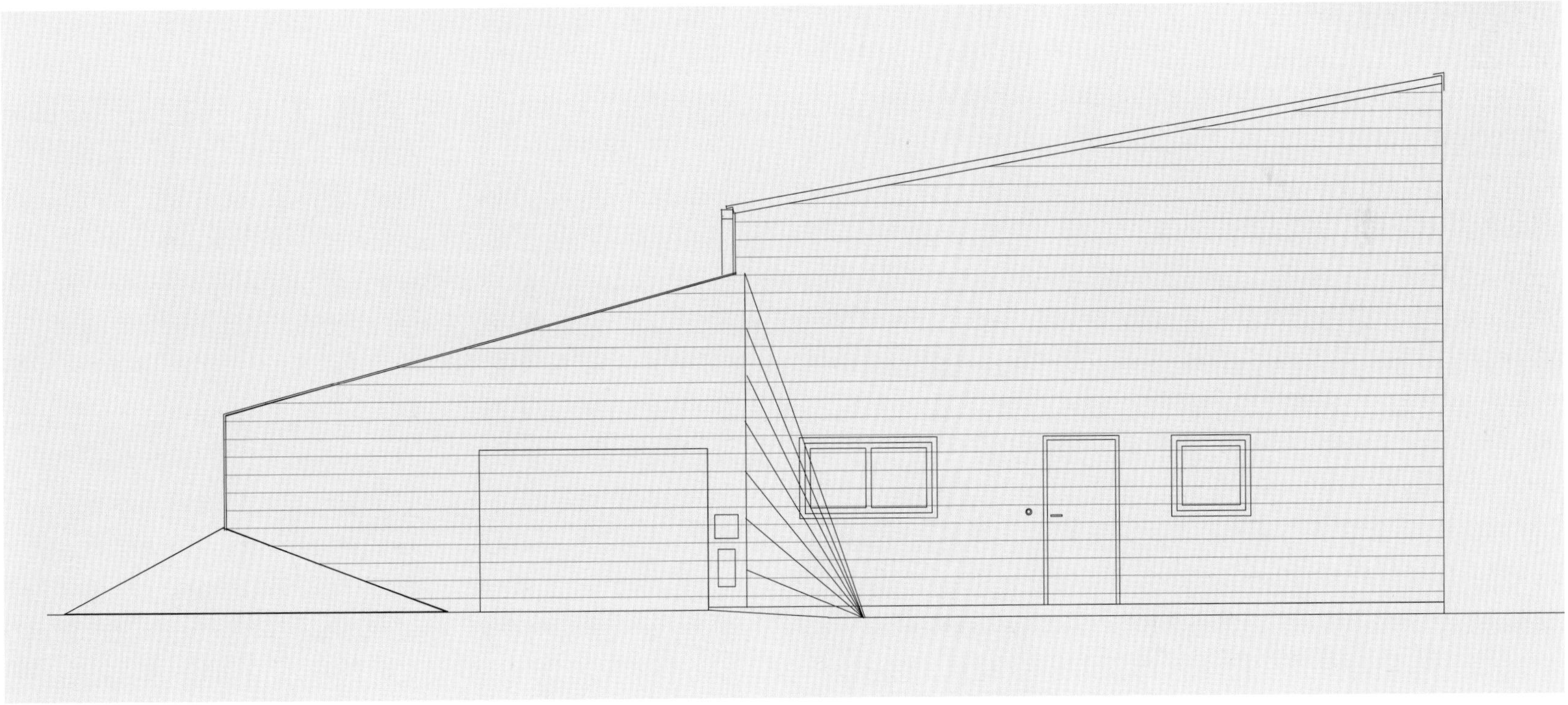

Top left: Open stairs enhance the transparency of the common areas.

Above: Side elevation of a maison talus.

Top right: Views from all windows are of vegetation.

Housing Group
Porto San Paolo, Sardinia 2000
Marco Petreschi

Above: By using traditional materials and incorporating existing trees, the architect has created a development that looks as if it has been there for years.

Top: Traditional techniques give a deliberately heavy feel to the houses, which have to cope with winter storms as well as summer heat.

Above: Timber-framed windows look out on to magnificent scenery.

A group of houses on Sardinia's Costa Smeralda shows it is possible for architects to embrace traditional techniques and designs without producing embarrassing pastiches – although having a beautiful natural setting does help. Architect Marco Petreschi certainly had such an environment. The Costa Smeralda is a glorious stretch of Sardinia's north-eastern coast that has been deliberately developed for a very particular type of tourism – to appeal to wealthy visitors who want all mod cons but in an idyllic and, as far as possible, unspoilt setting. Developed after being discovered by the Aga Khan, it has become a high-class tourist honeypot on this rugged island.

The building codes for the Costa Smeralda specify that houses should be constructed in indigenous materials, and in his scheme at Porto San Paolo, Petreschi has made use of granite and timber, and has echoed the traditional form of housing for this part of Sardinia, known as a *stazzu*.

Stazzu is apparently derived from the Latin *statio*, meaning farm. Typically the houses disappeared into the landscape, their heavy masonry walls, unfinished externally, becoming part of their surroundings in a manner akin to drystone walling. Normally a *stazzu* started off as just a large fireplace and a bedroom plus, sometimes, an external oven, and would be added to as the family grew. Petreschi is giving his residents a few more facilities than these, and has dispensed with the traditional pigsty, goats and bee hives.

In the grouping of his buildings he is echoing the traditional entity of the *cussoghja*, a social grouping connected by moral links called the *manialia*. This led families to help each other in major enterprises, such as threshing or the construction of a fence, although in today's houses they are more likely to be meeting over a glass of Sardinian wine or exchanging tips about the best restaurant or beach. However, the arrangement of the buildings, and the self-effacing way they blend into the landscape, is a homage to the way homes were traditionally grouped.

The first word that comes to mind when looking at the houses is 'heaviness'. Here there is no truck with structural gymnastics, or an attempt to do more with less. Instead, Petreschi has embraced traditional techniques, with the blocks of granite that form his walls and columns matching the large-section rafters of spruce that support the relatively shallow-pitched tiled roofs. But there is nothing crude about the construction. Indeed, one of its most interesting aspects is the manner in which the two elements meet, with the timber extending down from the rafters to form a handcrafted joint with the granite columns. Rather like a mathematical puzzle, they lock into each other in an intriguing geometric shape, and then are held together by sturdy metal bands.

As befits houses designed for holidays in a warm climate, as much attention is paid to the exterior as to the interior. There is a portico formed of spruce beams supported on granite columns and, at its outer edge, on timber columns, with a partial roof of latticed timbers that create intriguing shadows.

The setting could not be better, with not only the dramatic countryside and the famous emerald-coloured sea of the Costa Smeralda but also a view of the slab-shaped island of Tavolara.

The development is being marketed vigorously as one with all the facilities any holidaymaker could wish for. Life in the houses could scarcely be more different to that experienced by Sardinian peasants but, despite the element of make-believe, this is an attempt at working with tradition and the natural environment that should be applauded.

Above: As much consideration has been given to the external landscaping as to internal spaces.

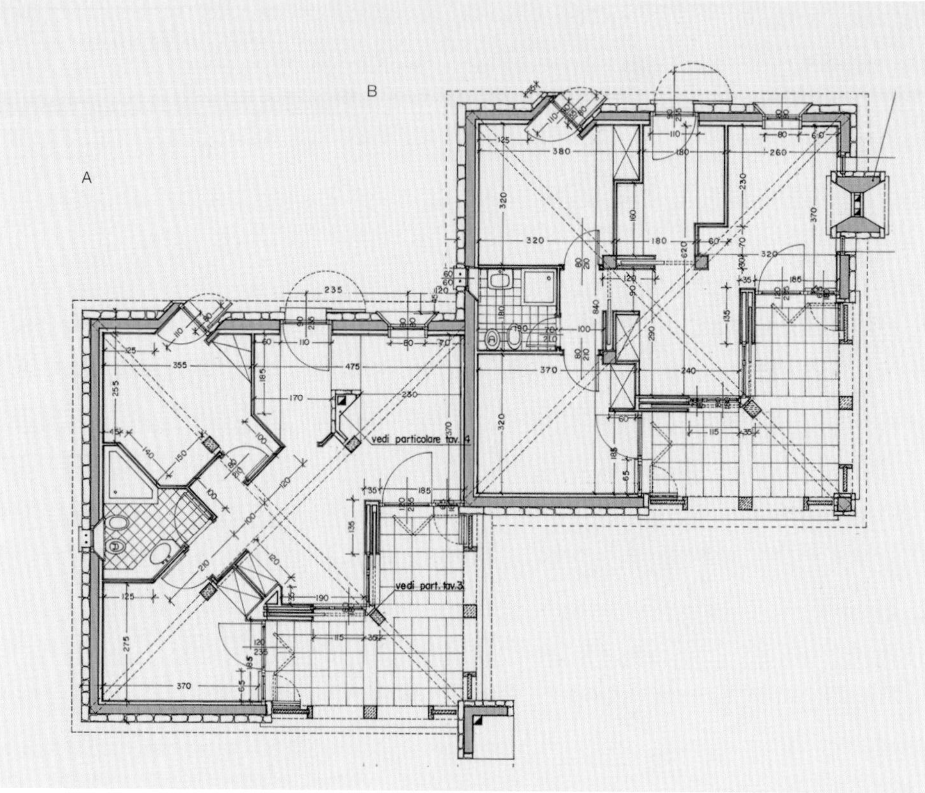

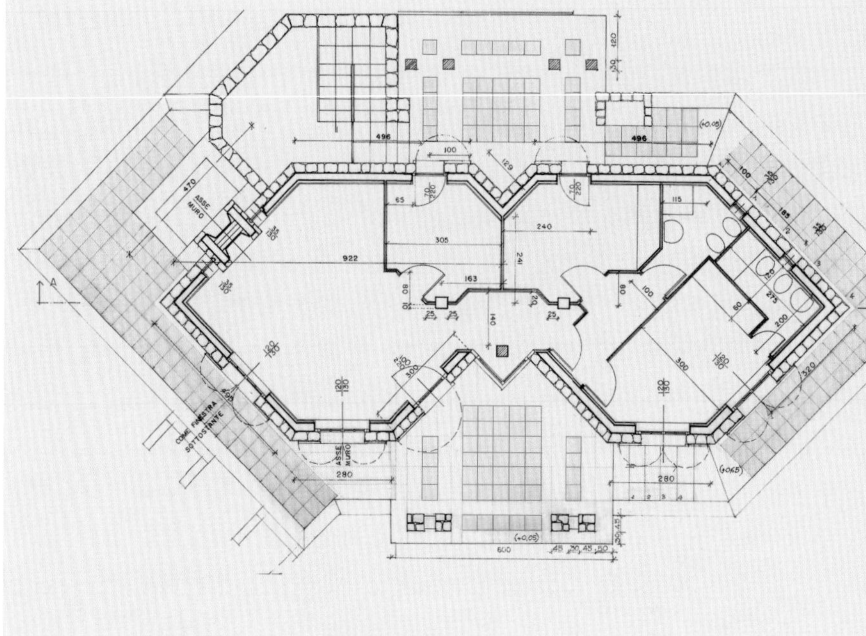

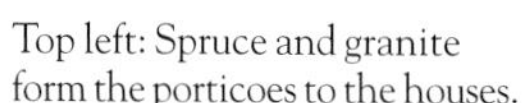
Top left: Spruce and granite form the porticoes to the houses.

Above left: Large-section spruce rafters support the roofs.

Top right: Plan of typical house types A and B. The old-fashioned sociability of the *cussoghja* is echoed in the relationship between neighbouring houses

Above right: By varying the plans of the house types, the architect avoids giving the development a feeling of excessive uniformity.

Top left: A simple but carefully considered joint links spruce and granite.

Above left: Architect's drawing of the joint detail.

Above right: Overall plan of the development.

House Extension

Paris, France 2004
Christian Pottgiesser
with Florian Hertwerk

Three timber elements play starring roles in a house extension in Paris by Christian Pottgiesser and Florian Hertweck. In a very smart part of the city, only 10 minutes from the Champs Elysées, this is one of those fantastically complex projects where the quantity of work seems to outstrip the amount of space gained. Only in a place where property prices are high, and the residents desperate to stay where they are, would such an enterprise be countenanced. But it does form a magnificent showcase for the ingenuity of a talented pair of architects.

The site has a curious history. In a road where the standard height of buildings is four to five storeys, an architect at the start of the last century managed to acquire a narrow strip of land, 8 metres (26 feet) wide, to the side of a house he had designed. Set to the back of this, he built a charming doll's-house home for his mistress. In order to preserve her views and space, he put a planning restriction on the site, which meant that no future development could be taller than a ground floor plus a single storey, and that it could not extend back more than 5.4 metres (17.5 feet) from the street.

Some extension took place when a couple of well-known singers bought the house and decided to extend the basement forward and create a garden on top with a living area, including a Turkish bath, below. When the present owners bought the property in 1997 they soon discovered that it was not large enough to accommodate them and their five growing children. They therefore contacted Pottgiesser and gave him their brief: they wanted as large as possible an increase in area, without losing any garden! Pottgiesser spent a long time working out the best solution with his client, and then went on to tussle with the planners. To add to the difficulties, there were two trees in the garden that had to be preserved: a lime right at the front and a Japanese alder towards the back. However, he eventually prevailed with a design that satisfied both client and planners.

His solution is certainly ingenious, based around an undulating reinforced-concrete deck. Beneath this the entire area of the site, including the basement of the existing house, is united into a large living space with natural light coming in from a central patio surrounded by glazed walls, and from a light well at the front of the building, near the street.

The street façade now consists at first-floor level of a screen of hand-sawn Noyon stone with, behind it, a guest area of 37 square metres (398 square feet). This area bridges a glazed 'ground floor' that in fact turns the pre-existing garden into a winter garden. Here the concrete deck slopes up to the right-hand side so that, to the left, the main entrance is at ground-floor level. There is then an upwardly sloping timber-clad face that, on the right-hand side, conceals the entrance to an underground garage.

Above left: The new façade, with the stone first floor 'floating' above the glazed ground floor, and the preserved lime tree poking through. The garage entrance is to the right.

Above: The Noyon stone on the façade creates a bridge between the conventional apartment blocks to either side.

Opposite: Untreated iroko suspended staircase, leading from the basement to the ground floor.

Left: The magically floating staircase leading up from the basement offers a view of the lime tree passing through an opening in the front façade.

The winter garden includes the preserved lime tree, just to the right of the front door. Encased in glass, it travels up through an opening in the floor of the upper level, and then out through the largest of the openings in the stone screen so that its branches poke out over the street. Other, carefully placed, openings in the screen are glazed and provide light for the guest space.

Two magnificent staircases, entirely of untreated iroko wood, lead up from the basement to the winter garden, then up from the winter garden to the guest room and up again to a rooftop garden. Two elements make them spectacular. The first is that they are suspended from above, so they do not touch the floor. Instead, you go up three concrete steps, then step across an air gap into the totally enclosed box of the staircase. The second spectacular element is that, in each case, the back of the box follows the line of the stairs, so that you see the stepped underside. The effect, therefore, is of a magnificent sculptural object.

In the guest room you exit this stair at the end of the box, but there is also an opening in its side, again accessed by three free-standing concrete steps, that takes you up and out onto the roof, so that the top part of the staircase enclosure becomes a cowl peeking out above the roofline.

The final structural timber element, also in the guest area, is a cubic box with a glazed end-face that projects over the patio. Large enough to contain a bed, it adds an important extra space to this very tight site.

Construction on this project was complex, with not only the tree roots but also a home cinema in the sub-basement having to be protected during excavation. And clever engineering was needed to conceal the beams that support the guest room above almost entirely glazed façades. The true achievement, however, is not in the structural ingenuity but in the puzzle solving, imagination and attention to individual elements that enabled the architect to make so much more of this very restricted site – in terms of not only usable area but also the pleasure it can give its inhabitants.

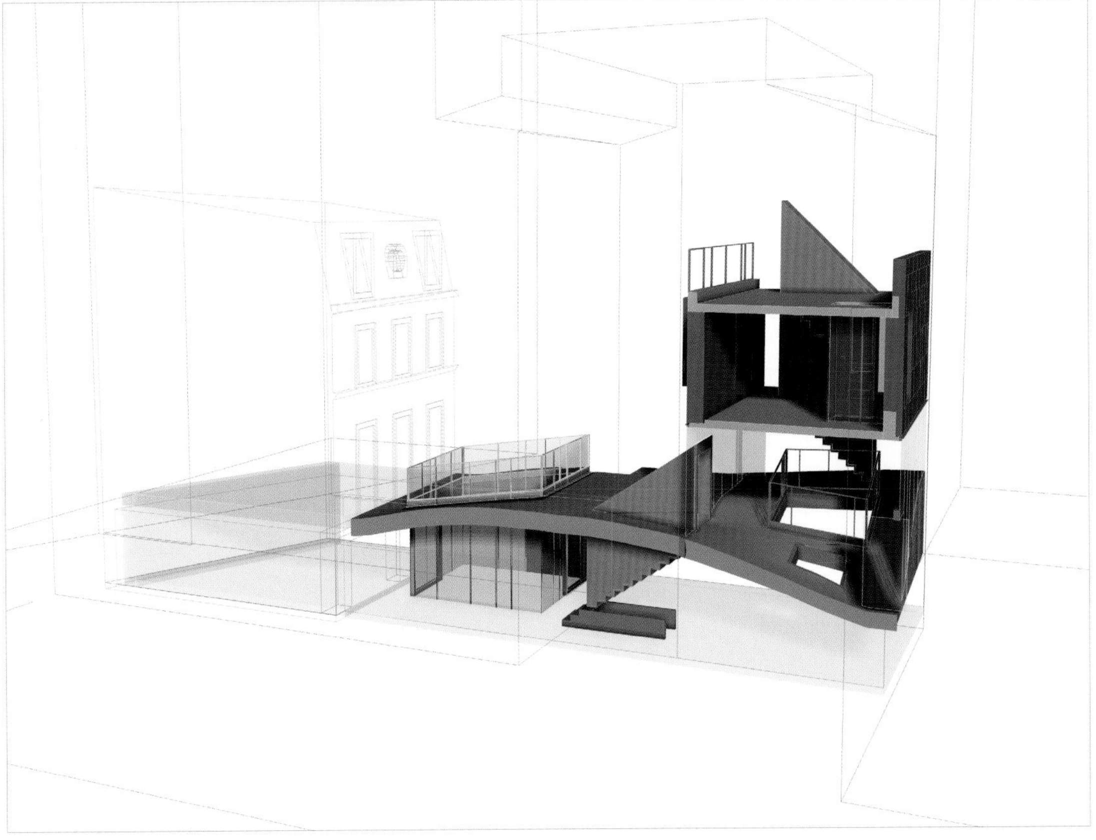

Top left: From the winter garden, with its central light well, one can see out to the 'doll's house' at the rear.

Above left: A cubic box projecting over the patio allows valuable space for a bed.

Above: This three-dimensional computer rendering gives a sense of the complexity of the project.

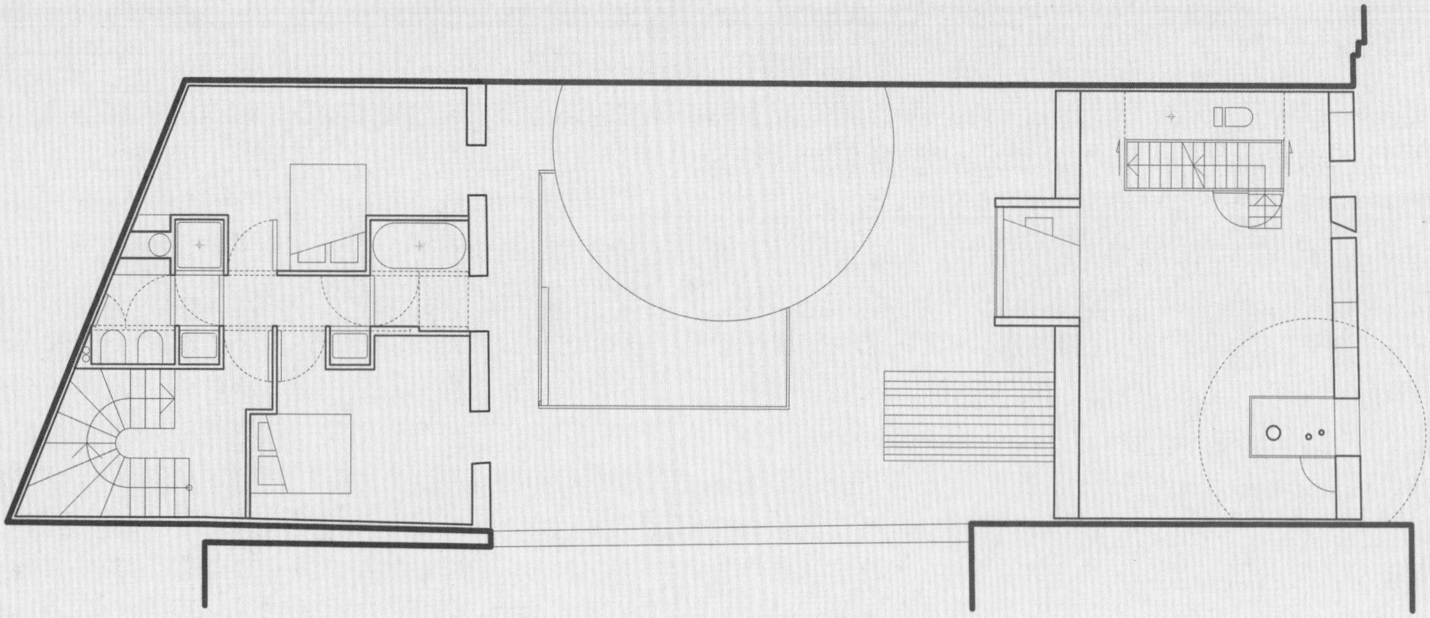

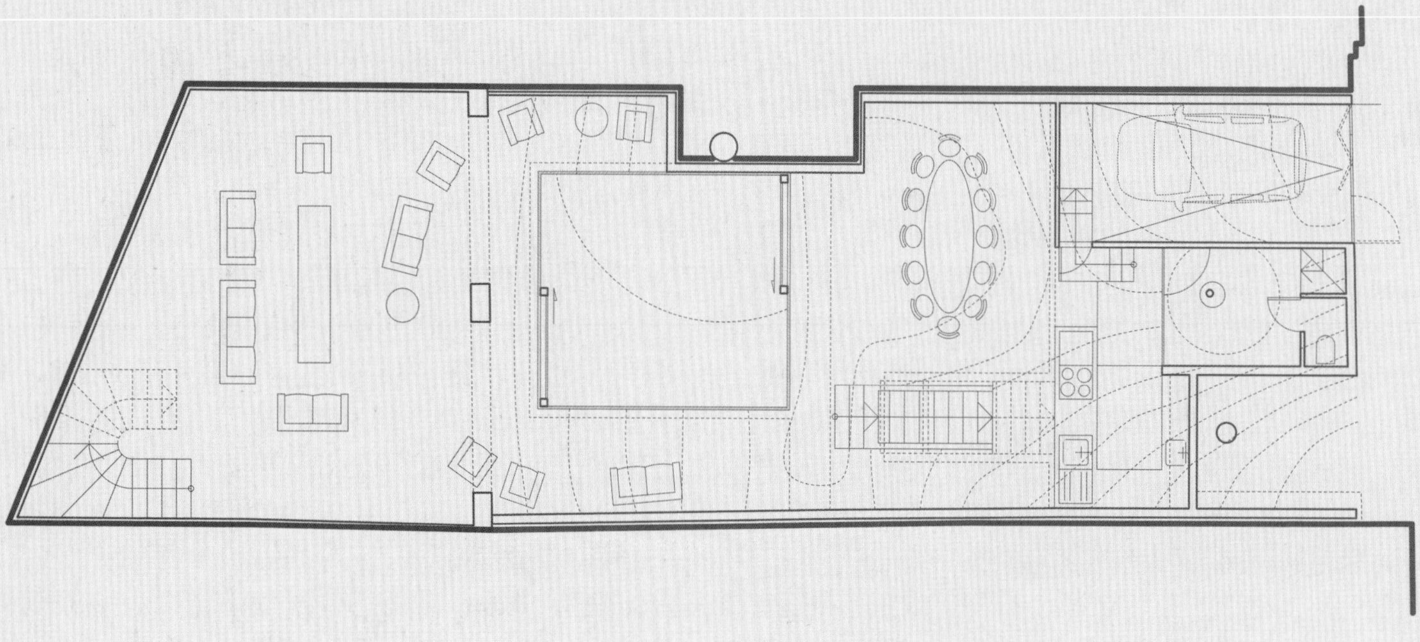

Opposite top: Upper-floor plan, showing the new guest room at the front of the building (right) and accommodation in the existing house at the rear (left).

Opposite bottom: Basement plan, showing the open, glazed courtyard at the heart of the building.

Above: The new guest room at the front of the building has a glazed enclosure for the preserved lime tree, and a staircase leading up to the roof.

Cargo Fleet
London, UK 2005
Chance de Silva

We hear a lot about changes in family structures and the way people work and live, but remarkably few houses reflect this in their design. One that does is Cargo Fleet in a neglected area of north London. It is difficult to define what this project is. Should it be called a house, or a pair of houses? This ambiguity is deliberate, as its architects were eager to create a pair of linked dwellings that could be used in a number of ways. They could be occupied by a couple living semi-detached lives, or one section could be dedicated to working and the other to living. Alternatively, the smaller part could be used as a granny flat or by a teenage child. The achievement is made greater by the fact that Cargo Fleet has not been built on a generous open space, but on a narrow, wedge-shaped corner site that would scare off many designers altogether.

However, the architects Stephen Chance and Wendy de Silva have a track record with this type of project. Both fully employed by other, larger architectural firms, they dedicate only a day a week each to their joint practice, Chance de Silva, yet have managed to complete a number of intriguing schemes. Just round the corner from Cargo Fleet is their most high-profile one – a tiny building, Venus House, that is a cross between a live/work space and a private art gallery. Architecture critic Hugh Pearman described it as, 'a habitable modern folly in the 18th-century tradition, built as much for fun as for any practical purpose.' With this project under their belts, the duo could not resist the opportunity to develop another, and similarly unloved, site. After Venus, even the mean dimensions of Cargo Fleet look generous.

London has become such an affluent city, where even areas that were previously down-at-heel are now refurbished and enjoying astronomical property prices, that it is surprising to find anywhere as neglected as Whistler Street in north London. It loops around a derelict former laundry, and is jammed between a railway line and rising ground. This, combined with the narrow and cobbled nature of the street itself, makes it more reminiscent of the industrial northern towns where Stephen Chance grew up than of the rest of London. And this, in turn, affected the design of the house and, in particular, the materials used.

Chance was keen to mirror 'the threatened industrial structure' around his home town of Redcar – an unusual brief for a house, but in Chance's case evidently a concept that had more of romance than depression about it. The result is a

Above left: Cargo Fleet fits tightly in its urban setting.

Above right: A conservatory and a courtyard link the two parts of the building.

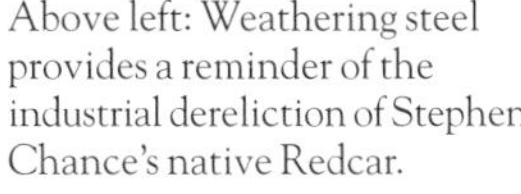

Above left: Weathering steel provides a reminder of the industrial dereliction of Stephen Chance's native Redcar.

Above right: Thanks to the slenderness of the timber frame, a staircase can squeeze in next to the party wall.

Top right: Larch cladding would have produced acid run-off that would have attacked zinc, so terne-coated steel was chosen instead for the conservatory roof.

building where the dominant cladding material is weathering steel – a form of steel that develops a protective patina of rust so that it is durable but weathers first to orange, then to purple and finally to a near-black.

However, if it is this steel that first catches the eye, timber also has an important role to play in the building. A timber frame, assembled on site, supports the house. According to the structural engineer Price & Myers it allowed the walls to be more slender than could have been achieved with any other construction technique. This advantage was essential in a building where space was at a premium.

Nor is all the structure clad with steel. One way of differentiating between the two 'houses' is that the rear part, linked to the front by a glazed conservatory, is faced not with steel but with rough-sawn larch. And this is echoed in a projecting loft 'box' clad in the same material, which is perched on top of the main house. Neither of these were the architect's original choices. At first, the architects intended to use cedar for the rear building and to make the loft box in concrete. But, in keeping with the rough-hewn aesthetic, they decided the cladding of these elements should resemble shuttering planks, and so alighted on larch. The large planks, running vertically, have square edges, and 6-millimetre (¼-inch) joints, which have insect protection behind them.

The use of larch led in turn to another change of material. Originally the conservatory link was to have had a zinc roof. However, in common with many timbers (although not spruce or pine), larch is highly acidic, with a pH below 5, and so its run-off will attack zinc. The architects therefore substituted terne-coated steel for the zinc.

This mutability in the use of materials reflects the architects' keen interest in the expression they can bring to a project. Another analogy they drew when considering the disposition of spaces was with the linked but separate studios of Diego Rivera and Frida Kahlo. Cargo Fleet, situated in one of London's meanest streets and evoking the industrial decay of the north of England, is far from the hot sun and torrid lives of the Mexican artists. But in a very different way, the project is to do with unconventional living and a challenge to accepted orthodoxy.

Like many architects who are relatively restricted in the amount they build, Chance and de Silva have poured a wealth of ideas into this tiny site. Cargo Fleet is not likely to be emulated on a large scale. But the concept of flexible accommodation is one that will become increasingly important as we move further away from the rigid idea that all homes must be designed for the stereotypical but rapidly disappearing nuclear family.

Top left: Staircase in the smaller, rear 'house'.

Above left: With two street façades and light brought in at the centre, this unusual arrangement makes the most of the narrow site.

Above right: Section through the two parts of the house.

Opposite: Plans of the ground and first floors. 1. conservatory; 2. shower/ bath; 3. bedroom; 4. courtyard; 5. living/dining/kitchen; 6. balcony.

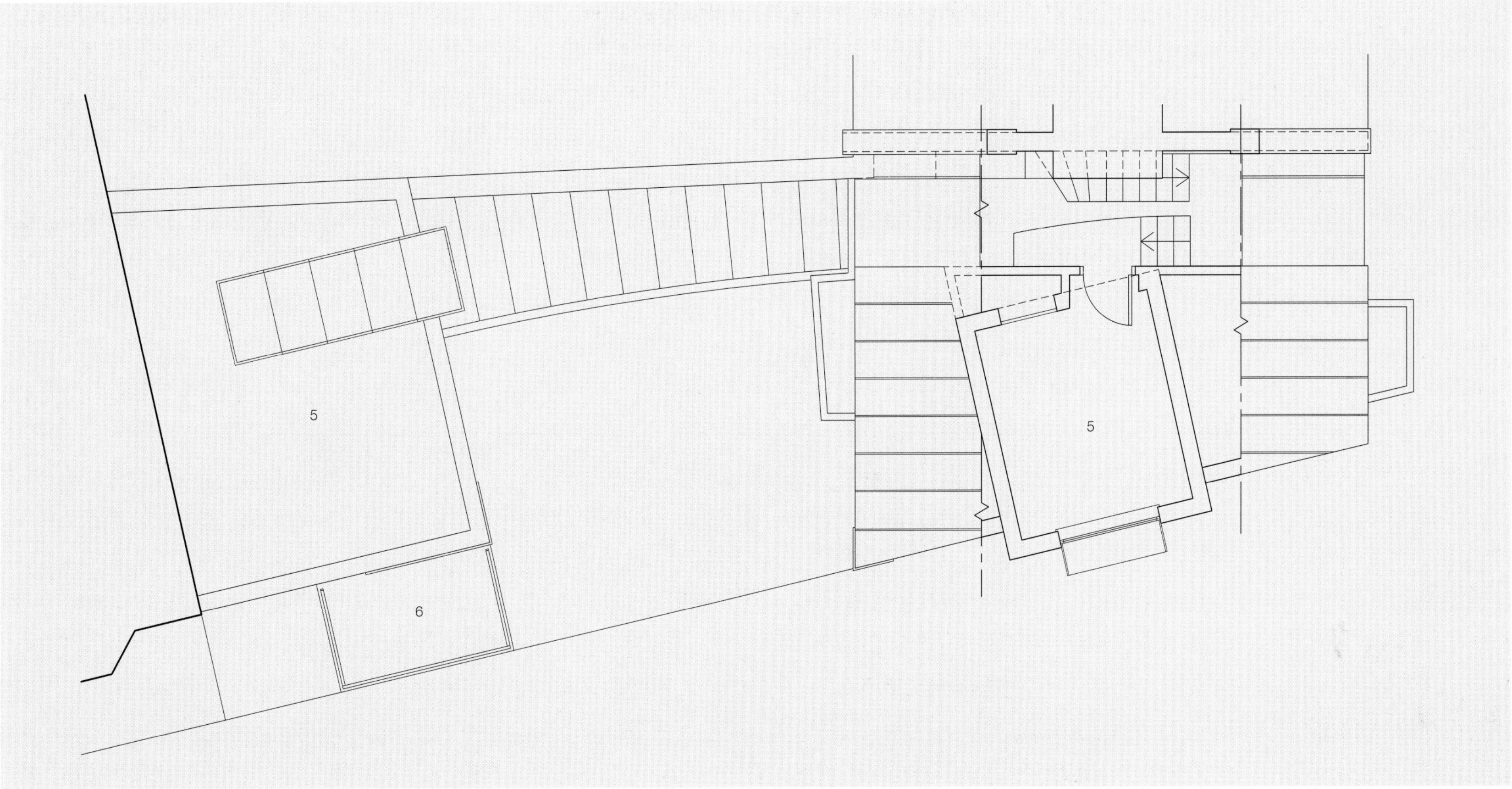

5
5
6

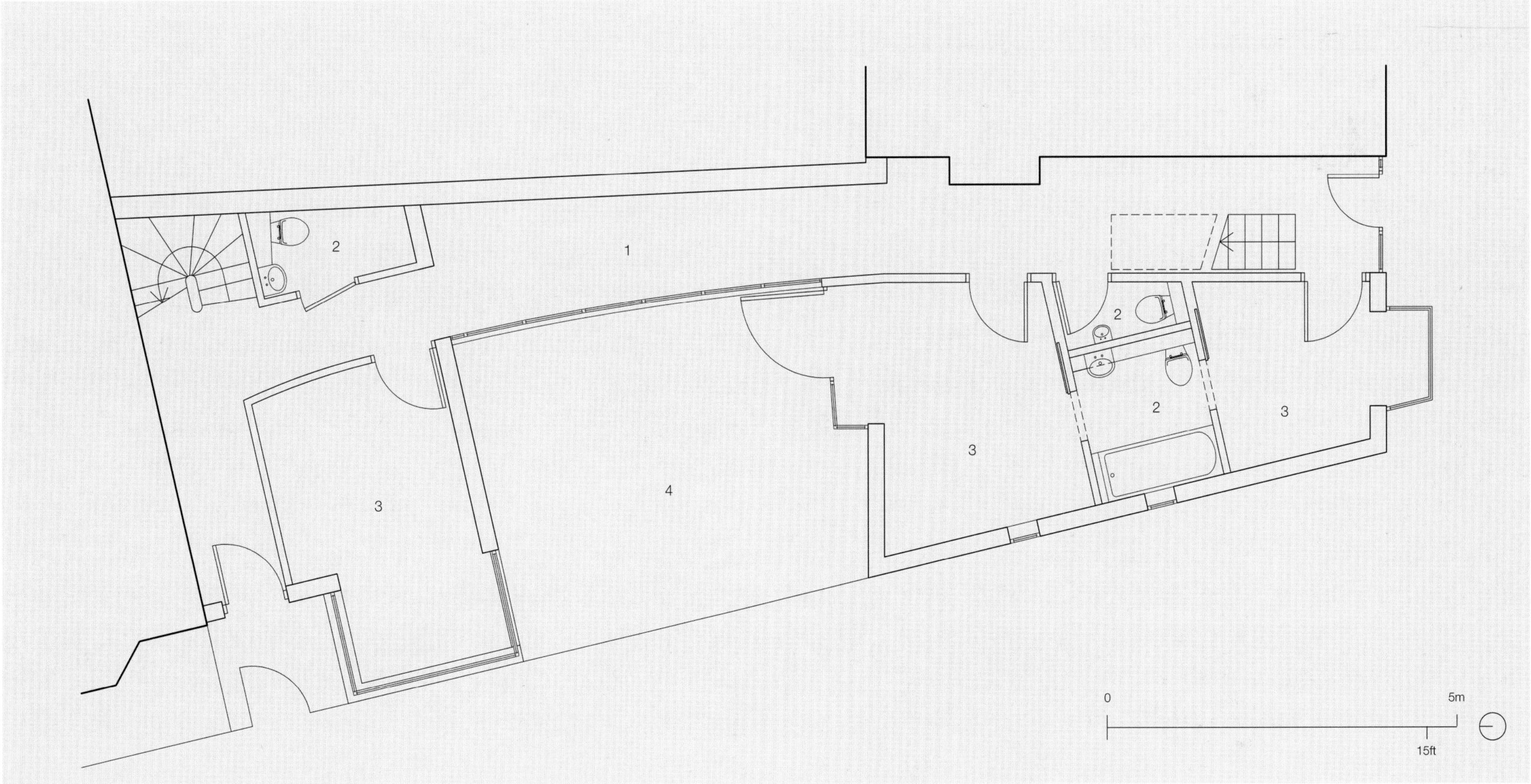

2
1
2
2
3
4
3
3

0
5m
15ft

Ebeling House
Dortmund, Germany 2001
ArchiFactory.de

Right: The blank front façade is accentuated by the fact that the entrance is through the underground garage.

Sometimes a lack of expression can be a statement in itself, and this is what ArchiFactory.de has achieved with their addition to a house in Dortmund. Although described as an extension it is to all intents and purposes a new building, sited next to the owner's original property and with a full set of functions.

It is a tall, thin wooden box, with none of the accoutrements that create the usual suburban landscape – no welcoming front door, no pitched roof, visible downpipes, projecting window sills or, heaven forbid, any decoration. Instead the block is entirely blank, with just four metal-framed windows set flush with the horizontal timber cladding, the disposition of the functions within remaining almost totally mysterious.

The sense of arrival is extremely muted – you sidle in through an underground garage before taking the stairs to arrive at the open-plan double-height living area at the rear of the building. Its window, also double height, includes a door that opens onto steps down to the rear garden. At the front is a kitchen/dining room, with a window on one of the side façades. On the first floor a study at the front, above the dining room, has a window overlooking the street. And the top floor has a bedroom at the rear. Doors open from both the bathroom and the landing onto an enclosed patio at the front. Effectively a five-faced timber box, with just the top face open to the sky, this is the most secret of the elements in this very uncommunicative building.

Decorated austerely internally, the house is an ideal environment for visitors who want a degree of independence, offering them not only a bedroom but also places to cook, eat, relax and work. Doubtless the study could, if necessary, offer additional sleeping space, but the general disposition comprises extremely generous accommodation for a single couple.

Standing slightly proud of its neighbours, right on the street frontage, the Ebeling House makes no effort to conform to their aesthetic. Only the texture of the timber cladding softens it a little, preventing it from being an entirely monolithic structure.

If you try to envisage streets of such houses the prospect is certainly forbidding, but in the midst of pleasant suburban architectural mediocrity its uncompromising nature is certainly refreshing. It is not surprising, then, that ArchiFactory.de represented Germany with this project at the Venice Biennale in 2004, and that it picked up an award for best façade in 2005. By almost entirely ignoring the concept of context, it has enhanced its surroundings to a considerable degree.

Above left: Double-height glazing at the rear includes a door leading to the garden.

Above right: The building stands proud of its neighbours, right on the street line.

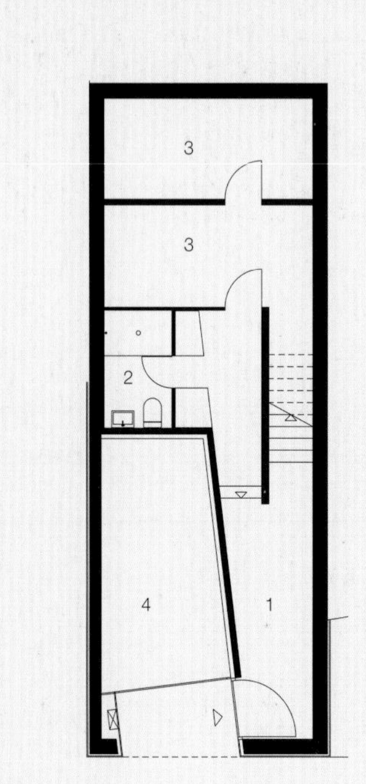

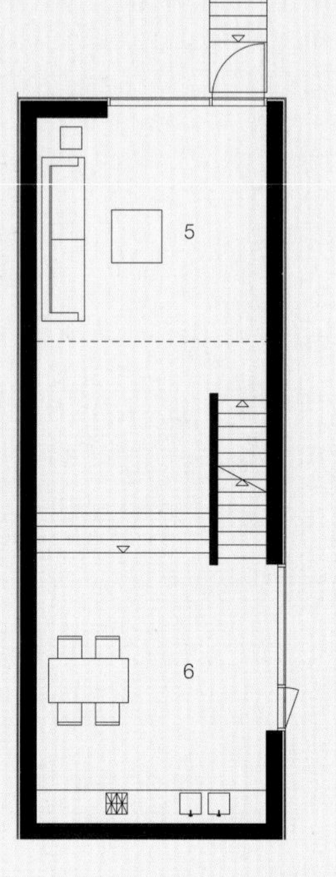

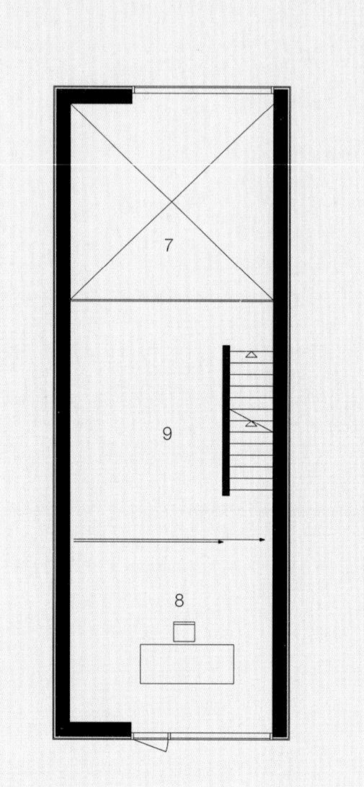

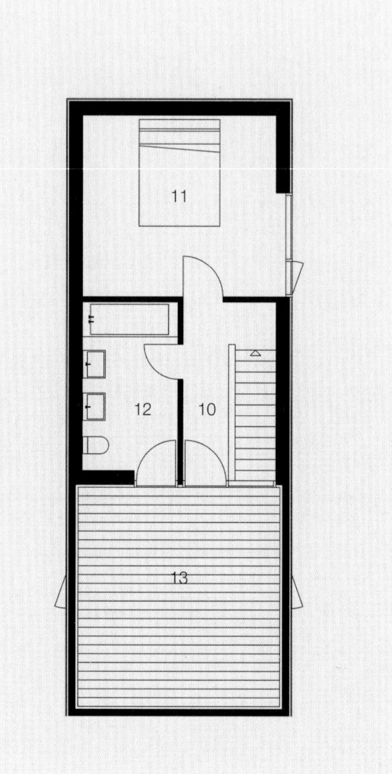

Top: An enclosed roof-top space at the front of the building is another of the house's secrets.

Above: Plans of the house, showing, from left to right: lower ground, ground, first and second floors. 1. entrance hall; 2. WC; 3. store; 4. garage; 5. living room; 6. dining room; 7. void; 8. study; 9. landing; 10. landing; 11. bedroom; 12. bathroom; 13. roof terrace.

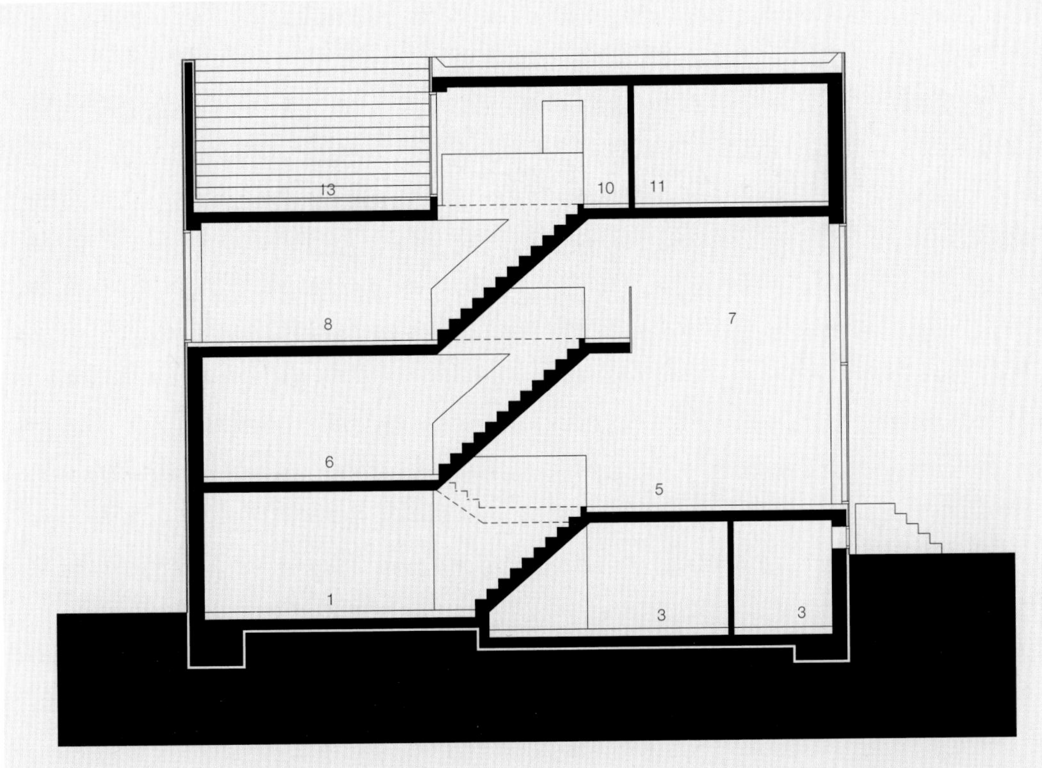

Top left: Long section.

Above left: The upper-ground floor dining room has a window looking out to one side.

Top right: Top-floor view, looking towards the roof terrace at the front.

Above right: Cross-section.

Housing Group
Trivières, Belgium 1998
Groupe Gamma

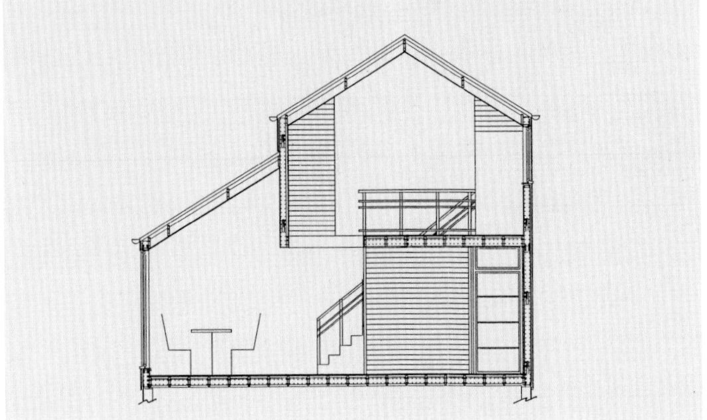

Top: By minimizing the roof overhang and taking the cladding right down to ground level, the architect has given the houses a taut containing skin.

Above left: Positions of entrances alternate to give some rhythm on the street façades.

Above right: Section through a typical house, showing the value of the rear 'extension'.

Semi-detached suburban housing is perhaps one of the most reviled of all forms, but at Trivières in Belgium (part of the old steel town of La Louvière) Groupe Gamma has redefined the type to create houses that are considerably more attractive and pleasurable to live in than their predecessors, while remaining affordable. It has also taken the idea to another site at nearby Mons, which includes the home of one of the Groupe Gamma architects, Françoise Godefroid. In neither case have as many houses been built as were originally envisaged, but general principles have been established: that it is possible to create a simple framework for the design of semi-detached housing that still allows variation from one pair to the next; that houses can be designed to be pleasurable to occupy and elegant from the outside; that this can be done with sustainably specified materials; and that timber can play an important role in the process.

The two-storey houses are framed in larch and clad in slender horizontal elements of the untreated wood. These are divided into bays by slim uprights, and the vertical emphasis is enhanced by the full-height glazing to the hall and landing at the front of the house. This serves both to bring light into the house, and to articulate the façade, with horizontal, timber glazing bars echoing the cladding strips.

Two major factors differentiate the houses from typical semi-detached dwellings. One is that each has a rear extension, something that happened frequently on an ad hoc basis on older city properties where, typically, utility rooms and bathrooms were added several decades after construction. By making the extensions part of the initial specification, the architect has acknowledged that most houses, in fact, need more space downstairs than upstairs; and has also moved away from the dull, rectangular box that defines so many suburban homes.

But what Groupe Gamma has given with one hand it has in part taken away with the other, with its second move. This is to create an inset entrance area, providing the shelter of the much maligned porch but without its usual 'stuck-on' quality. In addition, the front doors are no longer baldly facing the street, and there is some additional semi-sheltered space. By cutting into the plan – on some pairs at the centre of the semi-detached houses, on others at the corners – it also adds to its liveliness.

Part of the visual satisfaction comes from an approach that may have implications for durability. Ignoring the dictum that a 'good hat and boots' is crucial for the performance of a building, the architect has taken the timber cladding right down to ground level instead of, as is common practice, setting it on a plinth of more durable material. This is in contravention of normal Belgian building regulations, but was allowed here because of the argument that the area rarely has a snowfall. Similarly, the roof, of Eternit fibre-cement slates, has a minimal overhang.

But if the architect has traded some assurance of durability for aesthetics, there has been no compromise where the environmental specification is concerned. The weatherproof skin behind the panels is of wood-fibreboard, impregnated with an organic moisture-proofing material, and insulation is of cellulose made from recycled material.

In her own house, Godefroid has taken the use of timber further by using a series of stepped, timber cupboards as the basis for the staircase. This, however, is a very individual approach, to suit a particular occupier. What Groupe Gamma has shown otherwise in these modest houses (each has one double and one single bedroom) is that size, budget and location need be no impediment to good design.

Above left: Horizontal glazing bars on the windows echo the pattern of the larch cladding.

Above right: There is a simple but pleasing elegance to the houses.

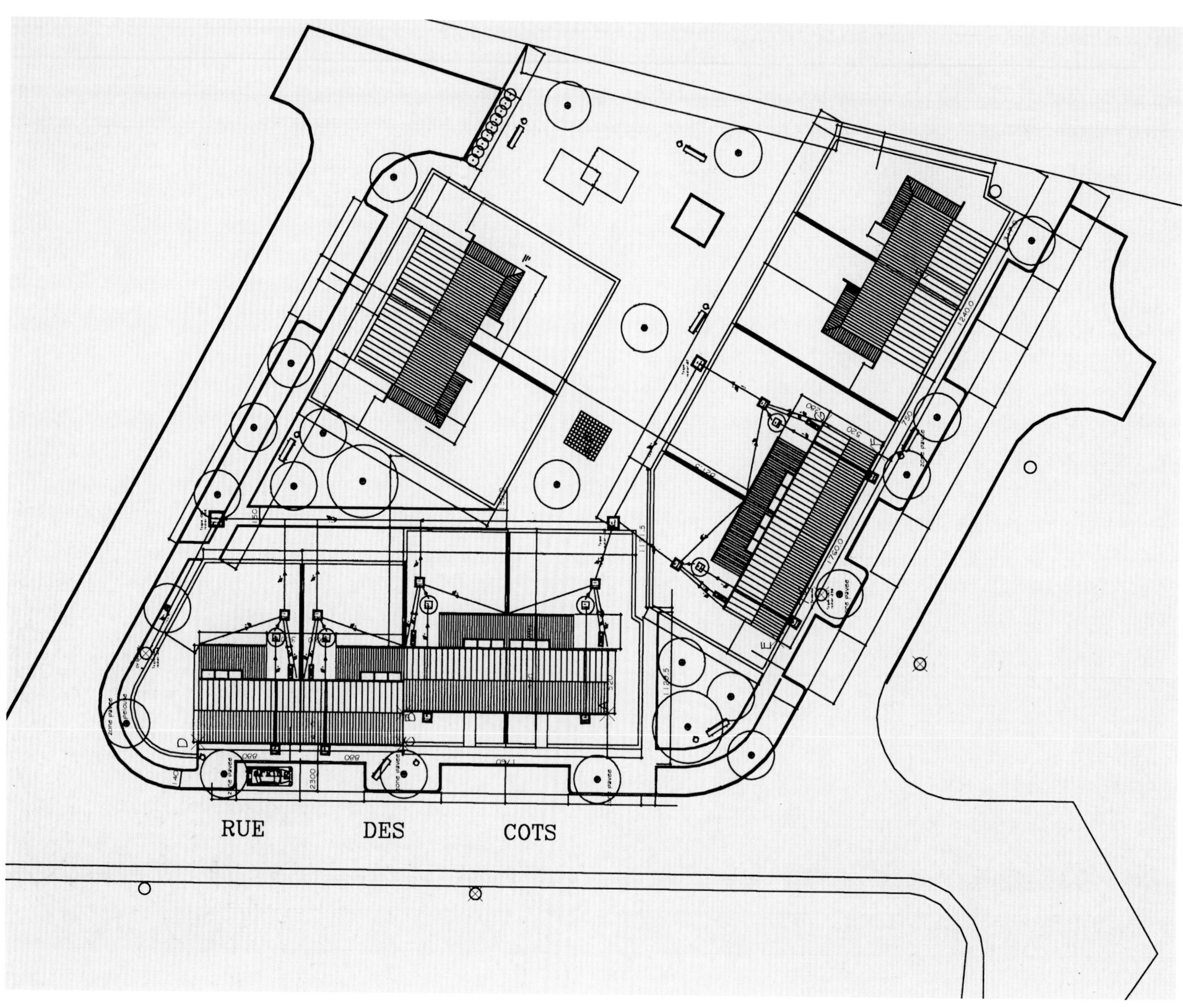

Above: Site plan, showing the effort to avoid uniformity.

Opposite top left: In her own house, Françoise Godefroid has built in cupboards under the stairs.

Opposite top right: Godefroid has used a variant on cathedral stairs in her own house.

Opposite bottom: Lower- and upper-level plans of a typical house.

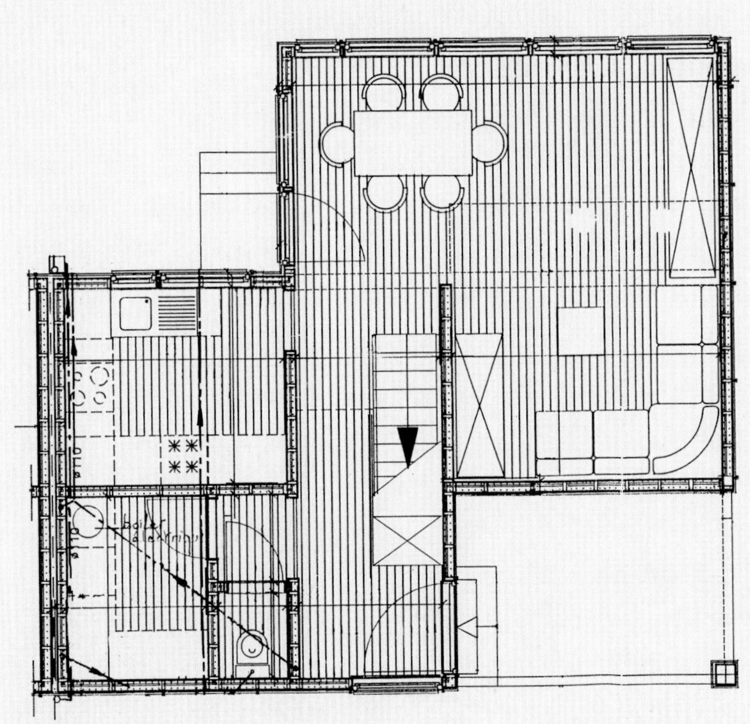

boiler

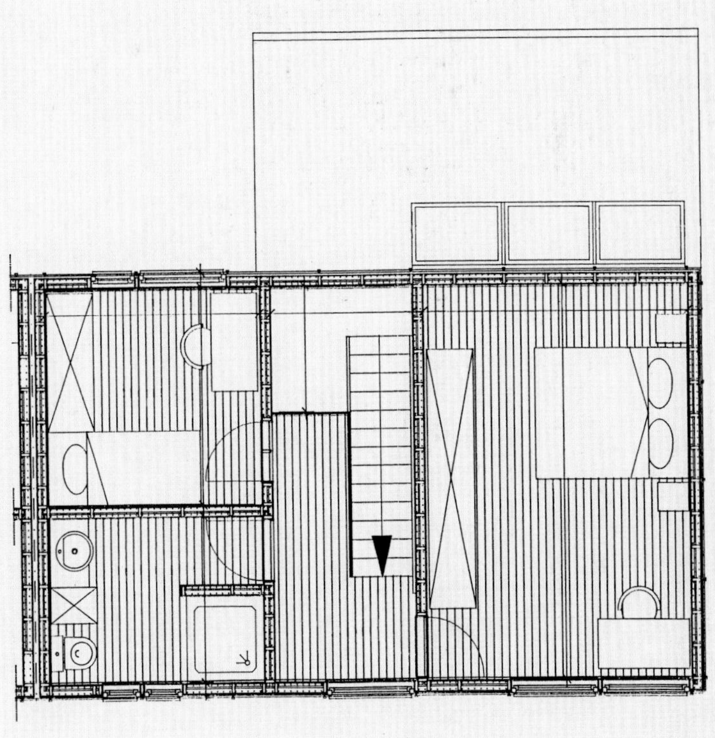

Template House
Beijing, China 2004
Michele Saee

Beijing is hardly the most beautiful of cities, although it is one of the fastest growing and changing. There is a great deal of sense, therefore, in making buildings inward-looking and in creating your own exciting environment in a city of stereotypes and rigid plans. This is what the California-based architect Michele Saee has done with his design for a template house, the fitting out of an apartment within a condominium at Beijing's Phoenix City. It was not created simply for this single space, but is one that the architect believes could be adapted and developed for other apartments.

He created the design, which banishes corners and straight lines in favour of curves and organic openings, for the Beijing architecture biennale that was held at the end of 2004. As part of this event, architects from around the world were invited to design apartments within the flourishing development of Phoenix City.

Saee describes his design as 'an attempt to produce a flowing space where everyday activities take place with the least amount of resistance and clutter. The new design, conceived as a "template house", unifies the space by joining the floor, walls and ceiling into a continuous space that accommodates functions and technical necessities of the new living organism.'

The result is entirely supported on a series of plywood ribs, either 20 or 25 millimetres (¾ or 1 inch) thick, shaped to the curves of the interior and fixed to the original walls of the structure. These support moulded wall panels and ceiling panels that each consist of two layers of poplar bending board with two layers of 'wiggle board' (a board scored on one side to make it flexible) sandwiched between them.

The floors are made up of an assembly of 6 millimetres (¼ inch) of self-levelling material, 6 millimetres (¼ inch) of cork for soundproofing, 20 millimetres (¾ inch) of plywood subfloor and 20 millimetres (¾ inch) of tongue-and-groove floor plywood. The overall result, with veneers beautifully matched so that they all run parallel, is of a kind of lightweight luxury, both pleasing and surprising but in no way oppressive. Sinuously curved contemporary furniture sits well there, and the underlying structure of the apartment is clearly apparent as curved cutaways reveal rectangular door frames plus the walls surrounding them.

Having looked carefully at the moulding and manufacturing process, Saee is confident that it should be possible to extend this idea to many other apartments, giving each one its own individual shape simply by modifying the forms.

As with many prototypes, the Template House may well remain an intriguing one-off, but the thinking behind it shows that even a seemingly bland interior can be entirely transformed by the use of imagination.

Top left: The cocoon-like nature of Template House deliberately isolates residents from the ugly world outside.

Above left: Moulded wall and ceiling panels create a variety of shapes.

Above right: With such a versatile material, the architect's imagination could run free.

Above: Beautifully matched veneers provide a luxurious finish that sets off contemporary furniture.

Above: In keeping with the need for repose, the bedroom has a less visually busy feel.

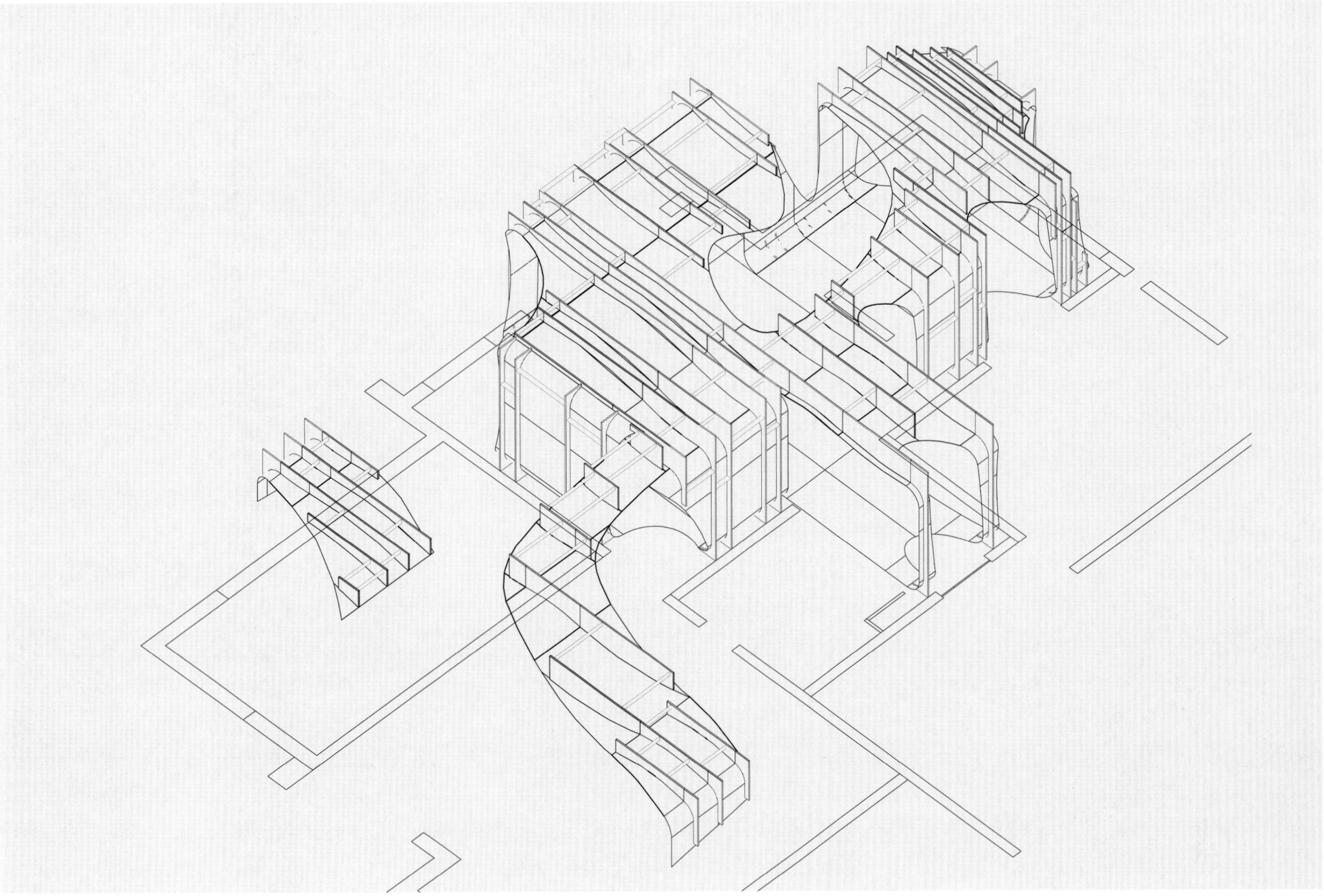

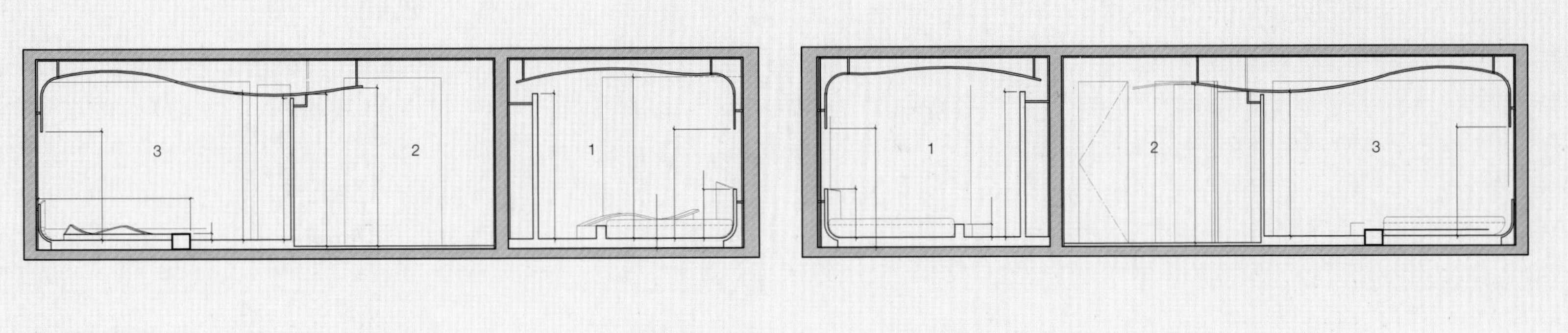

Top: Construction drawing showing the series of plywood ribs that form the structure.

Above: Sections through the apartment. 1. bedroom 1; 2. bedroom 2; 3. bedroom 3.

Jackson Meadow

Marine on St Croix, Minnesota, USA 2008
Salmela Architect

Marine on St Croix is the oldest settlement in Minnesota and so creating an extension in the nearby prairie land was a sensitive and ticklish issue. The solution – a collaboration between local architect David Salmela and landscape architect Coen + Partners (Coen + Stumpf at the time the work was done) – is a sensitive solution that has garnered praise from organizations as diverse as the American Institute of Architects and North American Wetland Engineering.

Drawing on the area's Scandinavian traditions, it is a development of surprising uniformity, as strict design rules determine the maximum size of houses, the materials used, the form of openings and other elements. But within these rules there is still a degree of flexibility, as if this cluster of houses has just evolved, constructed by people with a common building language.

The houses, although set in the vast prairie, are surprisingly close together. This is because the decision was taken, early on, to keep 70 per cent of the 59 hectares (145 acres) as open land. Combined with a large adjacent protected site, this gives the feeling of a real connection with nature.

In contrast to more undulating landscapes, with prairie there is no chance of disguising anything, or making any element look as if it has just grown. Even relatively small buildings stick out from the unending horizontal, and so the designers made the most of this effect, carefully placing the buildings as objects in the landscape.

All of the houses, which have pitched roofs, are clad in timber planks stained with the prescribed white stain. These contrast with the few buildings that have a semi-industrial function, housing such machinery as pumps for the water system. These, also of timber, are stained black, providing a pleasing modulation to what otherwise would be a monoculture of housing. After all, although the aim is to give a feeling of community, this is still a satellite suburb to a fairly small town, with none of its own facilities – no school, no shops, no sports halls. And, in fact, for most of the residents of what are pretty upmarket homes, the true focus of their lives is not on Marine on St Croix but on the twin cities of Minneapolis-St Paul, just half an hour's commute away.

This does not, however, remove the value from the project. It has ambitious environmental credentials, is providing a civilized way of living and manages the delicate balance of looking traditional without being folksy. There will be a total of 64 houses when the development is complete, placed carefully on their plots by Coen and designed with care by Salmela. The latter, an architect who qualified through working rather than at college, comes himself from a background of Finnish immigrants and draws on that for these designs. Having made a reputation for himself with relatively small one-off projects – right down to an award-winning family sauna – his work on this larger scale shows great confidence and skill.

Above left: Despite their relatively modest size, the houses form sculptural objects on the prairie.

Above right: As much attention was given to the external environment as to the houses themselves.

Top: By defining the pitch of the roofs, the nature of the cladding and the fenestration, the designers created a pleasing unity.

Above: Houses are not arranged in a regimented manner but, because of the common design features, there is no sense of disorder.

The rules include the fact that no house may be more than 7.3 metres (24 feet) wide. Given the fixed pitch of the roof, becoming any larger would make the building wildly out of scale. Also, restricting the width allows the interior to benefit much more from natural light. Similarly, every house has a basement, with at least one light well to ensure that it is not dark. By building down into the ground, the houses benefit from the natural insulating properties of the surrounding earth, so improving their thermal performance.

Every house-owner has the right to construct at least two outbuildings, although their form is regulated as strictly as it is for the main house. One of these will be a garage, since integral garages are banned. This is partly for health reasons – it is not considered desirable for petrol fumes to enter the house, but Salmela is also a great enthusiast for the way that the white walls of the outbuildings can reflect light towards the north faces of the houses.

Integral garages are popular in houses in America, especially in places where the winters can be as harsh as they are in Minnesota. But Shane Coen of Coen + Partners is positively evangelistic about the virtues of separation. 'If you live in a house with a detached garage, and you love your house, there's a relationship that happens on the walk from your garage,' he has said. 'You see your house, and you get to walk toward your house, and you feel grateful that you live in that house.'

People living in a less car-centred society may feel that the sense of connection with the outside world that comes from walking a few feet twice a day is exaggerated, but this is not the only way in which residents of Jackson Meadow can interact with their environment. Children regularly play outside, and there are paths through the prairie land, including one leading into Marine on St Croix. Many of these paths are simply mown rather than paved, part of a strategy that also includes putting substantial crowns on the roads so that rainwater can run off and soak away into the surrounding grassland. This is part of the environmental approach that seeks a less polluting alternative to the use of individual septic tanks with every house, the common approach for outlying settlements. Instead, water and sewage are collected centrally and filtered in a specially constructed wetland. It is the equipment to facilitate this that is housed in those handsome black utility buildings.

Houses at Jackson Meadow are relatively expensive, but Coen and Salmela believe that a similar approach could be used to facilitate less expensive housing in another location. It is a bold approach to development that in less skilful hands could have been depressing sprawl. Instead, the handsome white houses look equally right contrasting with the bright colours of summer or blending with the winter snows.

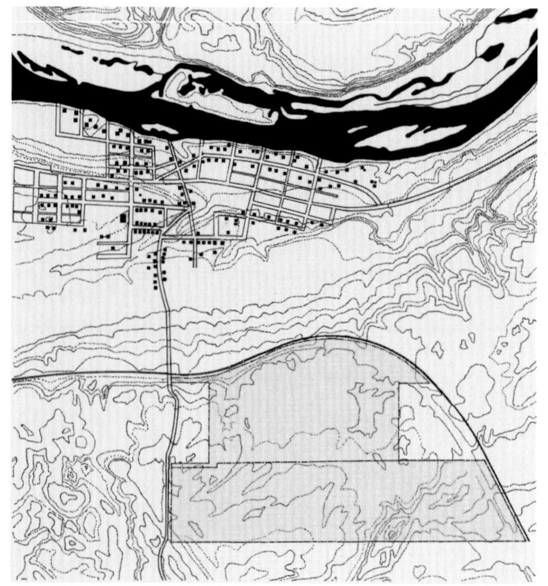

Above left: Plan of the new community, showing the importance of open space and walking trails.

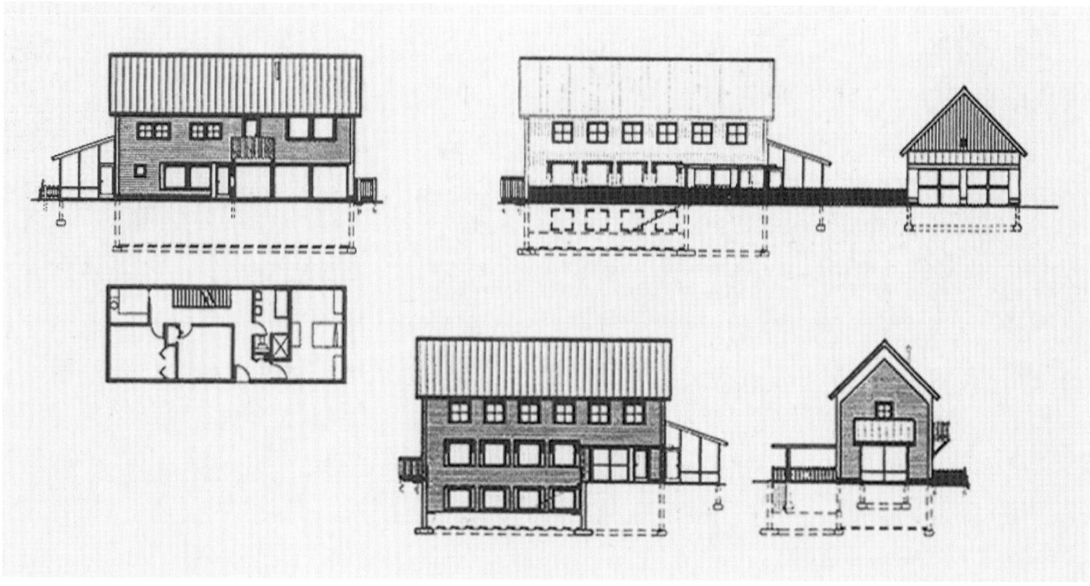

Above right: Drawings of some typical houses, showing the use of basements and of separate garages.

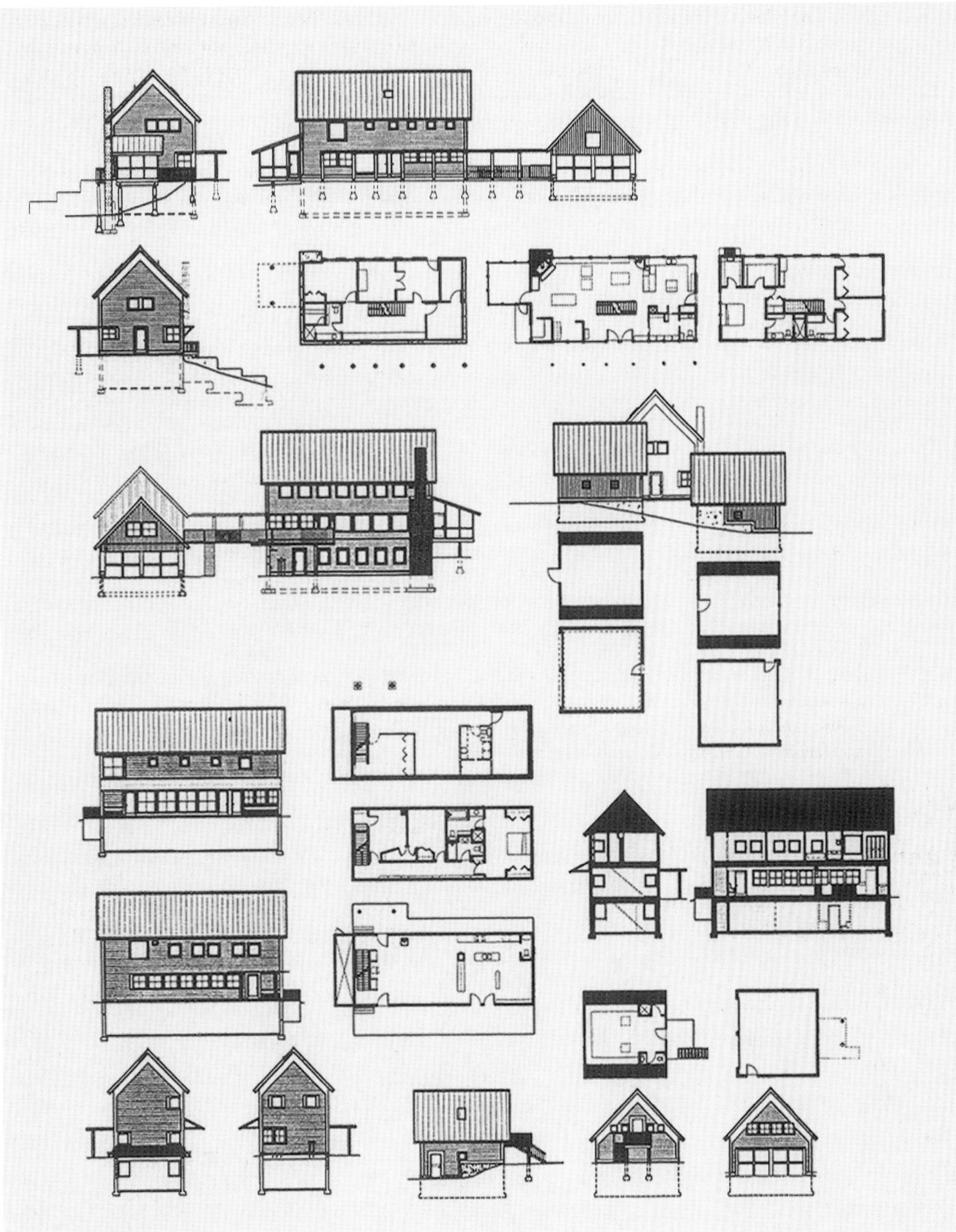

Above: Although the designers have laid down strict rules, considerable variation in the detailed design of houses is still possible.

Glossary

This is not intended as a comprehensive glossary of timber types. The timbers listed below are those referred to in the text of the book. For more information on many of these and on many other timber species, the following websites are excellent sources of information: in the UK, the Timber Research and Development Corporation (www.trada.co.uk); in the USA, Forest Products Laboratory (www.fpl.fs.fed.us); in France, www.bois-construction.org. Helpful websites related to other countries can be found at: www.alexschreyer.de/eng/w_res.htm.

Birch

Hardwood

There are two main types of birch, European birch and American birch, although several species are contained within each category.

In Europe, two forms are recognized, *Betula pendula* (silver or white birch), and *B. pubescens* (common birch). Although the trees appear different, the properties of the timber are very similar.

American birch consists of a number of species (*Betula papyrifera, Betula alleghaniensis, Betula spp, Betula lutea, Betula lenta*) and a confusing number of names: paper birch, yellow birch, betula wood (Canada), red birch, white birch (Canada), hard birch (Canada), American Birch (UK), Canadian yellow birch, Quebec birch. But there are only two types that are exploited commercially – paper birch and yellow birch. Yellow birch is about 20 per cent harder and stronger than European birch. Properties of paper birch are not as good as those of yellow birch.

European birch occurs throughout Europe. It penetrates further north than any other broad-leafed tree, being found in Lapland, but it also extends as far south as central Spain, since it can also cope with heat.

This is a fairly featureless wood, whitish to pale brown in colour. It is straight-grained and fine-textured, weighing about 670 kg/m3 when dried. The dried timber is similar to oak in most strength properties, and superior to that timber in compression along the grain, stiffness and toughness. An inexpensive wood, it is popular for use in plywood.

There is an exception to the generally bland appearance. The timber is sometimes attacked by the larvae of an insect called *Agromyzia carbonaria*. When these larvae burrow into the tree they create 'pith flecks', which are dark markings in the wood, and localized grain disturbances. Logs that have been attacked severely can, when rotary peeled, produce a highly decorative veneer known as masur birch, in which the irregular dark markings appear to stand out in relief against the white background. Flame birch and curly birch veneer are also created by grain deviations.

Cedar

Softwood

There are three main species. *Cedrus atlantica* is the Atlantic or Atlas cedar, native to Algeria and Morocco. *Cedrus libani* or *Cedrus libanotica* is the cedar of Lebanon, native to the Middle East. *Cedrus deodara* is the deodar, an important timber tree of northern India. All three species have been introduced into Britain where they are commonly planted for ornamental purposes.

Although the wood from all three timbers has a similar appearance, Atlantic and Lebanon cedars produce soft, brittle wood. Deodar is the only one with any importance for construction, with a similar bending strength and stiffness to European redwood, although lower shock resistance and tougness. The heartwood of the timber is a light brown, with strongly marked growth rings, and the grain is generally straight. The wood has a pungent, pleasing smell.

The main applications are in exterior joinery, interior joinery and furniture. However, the most commonly used form of cedar in construction is western red cedar (see below).

Cherry

Hardwood

The most commonly found species is European cherry (*Prunus serotina*), also known in the UK as gean or wild cherry, as kers in the Netherlands, ceriser in France and kirsche in Germany. In North America the same species is known as American cherry, black cherry or cabinet cherry.

In Europe the tree ranges southwards from Scandinavia to south-west Russia, as well as the UK. It also grows in western Asia and the mountains of North Africa. It is fairly widely distributed in North America, but does not grow in profusion anywhere on that continent.

Cherry wood, which weighs about 630kg/m3 when dried, has similar strength properties to oak. It has a tendency to warp when it is dried, which means that it is mostly used for specialist crafted furniture and for decorative work. These are applications where the medium-priced wood can shine, as it has an attractive appearance, with pale, pinkish-brown heartwood. The texture is fine and even, and the grain is generally straight.

Chestnut

Hardwood

In terms of construction, sweet chestnut (*Castanea sativa*) – not horse chestnut – is the species that people generally mean when they talk about chestnut wood.

The tree's range goes from southwest Europe, including the UK, to France and south-west Germany, as well as Australia, North Africa and Asia Minor.

The heartwood is yellowish-brown in colour, fairly closely resembling oak, but the wood is less hard and tough, with all properties inferior by about 20 per cent. The grain may be straight, but is more commonly spiral, particularly in wood from old trees. Chestnut wood weighs about 560 kg/m3 when dried. Because the timber is acidic, it will accelerate the corrosion of metals, particularly when moist. It also contains tannin, as a result of which blue-black discolourations are prone to appear on the wood when it comes into contact with iron.

Applications include structural use and external and interior joinery.

Cypress

Softwood

There are about 130 species of the genus *Cupressus* found throughout the world, including *Cupressus*, *Thuja* (*arborvitae*), *Calocedrus* (incense cedar), and *Juniperus* (juniper).

Cupressus lusitanica is used in New Zealand, and also grows on plantations in Kenya. It is a low-to-medium-density softwood with a speckled appearance. It weighs about 485 kg/m3 and is moderately stiff and strong, making it suitable for use in timber frame as well as in furniture.

In Australia, white cypress pine is a durable softwood timber with a natural resistance to insect attack that is often seen used as flooring, decking and weatherboarding in old houses. The flooring has a characteristic golden brown colour with highlights from pale creams to yellows and decorative tight knots. 'Cypress Pine' is in fact a collective name for several native Australian tree species of the genus *Callitris* (*Callitris glauca*, *Callitris columellaris*, etc). Of these, White Cypress is the main commercially exploited tree. Although it is not a true pine, the tree has a similar appearance to pine. It has been grown commercially in South Africa for about 80 years, and it has been naturalized in Florida in the USA, but there are no plantations in Australia. Because it is generally harvested from native forests, unless it is known that it has been harvested ethically, its use in Australia is not recommended.

Douglas fir

Softwood

A native of North America, Douglas fir has also been planted extensively in Europe, including the UK. It comes from one of the following species: *Pseudotsuga menziesii*, *Pseudotsuga taxifolia* or *Pseudotsuga douglasii*. It is also known in the UK as British Columbian pine or Columbian pine, and in the United States as Oregon pine. The timber is used structurally, for interior and exterior joinery, in plywood and for sea defences. Structural timber is often shipped to the UK from the USA and Canada in a 'Douglas fir– larch' mix, comprising *Pseudotsuga menziesii* and western larch (*Larix occidentalis*).

The heartwood is a light reddish-brown in colour, with prominent growth rings. Wood from trees grown in the UK appears to have less resin than North American wood, and to some extent is of more rapid growth. The average weight of dried timber from either source is about 530 kg/m3.

Compared with European redwood, Douglas fir is some 60 per cent stiffer, 40 per cent harder and more resistant to suddenly applied loads, and is 30 per cent stronger in bending and in compression along the grain.

Eastern white cedar

Softwood

Thuja occidentalis, also known as arbor-vitae, is one of the most decay-resistant of timbers.

It is typically found in areas where the underlying rock is limestone, and it can tolerate very dry soil, although it also grows in wet, marshy areas.

The timber is light brown, soft and weak, and very light in weight. This light weight, coupled with the resistance to decay, leads to its use in cladding shingles and sidings, as well as in fencing, poles, canoes and other boats.

European oak

Hardwood

There are more than 200 species of true oaks in the genus *Quercus*, most of them found in the northern hemisphere. They can be divided into three groups: the red oaks, the white oaks, and the evergreen oaks or live oaks; red and white oaks are deciduous.

In general, European oak can be divided into the sessile or durmast oak (*Quercus. Petraea*) and the pedunculate oak (*Quercus robur*). Both occur throughout Europe as well as in Asia Minor and North Africa, and have local names such as English, French or Polish oak, depending on the country of origin.

Wood from both species is similar in both appearance and properties, although these will be influenced by conditions of growth. Where growth is slower, the proportion of dense late wood in each growth ring is less, making the wood softer and lighter. This is reflected in the weight of the timber, which can vary between 720 kg/m3 for timber from the Baltic area, western Europe, and Great Britain, and 672 kg/m3 for timber from central Europe.

Oak heartwood is a yellowish-brown colour with clearly marked growth rings. Quarter-sawn surfaces show a distinct silver-grain figure.

Oak is high in strength. It dries very slowly and has a tendency to split and crack.

The timber is employed for heavy structural use, in cladding, interior and exterior joinery, furniture and flooring. In damp conditions, iron staining may occur, or corrosion of metals.

Brown oak is not a different species. Instead it is a colour change caused by a fungus attack by *Fistulina hepatica* on the growing tree. Another fungus, *Polyporous dryadeus*, may cause a yellow-coloured streak to appear in the wood. Since these fungi die after felling and drying, they do not affect the properties of the timber. Brown oak may be specified for its visual appeal.

Iroko

Hardwood

This consists of two African species with similar properties. *Milicia. excelsa* is widely distributed in tropical Africa, from Sierra Leone in the west, to Tanzania in the east. *Milicia regia* grows only in West Africa. The wood has a number of different local names, including kambala (Zaire), tule or intule (Mozambique), odum (Ghana and Ivory Coast), moreira (Angola), mvule (East Africa) and bang (Cameroon).

The heartwood of iroko, initially a yellow colour, quickly becomes golden-brown on exposure to light. It has an interlocked grain and a coarse but even texture. The wood weighs an average of 660 kg/m3 when dried and has excellent strength properties. It is used in garden furniture, boat-building, flooring and joinery.

Iroko is listed in the IUCN Red List of Threatened Species as being 'LR' of Lower Risk (near threatened). Care should therefore be taken with specification and sourcing.

Larch

European larch is of the species *Larix decidua* or *Larix europaea*. Its natural habitat is in mountainous areas going up to high elevations, from the Bavarian to the Swiss Alps, through western Poland and the Moravian Heights to the Carpathians. Although larch has been planted extensively elsewhere, the wood will not ripen thoroughly without long cold winters. Therefore larch grown in the UK, for example, is inferior in properties to larch grown on mountains.

The heartwood is pale reddish-brown to brick-red in colour, with clearly marked annual rings, a straight grain, and a fine, uniform texture. The wood is very resinous. It weighs 590 kg/m3 when dried.

Larch is a hard, tough timber, about 50 per cent harder than Scots pine and slightly stronger in bending and toughness; in other strength categories it is about the same as Scots pine. It is inexpensive and is used for cladding and as an all-purpose timber.

Live oak
Hardwood
Live oak is the term used to describe any native American evergreen oak. For example, the species *Quercus virginiana* grows on the lower coastal plain of the United States, from south-eastern Virginia to southern Florida and southern Texas, mostly on sandy soils. It is the Georgia state tree.

The yellowish-brown wood is hard, heavy (55 pounds per cubic foot when dry), tough and strong. It is used for structural beams, shipbuilding, posts, and in applications requiring strength and durability.

Lodgepole pine
Softwood
Known also as the contorta pine, *Pinus contorta* grows in North America, extending from the Yukon territory over most of British Columbia, and also growing in parts of Alberta, Montana and Colorado.

It is often shipped to the UK in a mix comprising black spruce (*Picea mariana*), Engelmann spruce (*Picea engelmannii*), red spruce (*Picea rubens*), white spruce (*Picea glauca*), jack pine (*Pinus banksiana*), lodgepole pine (*Pinus contorta*), ponderosa pine (*Pinus ponderosa*), alpine fir (*Abies lasiocarpa*) and balsam fir (*Abies balsamea*).

The timber is a pale yellow colour, with a soft, straight grain and a fine texture. It weighs about 470 kg/m3 when dried. The wood has small, tight knots. Because lodge pole pine trees are fairly small, they do not produce much high-grade timber. Strength is similar to that of European redwood.

This inexpensive timber can be used for heavy structural use, exterior joinery and interior joinery.

Maple
Hardwood
There are ten species of the genus *Acer* in the *Aceraceae* family, which is found in North America. Only five are important sources of timber, and two of these, *Acer saccharum* and *Acer nigrum*, produce rock maple, which is also known as hard maple, sugar maple, or black maple. These trees grow mainly in Canada and the eastern USA. They produce a heartwood that is light reddish-brown with deeper-coloured late-wood bands, and a white sapwood that is an attractive timber for special applications. Density of rock maple is 740kg/m3, and the timber is strong and hard, with a straight grain and a fine texture. It is highly resistant to abrasion, making it suitable for flooring. Other applications include furniture and sports goods.

The bending strength of rock maple is equivalent to that of European beech but it is considerably harder and has more resistance to shocks and to splitting.

Soft maple, which comes from the species *Acer rubrum* and *Acer saccharinum*, has considerably inferior properties. It is also known as silver maple and red maple.

Oak
See European oak, white oak. Other types include American red oak, Japanese oak, and Tasmanian oak (which is not an oak at all but a number of species of Eucalyptus – *see* stringybark).

Oregon pine
This is another name for Douglas fir.

Pine
Softwood
Vast number of timbers are categorized as pine, including Douglas fir. The most common kind, *Pinus sylvestris*, is characterized in Europe as European redwood. It has a plethora of other names, including Polish redwood, Baltic redwood, Russian redwood, Finnish redwood, Archangel redwood, red deal and yellow deal. In the UK, the names 'Scots pine' and 'European redwood' are used to differentiate between home-grown and imported *Pinus sylvestris*.

As the abundance of names suggests, this tree is widely distributed in Europe and northern Asia. It is found in the mountains of Spain and in the UK, especially in Scotland, at its westerly limits, in the north-west of Norway in a northerly

direction, spreading east through northern Europe into Asia, and reaching the Verkhoyansk Range. Its extreme southerly point is in Spain, in the Sierra Nevada in Andalucia. It also grows in the Maritime Alps in France, and in the eastern Pyrenees, and in the Caucasus and Transylvanian Alps. It is the only true pine indigenous to the British Isles, being native to Scotland and just over the border; elsewhere in the UK the forests are generally the result of planting.

The heartwood of European redwood is pale yellowish-brown to reddish-brown and resinous. Growth rings are clearly marked.

Because the trees are so widely distributed in such a mix of environments, considerable variations in timber properties result from the effect of climate, soil and elevation. The weight of dried timber is about 510 kg/m3.

For its weight, the timber is strong and moderately hard, although UK plantation-grown timber is generally slightly softer and weaker than that from other sources. Pine is an inexpensive timber that is used structurally, as well as in furniture and interior joinery.

Pitch pine
Pinus rigida is a small-to-medium sized (6–30 metre/19½–98 foot) tree, often contorted due to fire or weather, that grows mainly in the north-eastern United States, from Maine and Ohio to Kentucky and northern Georgia. Some trees also grow in southern Quebec and Ontario. Habitats vary and the tree can survive in very poor conditions. The heartwood is a reddish-brown colour, and the timber is very heavy, strong, stiff and hard.

Because of its size, the fact that it often has multiple or twisted trunks, and that it grows relatively slowly, pitch pine is not a major source of timber today. In the past, because it would grow in places where little else could be grown, it was used for mine timbers, and railroad ties. Today it is more likely to be used for rough construction, as pulp, in crates or for fuel.

Poplar
Hardwood
Poplars growing in the British Isles and Europe include black poplar (*Populus nigra, Populus robusta*), aspen (*Populus tremula*), Lombardy poplar (*Populus italica*), grey poplar (*Populus canescens*), white poplar (*Populus alba*) and black Italian poplar (*Populus canadensis*).

All of these produce soft, fine-textured woods with a straight grain. Density is typically 450 kg/m3, although grey poplar is a little heavier. Quality varies, with aspen often the best, and with white and grey poplars the poorest.

Poplar has only about half the hardness and shear resistance of European oak, but in other respects its properties are only about 15 to 30 per cent lower than those of oak – a creditable performance considering the timber's low weight.

Applications include plywood, flooring, interior joinery and furniture.

Spruce
Softwood
Often known as whitewood, this is the most general-purpose softwood. There is some distinction to be made between Canadian spruce, Sitka spruce, and European whitewood.

What is sold as Canadian spruce usually consists of a mix of three species. *Picea glauca* (white spruce) dominates, but is usually accompanied by some *Picea rubens* (red spruce) and *Picea mariana* (black spruce). For structural use, it is also common to find a mix of 'spruce-pine-fir' which also includes jack pine, lodgepole pine, ponderosa pine, alpine fir and balsam fir.

Canadian spruce is very widely distributed, growing from Alaska to as far south as Michigan. The wood is pale, with a straight grain and it has strength properties similar to those of European redwood. Density is typically 416 kg/m3.

Sitka spruce, also known as silver spruce, tideland spruce or Menzies spruce, is *Picea sitchensis*. It grows in the coastal belt of British Columbia, as well as in Washington and California. The heartwood has a pinkish tinge and a very straight grain. Density is typically 450 kg/m3, with a very high strength to weight ratio. It is about 25 per cent stiffer than European redwood. 'British spruce' is a mixture of Norway spruce and Sitka spruce.

Applications of Sitka spruce are commonly for structural use or interior joinery.

European whitewood is in fact a mixture of Norway spruce (*Picea abies*) and silver fir (*Abies alba*). Norway spruce grows throughout Europe, with the exception of Denmark and the Netherlands. The timber is pale, with a straight grain and fine texture. Density is typically 470 kg/m3, although lower for timber grown in the UK and south-eastern Europe. Strength is similar to that of Scots pine.

Silver fir is a native of central and southern Europe, and also grows in northern Spain, in Corsica and in the Balkans. Despite its different geographical origins, the timber is very similar in appearance and properties to Norway spruce.

Stringybark

A number of Australian eucalyptus, including *Eucalyptus obliqua*, *Eucalyptus regnans* and *Eucalyptus delegatensis*, make up the stringybarks. The standard UK name is, misleadingly, Tasmanian oak, although the trees bear no botanical relationship to true oaks. Other common names include gum-top, brown-top stringybark, Australian oak, white-top, stringybark, alpine ash (Australian standard), white top stringybark, woollybutt, and gum-top stringybark. There are different common names for particular species, but in fact the trees are fairly similar and so are the qualities of the timber, although there are some differences in appearance. Average densities vary from about 610kg/m3 to 710kg/m3, depending on the species.

The timber varies in quality but is in general tougher, stiffer and stronger in bending than true oak. Main uses are for interior joinery and furniture.

Western red cedar

Softwood

The most commonly specified and used cedar in construction, *Thuja plicata* is a native of North America, growing in the northern Rocky Mountains and the Pacific North-west. It has been planted in the UK, where it produces timber of similar properties except that the North American timber is rated as durable whereas that grown in the UK is only considered moderately durable.

The heartwood of the tree is reddish-brown and, immediately after felling, may be variegated, but after drying the colour becomes uniform. With long exposure to weather, it becomes a silver-grey colour. If this is not desired, the wood is also very easy to stain.

It is non-resinous, straight-grained, with a fairly coarse texture and quite prominent growth rings. Weighing 390 kg/m3 when dried, the wood is soft, quite brittle and aromatic. Because the timber is fairly acidic, it can corrode metals under damp conditions and cause damp staining. The main use is for cladding.

White oak

The white oaks commonly used in construction are often generally described as American white oak. They include chestnut oak (*Quercus Montana*, *Quercus prinus*), overcup oak (*Quercus lyrata*), American white oak (*Quercus alba*) and swamp chestnut oak (*Quercus michauxii*). Growing in North America from southern Quebec to Ontario and southward to eastern Minnesota and Iowa, their range extends to the Atlantic and southward through the lower western slopes of the Allegheny and Appalachian Mountains.

American white oak is more variable in colour than European oak, ranging from pale yellow-brown to pale reddish-brown, often with a pinkish tint. These oaks show a more prominent and attractive silver-grain figure on quarter-sawn surfaces. The grain is generally straight, and the texture varies from coarse to medium coarse. Quality will depend on the conditions of growth, and the timber weighs about 770 kg/m3 when dried.

Although there is not much difference, the greater weight tends to give American white oak slightly higher strength than European oak. The finer oaks will be used for furniture and veneers, the coarser ones for heavy structural use, for joinery and flooring.

As with European oak, this is an acidic timber, so iron staining may occur in damp conditions, and it may corrode metals.

Project credits

Messenger House II
Client: Mary and John Messenger
Project team: Brian MacKay-Lyons, Trevor Davies, Chad Jamieson, Peter Blackie
www.bmlaud.ca
Structural: Campbell Comeau Engineering
Builder: Gordon MacLean

Summer House, Jutland
Architect: Schmidt, Hammer & Lassen/Bjarne Hammer
www.shl.dk
Client: Bjarne Hammer

Onominese Retreat
Client: Cornelius and Dorothy Alig
Architect: Betsy Williams, Ann Arbor, MI and Cornelius Alig, Indianapolis, IN
Structural engineer: SDI, Ann Arbor, MI
General contractor: David Webster Construction, Inc., Traverse City, MI

Cabin at Elbow Coulee
Owners: Tom Lenchek & Mary Drobka
Architect: Balance Associates, Architects
www.balanceassociates.com
Design Team: Tom Lenchek AIA, Principal, Marcus Schott, Scott LaBenz AIA
General Contractor: Rhinehart Construction
Structural engineer: Jay Taylor PE, Magnusson Klemencic Associates

Accordion House
Architect: 24H > architecture, Rotterdam
www.24h-architecture.com
Client: Zeisser family
Design: Maartje Lammers, Boris Zeisser with Olav Bruin, Jeroen ter Haar, Sabrina Kers, Fieke Poelman
Structural engineering: ABT: Walter Spangenberg & Wiljan Houweling
Construction: 24H > construction with Rolf van Gils, Paul Rutten, Rowan van Wely, Gerben Pakkert, Mijke Teeken, Bart Cuppens, Marcus Lorenz, Olav Bruin, Wouter Homs, Freek Speksnijder

Summer House, Åland
Architect: Todd Saunders & Tommie Wilhelmsen
www.saunders-wilhelmsen.no
www.saunders.no
www.tommie-wilhelmsen.no
Construction Firm: Mats Odin Rustøy

Terrace House
Architect and builder: Rockhill and Associates
www.rockhillandassociates.com

Maison Goulet
Architectural practice: Saia Barbarese Topouzanov architectes
www.sbt.qc.ca
Lead design architect: Mario Saia, architect: Marc Pape
Client: Ms. Marlène Goulet
Builder: Michel Riopel
Structural engineer: Jean Saia
Graphic design: Nadia Meratla

Family House
Architect: Brückner & Brückner Architekten, Tirschenreuth
www.architektenbrueckner.de
Project management: Christian Brückner, Peter Brückner
Client: Sabine & Andreas Rösch
Project team: Robert Reith, Wolfgang Herrmann
Structural engineer: Klaus-Peter Brückner, Brückner & Brückner Ingenieure, Tirschenreuth
Electrical services: Elektro Schuller, 95643 Tirschenreuth
Plumbing: Klaus Schmaußer, 95643 Tirschenreuth
Heating: Heizung Werner, 95695 Mähring
Quantity surveyor: Christian Brückner, Peter Brückner
Stone façade: Willibald Roth
Timber façade: Robert Fröhlich, Wiesau
Roof: Robert Fröhlich, Wiesau and Karl Söllner, Tirschenreuth
Windows / doors: Tischlerei Rosenberger, Waldershof
Furniture: Sana Innenausbau GmbH, Weiden

The Lodge
Architect: James Gorst Architects Ltd.
www.jamesgorstarchitects.com
Quantity surveyor: Holpen Associates
Structural engineer: Alan Conisbee & Associates
Contractor: Ceecom

Bunch Residence
Owners: Marjorie Caldwell and Carl C. Bunch
Architect: Turnbull Griffin Haesloop Architects
www.tgharchs.com
Project team: William Turnbull, Jr., Mary Griffin, Eric Haesloop, Sean Culman, Andrew Mann
Contractor: Sawyer Construction
Structural engineer: Richard Hartwell Co.
Landscape architect: Lutsko Associates

Casa del Sole di Mezzanotte
Client: Sting and Trudie Styler
Designed by Roderick J. W. Romero, Romero Studios
www.romerostudios.com
Built by Roderick J. W. Romero and Wolfgang Rain

Box House and Collopy House
Architect: Nicholas Murcutt

Split House
Client: Red Stone Industrie Co. Ltd.
Architect: Atelier Feichang Jianzhu
www.fcjz.com
Project designer: Yung Ho CHANG
Project team: LIU Xianghui, LU Xiang, Lucas Gallardo, WANG Hui, XU Yixing
Structural consultant: XU Minsheng

House in Savoy
Architect: Tectoniques
www.tectoniques.com
Wood supplier: Favrat

House in Pedralbes
Project and execution: Tito Dalmau, architect (BDM Arqtos.)
Project assistant: Mar de Bobes, architect
Execution assistant: David Chayle, architect
Technical supervisor: José Ma Español
Industrial Coordinator: José Ma Garcia Vallés (I+I)
Carpenter: Industrias Muntané, s.a.

Mann Residence
Architect: Fernau and Hartman Architects, Inc.
www.fernauhartman.com
Design Team: Richard Fernau and Laura Hartman (partners in charge) Richard Fernau, Laura Hartman, Jeff Day (house design team)
Randy Hellstern (construction phase project architect)
Alexis Maznick (project team)
Structural engineer: Richard Hartwell and Jon Brody
Lighting: Peters & Myer
Cooling: Davis Energy Group
Contractor: Jeff F. Nimmo

Riddell Residence
Architect: Will Bruder Architects, Ltd.
www.willbruder.com
Design: Will Bruder
Design team: Richard Jensen, Michael Crooks
Clients: Lee and Ed Riddell
Structural engineer: Rudow & Berry, Inc. (Mark Rudow)
Mechanical engineer: Otterbein Engineering (Roy Otterbein)
Electrical engineers: Martin Heating, design-build, ca energy designs (Charles Avery)
Landscape architect: Mother Nature
Contractor: Continental Construction (Quinn Heiner and Deon Heiner)

House in the Orchard
Architect: Damien Carnoy
www.carnoy-crayon.be
Client: Mr & Ms Simon

Villa B
Architect: Fink + Jocher
www.fink-jocher.de
Project team: Elfriede Matt, Katrin Möller, Peter Scheller

Hangar House
Architect: Sylvain Gasté, Michel Bazantay, Nantes, France

House in Fontainebleau
Architect: Sinikka Ropponen-Brunel, Architect Atelier Brunel Paris

Milanville House
Client: Jane Cyphers and Joe Levine
Architect: Joe Levine, Bone/Levine Architects, NY
www.bonelevine.net
Project Team: Barbara Wronska-Kucy, Koon Wee, Paul Deppe
Structural Eng: Edy Zingher, ETNA Consulting, NY
Builder: Larry Braverman, Beach Lake, PA

Prefabricated Housing
Client: Baugesellschaft Wolkenstein, Merano
Architect: Holzbox ZT GmbH & DI Anton Höss, Innsbruck
www.holzbox.at
Structural engineers: Vorarlberger Ökohaus GmbH, Ludesch and Erich Huster, Bregenz
Wood constructions: Vorarlberger Ökohaus GmbH, Ludesch
Steel constructions: Mark Stahlbau GmbH, Ludesch

Garriga-Poch House
Client: Xavier Garriga and Conxita Poch
Architect: Arturo Frediani Sarfatí
Technical architect: Mercé Martín Valls
Collaborators: Francesc Oller Figueras, Jordi Ramos
Structure: Gerardo Rodríguez (static engineering)
Construction company: Peipoch SL, Joseph Maria Peipoch, Castellar d'en Hug (bcn)
Carpentry: Jesús Borrellas from carpentry El Pí, Bagà (bcn)
Metalwork: Josep Flores, Ferros Buscall SL, Berga (bcn)

Self-build House
Construction: Nick Fisher with directly contracted labour
Design: Jo Jordan and Nick Fisher

Modular2
Architect and builder: Studio 804
www.studio804.com

Garden City
Architect: bcde architecture

Housing Group, Porto San Paolo
Architect: Marco Petreschi (Principal) with Giulia Amadei

House Extension
Architect: Christian Pottgiesser
Architect's assistant: Florian Hertweck

Cargo Fleet
Architect: Chance de Silva
www.chancedesilva.com
Contractor: TBA Contractors, Ltd.
Engineer: Price and Myers
Quantity surveyor: Chris Payne
M & E consultants: EDC
Party wall: Watkinson and Cosgrave
Cor-ten steel cladding: Roles LLP and Rannila, Ltd.
Metalwork: Crovin Metalworks, Ltd.
Glass: Kirsty Brook
Photographs: Frank Watson
Computer visualization: June Raby
Model: Mona Kvanka

Ebeling House
Client: Sabine Ebeling
Architect: ArchiFactory.de
www.archifactory.de
Project Team: Matthias Herrmann, Matthias Koch, Till Roggel
Construction management: ArchiFactory.de
Structural engineer: Assmann - Beraten und Planen, Dortmund
Garden: ArchiFactory.de

Housing Group, Trivières
Architect: Groupe Gamma, Atelier d'architecture & d'urbanisme

Template House
Template house
Architect: Michele Saee
www.michelesaee.com
Project team: Franco Rosete, Zhang Haitong
Owner: CRLand (China Resource Land Company)

Jackson Meadow
Architect and co-planner: Salmela Architect
Landscape architect and co-planner: Coen + Partners
Developer and visionary who started the project: Harold Teasdale
www.jacksonmeadow.com

Index

Page numbers in *italics* refer to picture captions

Picture credits

6 © Jiri Havran
7 by permission of the British Library (shelf mark: Add. 18850 f.15v)
8 © Alan Weintraub/Arcaid/©ARS, NY and DACS, London 2006
9t M. Kapanen/Alvar Aalto Museum
9b Maija Holma/Alvar Aalto Museum
11t Tom Church
11b Canada Mortgage and Housing Corporation (CMHC). Canadian wood-frame house construction (CD). 2001.
12 © Donald Corner & Jenny Young / GreatBuildings.com
13t Architype Architects (photo: Leigh Simpson)
13b by kind permission of the Building Research Establishment Ltd
15 Hayball Leonard Stent Pty Ltd Architects (photo: Peter Clarke)
16 Fritz Busam
17 © Raf Makda/VIEW & Bill Dunster Architects
19t Andrew Lee
19bl Jens Lindhe
19br Espen Grønli
20–22 © James Steeves
23–24 Steven Evans
25t Steven Evans
25b © James Steeves
26–29 larsenform.com
30 ©Peter Tata
31l ©Peter Tata
31r Betsy Williams
32–33 ©Peter Tata
36 Balance Associates, Inc.
37–41 Steve Keating
42–45 © Christian Richters
48–49 courtesy of the architects
50 Michael Davies
52–57 Dan Rockhill
59t Mark Fiennes
59bl Ahadu Abaineh
59br Ebner : Grömer Architekten
60–61 Frédéric Saia
62–63 Marc Cramer
66–68 Peter Manev
70–73 David Churchill
74–76 © Matthew Millman
78–81 © Manuel Vecchina
83t Hufton & Crow (www.retreathomes.co.uk)
83bl Simon Scally
83br Jong Oh Kim
84–91 Brett Boardman
92–93 Satoshi Asakawa
94l Satoshi Asakawa
94r FU Xing
95 FU Xing
96–97 FU Xing
100–103 Erick Saillet
104–109 Tito Dalmau
110–113 John Linden
114–117 Bill Timmerman
118–121 Damien Carnoy
122–127 Simone Rosenberg fotografie
129t Huf Haus
129bl Rubner
129br Haiku Houses
130–133 © Philippe Ruault
134l Patrick Tourneboeuf
134r Sinikka Ropponen-Brunel, Architect Atelier Brunel
135t Sinikka Ropponen-Brunel, Architect Atelier Brunel
135b Patrick Tourneboeuf
136 Jack M. Kucy
137l Jack M. Kucy
137r Joe Levine
138–139 Jack M. Kucy
140 Joe Levine
142–144 Manuela Tessaro, Bozen
146l Eugeni Pons
146r akme
147 Eugeni Pons
148t akme
148bl Eugeni Pons
148br akme
150–153 © Brian Benson
154–159 Courtesy of Studio 804
16tl Thomas Spiegelhalter
161bl Duncan Baker-Brown
161br Matti Karjanoja (ARRAK Arkkitehdit Oy)
162–167 bcde architecture
168–171 Marco Petreschi
172–177 Gert von Bassewitz
178–179 © Timothy Soar
180t © Timothy Soar
180bl 3D visualizer, June Raby
182 Gernot Maul
183l Gernot Maul
183r ArchiFactory.de
184 Karin Hessmann
185t Gernot Maul
185b ArchiFactory.de
186–187 Eternit
189 Françoise Godefroid
190–192 Chen SU
194–195 Peter Bastianelli Kerze

Acknowledgements

I would like to thank everybody who helped with information, ideas and the production of this book. I should also thank my colleagues at *The Architects' Journal* for their forbearance and advice, my father who always believed I would write books, and Barry Evans for limitless moral support and meals.

Thanks also to research coordinator Fredrika Lökholm and designer Neil Pereira, and to Philip Cooper, Liz Faber and Kim Sinclair at Laurence King Publishing.